Farewell to Farms

Farewell to Farms

De-agrarianisation and Employment in Africa

Edited by
Deborah Fahy Bryceson and Vali Jamal

African Studies Centre
Research Series 1997/10

Routledge
Taylor & Francis Group
LONDON AND NEW YORK

Research Series of the African Studies Centre, Leiden

Vol. 1 *Tied to the land. Living conditions of labourers on large farms in Trans Nzoia District, Kenya*
Dick Foeken & Nina Tellegen, 1994

Vol. 2 *Asylum or Aid? The economic integration of Ethiopian and Eritrean refugees in the Sudan*
Tom Kuhlman, 1994

Vol. 3 *Quest for self-esteem. State, Islam and Mundang ethnicity in Northern Cameroon*
Kees Schilder, 1994

Vol. 4 *Taking the waters. Soil and water conservation among settling Beja nomads in Eastern Sudan*
Johan A. van Dijk, 1995

Vol. 5 *Gender and class in the tea estates of Cameroon*
Piet Konings, 1995

Vol. 6 *Passing on the rites of passage. Girls' initiation rites in the context of an urban Roman Catholic community on the Zambian Copperbelt*
Thera Rasing, 1995

Vol. 7 *Seasons and nutrition at the Kenya coast*
Jan Hoorweg, Dick Foeken & Wijnand Klaver 1995

Vol. 8 *Tropical Africa's emergence as a banana supplier in the inter-war period*
John A. Houtkamp, 1996

Vol. 9 *Nomads and the state in Africa: the political roots of marginality*
Victor Azarya, 1996

In memory of Mboya Bagachwa

First published 1997 by Ashgate Publishing

Reissued 2018 by Routledge
2 Park Square, Milton Park, Abingdon, Oxon, OX14 4RN
52 Vanderbilt Avenue, New York, NY 10017

Routledge is an imprint of the Taylor & Francis Group, an informa business

Cover design: Peter Stroo

ISBN 13: 978-1-138-33550-9 (hbk)
ISBN 13: 978-1-138-33553-0 (pbk)
ISBN 13: 978-0-429-44267-4 (ebk)

Contents

Acknowledgements

This book is the product of the effort and creative thought of a large number of people. Its origins date back to a workshop held at the Afrika-Studiecentrum, Leiden in May 1994 funded by the Ministry of Development Cooperation of the Dutch Government and the International Labour Office, Geneva. The papers in this book have benefited greatly from the face-to-face encounters of workshop discussions. Since then, the production of this book has been 'globalised'. Vali Jamal's work commitments at the International Labour Office took him to Bangkok, so three-way dialogues between editors in Europe and Asia and authors in Africa and Europe proceeded by whatever form of communication was available, ranging from press of a button e-mail messages to crackly telephone lines and dodgy postal services. Ann Reeves directed the traffic and copy editing work with enormous skill and practicality from Leiden. The book layout and cover design benefited from the creative talents of Adri van den Berg and Peter Stroo. The Afrika-Studiecentrum provided the infrastructural support and funding for seeing this book through to publication. We are grateful for the help and advice of all those involved.

The Editors
Leiden and Geneva

I

INTRODUCTION

1

De-agrarianisation in Sub-Saharan Africa: Acknowledging the Inevitable

*Deborah Fahy Bryceson**

It is generally assumed that Africa is the world's most agrarian continent. Vast deserts, forests, and savannah lands populated by wild animals and farmers with rudimentary technology of the hoe or plough is the image conjured up by the mention of Sub-Saharan Africa. African farming has a tinge of the frontier about it in both spatial and technological terms. Another image, less bucolic but perfectly compatible, is that of starving people in wasteland settings. The two images put together suggest to many outsiders that the solution to Africa's problems lies in African farmers modernising their agriculture. African farmers, voting with their feet, are not as sure.

This book is about people, male, female, young, middle-aged, and old, who in one way or another are easing away from a strictly agrarian existence. They are choosing non-agrarian livelihoods in the rural areas or more urbanised existences. Their decisions are rational in economic, social, political and psychological terms. In many cases, they are not only beneficial to the individual directly involved but function for the 'common good' of the household, community, region and nation-state. The negative connotations that de-agrarianisation may hold for the outside observer are generally biased. The title of this book, *Farewell to Farms*, has been deliberately chosen to challenge the unwarranted assumption that the African continent's destiny is *necessarily* rooted in peasant agriculture. It refers to an on-going process in which the continent's population is becoming less agrarian in nature year by year.

This chapter defines de-agrarianisation and cites official statistics demonstrating that a process of de-agrarianisation is currently under way in Africa and has been on-going for several decades. Reasons why western opinion, particularly that of donor agencies, has been averse to de-agrarianisation are explored through a review of western social science concepts of African development. The utility of the 'informal sector' concept is considered before outlining the general focus and sectional breakdown of the remainder of the book.

Defining and Discerning De-agrarianisation

De-agrarianisation is defined as a long-term process of: (1) occupational adjustment, (2) income-earning reorientation, (3) social identification, and (4) spatial relocation of rural dwellers away from strictly peasant modes of livelihood (Bryceson 1996). Not all facets of de-agrarianisation necessarily unfold simultaneously. Rather, asynchronic development is the norm. Some countries have experienced periods when migration to urban areas, i.e. (4), has been rapid, leading to a marked change in rural life vis-a-vis the other facets. At times, physical movement of people from rural areas or noticeable transformations of social identities have been minimal although rural-based diversification into non-agricultural activities is taking place and leading to measurable differences in individual and household sources of income. There are innumerable permutations of the de-agrarianisation process, as illustrated by the case studies in this book, so much so that the overall tendency can be masked by the variations. Nonetheless, broad continental tendencies towards residential and occupational change are clearly evident in available statistics (Table 1).

Table 1 shows data from censuses which capture the swell of residential movement from rural to urban areas between 1960 and 1990. As with so many published African statistics, tallies of urban population and growth rates should be viewed as indicators rather than precise measures of urbanisation.[1] Growth rates vary from country to country, and indeed intercensal rates within individual countries also vary widely, but within such variations, rapid urbanisation comes through clearly all the same.[2]

Occupational change is by no means restricted to urban areas. National statistics, while indicating a gradual decline in the numbers employed in the agricultural sector, cannot convey the full extent of this phenomenon since detailed occupational and income changes, especially within rural areas, are not adequately captured, while social identity changes escape altogether. It is thus from social science research, notably quantitative surveys and qualitative data collection techniques, that a more well-rounded and more nuanced picture of the de-agrarianisation process can be gained.

A growing number of surveys over the past two decades have signalled the widespread appearance of 'income diversification' and, by implication, occupational shifts in both rural and urban households.[3] Borders between urban and rural areas have blurred in the process, as some urban households resort to farming and in turn rural households are increasingly engaged in non-agricultural activities.[4] But there is no mistaking that the direction of overall change is towards a growing preponderance of non-agricultural activities, as the chapters in this book testify.

The non-agricultural activities pursued in rural areas span a wide spectrum including: water, firewood, charcoal and fodder sales, the food and beverage trade, especially beer brewing, trade and transport activities, tailoring, brickmaking, carpentry, metal working, mineral excavation, leather goods production, and pottery. It is difficult to characterise these goods and services and hence the literature has resorted to labels, not all of which are overly accurate or helpful. 'Small-scale industries' and 'rural industries' conjure up the notion of an industrialisation process which is unwarranted as Livingstone hints in Chapter 12. 'Rural non-farm employment' (RNFE), 'non-farm activities' (NFA) or 'off-farm activities' are also terms found in the literature, which add the locational dimension of employment outside the confines of the family farm, but which still fail to capture the diversity of labour processes involved (Tellegen 1993 and 1997).

This chapter utilises the term 'non-agricultural rural employment' (NARE) to emphasise the 'non-agricultural' character of the diversified activities and to distinguish the de-agrarianisation approach from other terminologies with different analytical objectives. Non-agricultural rural employment refers to the gamut of economic activities that are performed by rural dwellers outside farming and maintenance of household subsistence needs. Thus, NARE excludes 'farming' defined as plant or animal husbandry for the production of raw materials directly consumed or exchanged by the producers themselves and the peasant subsistence sector, widely defined, including all non-agricultural activities which are not destined for the market such as house building, sewing, etc. for household members' direct usage.

Significance of Non-agricultural Rural Employment

Why has occupational and income diversification become so widespread in rural Africa over the last two decades? Looking at changes in rural communities over the past fifty years which might generate a supply of labour for NARE, one is immediately aware of the influence of population growth. The increasing

Table 1: African De-agrarianisation Statistical Indices

Country	Nat.'l pop. million 1990	GPD per capita 1989	Annual PGR % 60-90	Urban PGR % 60-90	Rural population % of total 1960	1990	Percentage of labour force in: Agriculture 1965	Agriculture 86-89	Industry 1965	Industry 86-89	Services 1965	Services 86-89	Labour force % of pop. 88-90	% of population in agricultural labour force 1965	86-89	Migration rate* 60-90
Angola	10.0	1225	2.5	5.9	90.0	72.0	79.0	73.8	8.0	9.5	13.0	16.7	41.4	32.7	30.6	3.4
Benin	4.6	1030	3.2	7.4	91.0	62.0	83.0	70.2	5.0	6.6	12.0	23.1	34.5	28.6	24.2	4.2
Botswana	1.3	3180	3.4	13.5	98.0	72.0	89.0	43.2	4.0	4.8	8.0	52.0	34.9	31.1	15.1	10.1
Burkina Faso	9.0	617	2.4	4.6	95.0	91.0	89.0	86.6	3.0	4.3	7.0	9.1	51.1	45.5	44.3	2.2
Burundi	5.5	611	2.1	5.5	98.0	94.0	94.0	92.9	2.0	1.6	4.0	5.5	55.5	52.2	51.6	3.4
Cameroon	11.8	1699	2.7	6.5	86.0	59.0	86.0	74.0	4.0	4.5	9.0	21.5	38.5	33.1	28.5	3.8
Cape Verde	0.4	1717	2.1	4.1	84.0	71.0	na	52.0	na	23.0	na	25.0	33.8	na	17.6	2.0
Central African Rep.	3.0	770	2.3	3.6	77.0	53.0	88.0	83.7	3.0	2.8	9.0	13.5	48.4	42.6	40.5	1.3
Chad	5.7	582	2.1	7.1	93.0	70.0	92.0	83.2	3.0	4.6	5.0	12.0	37.4	34.4	31.1	5.0
Comoros	0.6	732	3.2	6.8	90.0	72.0	na	83.0	na	6.0	na	11.0	38.0	na	31.5	3.6
Congo	2.3	2382	2.8	3.6	68.0	60.0	66.0	62.4	11.0	11.9	23.0	25.6	39.8	26.3	24.8	0.8
Cote d'Ivoire	12.0	1381	3.9	6.5	81.0	60.0	81.0	65.2	5.0	8.3	15.0	26.5	37.6	30.5	24.5	2.6
Djibouti	0.4	730	5.6	7.3	50.0	19.0	na	na	na	na	na	na	na	na	na	1.7
Equatorial Guinea	0.4	706	1.1	1.5	75.0	71.0	na	66.0	na	11.0	na	23.0	39.2	na	25.9	0.4
Ethiopia	49.2	392	2.4	4.8	94.0	87.0	86.0	79.8	5.0	7.9	9.0	12.3	42.7	36.7	34.1	2.4
Gabon	1.2	4735	3.0	6.3	83.0	54.0	na	75.5	na	10.8	na	13.7	48.2	na	36.4	3.3
Gambia	0.9	886	3.0	5.2	87.0	77.0	na	84.0	na	7.0	na	9.0	36.2	na	30.4	2.2
Ghana	15.0	1005	2.7	3.9	77.0	67.0	61.0	59.3	15.0	11.1	24.0	29.6	38.1	23.2	22.6	1.2
Guinea	5.8	602	2.0	5.3	90.0	74.0	87.0	78.1	6.0	1.3	7.0	20.6	39.1	34.0	30.5	3.3
Guinea-Bissau	1.0	820	1.9	3.2	86.0	80.0	na	82.0	na	4.0	na	14.0	30.0	na	24.6	1.3
Kenya	24.0	1023	3.6	7.7	93.0	76.0	86.0	81.0	5.0	6.8	9.0	12.1	40.3	34.7	32.6	4.1
Lesotho	1.8	1646	2.4	8.6	97.0	80.0	92.0	23.3	3.0	33.1	6.0	43.6	46.3	42.6	10.8	6.2
Liberia	2.6	937	3.1	6.2	81.0	54.0	79.0	74.2	10.0	9.4	11.0	16.4	36.2	28.6	26.9	3.1
Madagascar	12.0	690	2.8	5.6	89.0	76.0	85.0	80.9	4.0	6.0	11.0	13.2	42.6	36.2	34.5	2.8
Malawi	8.8	620	3.1	6.5	96.0	88.0	92.0	81.8	3.0	3.0	5.0	15.2	42.0	38.6	34.4	3.4
Mali	9.2	576	2.5	4.4	89.0	81.0	90.0	85.5	1.0	2.0	8.0	12.5	31.8	28.6	27.2	1.9
Mauritania	2.0	1092	2.4	9.8	94.0	53.0	89.0	69.4	3.0	8.9	8.0	21.7	33.4	29.7	23.2	7.4

Country	Nat.'l pop. million 1990	GPD per capita 1989	Annual PGR % 60-90	Urban PGR % 60-90	Rural population % of total 1960	1990	Percentage of labour force in: Agriculture 1965	86-89	Industry 1965	86-89	Services 1965	86-89	Labour force % of pop. 88-90	% of population in agricultural labour force 1965	86-89	Migration rate* 60-90
Mozambique	15.7	1060	2.5	9.5	96.0	73.0	87.0	84.5	6.0	7.4	7.0	8.1	54.6	47.5	46.1	7.0
Namibia	1.8	1500	2.6	4.8	85.0	72.0	na	43.5	na	21.9	na	34.8	29.1	na	12.7	2.2
Niger	7.7	634	3.2	7.4	94.0	81.0	95.0	85.0	1.0	2.7	4.0	12.3	51.4	48.8	43.7	4.2
Nigeria	108.5	1160	3.2	6.3	86.0	65.0	72.0	44.6	10.0	4.2	18.0	51.2	30.3	21.8	13.5	3.1
Rwanda	7.2	680	3.3	7.4	98.0	92.0	94.0	92.8	2.0	3.0	3.0	4.3	49.2	46.2	45.7	4.1
SaoTome	0.1		2.4	na	na	67.0	na	na	na	na	na	na	na	na	na	na
Senegal	7.3	1208	2.8	3.5	68.0	62.0	83.0	80.6	6.0	6.2	11.0	13.1	33.5	27.8	27.0	0.7
Seychelles	0.1	3892	na	na	na	na	na	na	na	na	na	na	44.0	na	na	na
Sierra Leone	4.2	1061	2.1	5.2	87.0	68.0	78.0	69.6	11.0	14.1	11.0	16.4	35.5	27.7	24.7	3.1
Somalia	7.5	861	3.2	5.8	83.0	64.0	81.0	75.6	6.0	8.4	13.0	16.0	29.4	23.8	22.2	2.6
South Africa	35.3	4852	2.4	3.2	53.0	40.0	32.0	13.6	30.0	24.4	39.0	62.0	36.0	11.5	4.9	0.8
Sudan	25.2	1042	2.8	5.4	90.0	78.0	82.0	63.4	5.0	4.3	14.0	32.3	35.1	28.8	22.3	2.6
Swaziland	0.8	2405	3.0	10.5	96.0	67.0	na	74.0	na	9.0	na	17.0	35.5	na	26.3	7.5
Tanzania	27.3	557	3.4	10.3	95.0	67.0	92.0	85.6	3.0	4.5	6.0	9.9	46.8	43.1	40.1	6.9
Togo	3.5	752	2.9	6.2	90.0	74.0	78.0	64.3	9.0	6.3	13.0	29.4	41.0	32.0	26.4	3.3
Uganda	18.8	499	3.6	6.1	95.0	90.0	91.0	85.9	3.0	4.4	6.0	9.7	44.6	40.6	38.3	2.5
Zaire	35.6	380	2.8	4.8	78.0	61.0	82.0	71.5	9.0	12.9	9.0	15.6	36.9	30.3	26.4	2.0
Zambia	8.5	767	3.4	7.1	83.0	50.0	79.0	37.9	8.0	7.8	13.0	54.9	31.5	24.9	11.9	3.7
Zimbabwe	9.7	1469	3.2	5.9	87.0	72.0	79.0	64.7	8.0	5.6	13.0	29.7	40.6	32.1	26.3	2.7
Sub-Saharan Africa	500.0	475	2.8	5.2	85.0	69.0	79.0	67.6	8.1	7.7	12.9	24.7	38.6	30.5	26.1	2.4
Least Developed C'tries	440.0	237	2.5	5.3	92.0	78.0	83.2	72.4	5.8	7.5	11.0	20.1	38.8	32.3	28.1	2.8
Developing Countries	4070.0	770	2.3	4.0	78.0	63.0	72.0	60.9	11.3	12.7	16.7	26.4	43.9	31.6	26.7	1.7
Industrial Countries	1210 0	17017	0.8	1.4	39.0	27.0	22.2	11.0	36.4	26.9	41.4	62.1	48.8	10.8	5.4	0.6
World	5280.0	3836	1.8	2.9	66.0	55.0	56.5	48.5	19.0	16.3	24.5	35.2	45.0	25.4	21.8	1.1

Source: UNDP, Human Development Report 1992

* Urban Population Growth minus Population Growth Rate

population density of most rural areas has, in many cases, led to constraints on land availability. The economic crisis of the past decade and a half, and the structural adjustment programmes (SAP) that have followed, have caused a contraction of urban employment opportunities for would-be rural emigrants. Due to investment in primary and secondary education many of the youth now remaining in the countryside are better educated than their parents' generation and often less satisfied with a strictly agrarian life.

Similarly, fundamental changes in rural communities have, it could be argued, influenced demand for NARE. In the transition from long forest fallow to shorter bush fallow, shifting settlement patterns and agricultural systems have given way to the establishment of permanent villages and more intensified agricultural techniques. Houses, roads, mills, and other village infrastructure have been built, generating employment in construction, operation and maintenance. Because of the increase in rural population density, there is now pressure on the availability of natural resources as well as land. The transition from freely available to scarce, market-mediated natural resources such as water and wood is increasingly taking place, giving rise to 'renewable' consumer goods to meet basic needs. Furthermore, under structural adjustment programmes, government and parastatal provision of rural social services and productive infrastructure, as well as wholesale and retail marketing services have been severely curtailed, often leaving demand suspended until a local market response is mustered. Rural demand for health, education, agricultural marketing services and productive inputs, as well as transport infrastructure all provide entry points for the development of NARE.

More revealing are the reasons rural households themselves give for resorting to NARE. Wealthier households often mention 'profit-maximisation', whereas middle and lower income households - i.e. the majority - emphasise 'risk-minimisation' and 'income stabilisation'. Risks are perceived primarily in terms of the vagaries of climate and market prices for agricultural produce, but also relate to socio-political risks, such as changing access to land, personal misfortune, illness and war. The mere fact that household economic activities span a wide array of employment activities with varying rates of return, reduces the risk of total income failure. Furthermore, each activity is likely to offer different payment schedules. Thus, NARE may provide sources of income in the off-agricultural season.

Berkvens' (1996) in-depth study of rural dwellers in a Zimbabwean communal area is illustrative, revealing a combination of long-, medium- and short-term considerations influencing engagement in NARE. Long-term population pressure and drought conditions gradually undermined people's confidence in agriculture as a provider of livelihood. Over the medium-term, government structural adjustment policies caused retrenchment and contraction of job opportunities in the cities, whereas households' short-term objectives of risk minimisation, income stabilisation and/or profit maximisation resulted in the juggling of agrarian and non-agrarian opportunities resulting from seasonal climatic and market fluctuations.

The question is why people continue to engage in agricultural activities at all. In Berkvens' case study the answer encompassed: the relatively high cost of purchased food, drastic cutbacks in government social service provisioning and the declining value of ex-migrant workers' pensions which made village life and an agrarian livelihood a vital refuge, and people's attachment to the cultural values of their agrarian ancestors. Rural areas are considered by the inhabitants to offer a more moral environment for raising children and caring for the elderly.

This moral preference for village life and agrarian pursuits leads to the question of the changing social identity of individuals and households involved in the de-agrarianisation process. Since the 1960s there has been a strong emphasis on the impact of urbanisation on changing identities. Particular attention has been accorded to the way ethnicity is redefined, if not created, to enhance the security or status of the individual in new urban and political settings (e.g. Cohen 1969, Obbo 1982). However, there is very little documentation on the effect of occupational change *per se* on social identity. Does income diversification result in the reformulation of social identity? The question has as yet not been addressed in the literature, and the answer can only be surmised.

To the extent that youth are often the most prominent segment of the population involved in the move away from strictly agrarian occupational pursuits in rural village life, the projection of their social identity as something other than farmers or future farmers could be established on actual occupational grounds. Furthermore, there may be a willingness, if not eagerness, to distance themselves from being identified as farmers. They are greatly influenced by western lifestyles exhibited in the media which now percolate into African village life and the growth of consumerism associated with current economic liberalisation policies. These relatively new influences most likely combine with age-old tensions between generations. In so doing, generational change increasingly takes the form of a youthful rejection of parents' values and an adoption of distinctive fashions and lifestyles, not unlike that experienced in the West.

On the other hand, middle-aged rural dwellers involved in occupational change are less likely to project a new social identity based on occupational grounds and may even attempt to mask their non-agrarian activities. They have been born and reared in rural societies where farming was the main, sometimes exclusive, occupation and way of life. They are integral members of a society whose psyche and morality are rooted in an agrarian perspective. To project a different social identity based on occupational change in these circumstances would put the individual at risk of social ostracism, as suggested by Bank in Chapter 11. Thus, they engage in elaborate efforts to reconfirm their agrarian roots, which is not surprising in rural settings where business cycles are still heavily influenced by the boom and bust of annual harvests, and principles of mutual support are premised on social conformity to community norms. More than that, farming is considered the most respectable and honourable rural occupation, and thus has a moral compulsion as the community members' 'essential identity'.[5]

There is of course one additional obstacle to social identity transformation based on changing rural occupations. In the vast number of cases, occupational change has not involved occupational specialisation. Income diversification has caused its individual practitioners to become jugglers of several different occupational pursuits, such that no one activity gains prominence in their purses let alone their minds (Seppällä 1996). Thus, the lowest common denominator principle works. Those engaged in income diversification retain their identity as farmers since that is their fallback and one of their most vital economic activities in terms of household self-provisioning. In other words, they are still subsistence farmers in the last instance.

Whether or not individual villagers are directly engaged in NARE or identify themselves as practitioners of new occupations, villagers generally throughout Sub-Saharan Africa are experiencing the effects of de-agrarianisation as consumers. If one focuses on what non-agricultural activities mean for village consumers, one finds three main tendencies at work: the replacement of 'free goods' with market-provisioned goods; changing demand for traditional handicraft products; and the development and proliferation of a local service economy. The first is clearly the case with regard to water, energy and fodder products which have become commodified goods in many places experiencing increasing population pressure. Secondly, traditional African handicraft skills were not necessarily part of any market exchange, usually being produced for domestic usage or ceremonial purposes. Thus, in some cases where these uses have been displaced, handicraft skills may be revitalised and reshaped by commodification. On the other hand, they may be crushed by increasing market influence and changing demand patterns at the local level associated with income diversification and NARE expansion.

The third tendency, that of mushrooming service activities especially petty trade, dominates NARE activities in many areas, whether its incidence is measured in terms of time taken in performing the activities, numbers of individuals involved, or income generated. This is related to the fact that petty trade tends to be the easiest entry occupation not requiring high educational attainment or specialised training, and is amenable to being combined with agricultural or other non-agricultural economic activities depending on the season. Even in the absence of entrepreneurial traditions, traders may surface in rural areas who fashion endogenous ideologies and exchange practices to create a new occupational niche, as Bank describes in Chapter 11. Exogenously, liberalisation policies of many African governments have facilitated the movement into trade. Besides noting the association trade has with the micro-level calculations of individual economic agents' and meso-level government policies, it is important to stress that the growing dominance of trade and service activities more generally has a profound macro-level consequence, namely it constitutes a pronounced sectoral shift from agriculture to services. This shift is in conformity with a worldwide tendency for the service sector to increase (Table 1).[6] However, in industrialised countries, the growth of the service sector has arisen from a shrinkage of the industrial sector, i.e. 'de-industrialisation', whereas in Africa the small industrial sector has remained virtually stagnant in size while the agricultural sector has given way to services.

Turning a Blind Eye to De-agrarianisation

De-industrialisation has been a recognised tendency in industrialised countries since the late 1970s and has engendered a great deal of policy concern as well as new creative visions of post-industrial economies for the 21st century (e.g. Singh 1977; Blackaby 1987). By stark contrast, *de-agrarianisation* in Africa has been ignored, despite its longer duration and current intensification. The policy recommendations emanating from the World Bank and other international and national agencies over the past decade have been rooted in the stale assumption dating back to the colonial period that Africa is fundamentally an agrarian continent whose interface with the world market now and for the foreseeable future is in agricultural commodity exchange. Why has western literature so determinedly avoided acknowledging de-agrarianisation as a process, let alone confronting its policy implications?

The answer may lie in the straightjacket of theoretical concepts, models and indeed moral imperatives that have underpinned development thinking over the past forty years, particularly the notion of sectoral development as a trajectory leading from agriculture to industry. Since Adam Smith, the expansion of non-agricultural activities has been primarily seen in terms of a changing relationship between agriculture and industry. Most development policy since the 1950s has centred on the 'right' relationship between the two, i.e. whether agriculture or industry is the lead sector, or alternatively whether it is possible to engender a balanced development of them both simultaneously. From Marx's use of England as the classic example of 'primitive accumulation' in agriculture and industrialisation, to debates about Soviet industrialisation and the role of 'heavy' industry, to the Latin American debate about the role of 'import substitution' industry, in all cases, successful industrialisation was depicted as the road to achieving development and its attendant higher standard of living for the general populace. Urbanisation was seen as a corollary of industrialisation.

Lewis (1954) assumed that marginal productivity of labour in densely populated rural settlements of the developing world was zero or near zero, such that a transfer of labour from rural agriculture to urban industry could occur without a decline in agricultural productivity. In the 1950s and 1960s, labour migration studies proliferated (Gulliver 1955; Mitchell 1957; Elkan 1960). Originally they focused on the implications of 'stabilising labour', i.e. the cessation of circular migration and the permanent settlement of labourers and their families in urban areas. By the mid-1960s, concern had switched from 'stabilising' to 'curtailing' urban labour migration. Researchers recognised that the educational levels of urban migrants were rising while job availability was declining. The so-called 'school-leaver problem' encapsulated the unbridgeable gap between the material expectations of the populace and the delivery of jobs. Economic analysts and government policy makers converged on the view that migration from the countryside was depleting agriculture.

'Informal sector' studies came to the fore beginning with the now famous ILO mission report on Kenya (ILO 1972). They constituted a challenge to the colonial notion that urban economic activities necessarily had to be conducted within the formal economy. Subsequent studies raised severe doubts about the development potential of the informal sector, arguing that its activities were marginal and destined to remain marginal. It was in the context of such mixed judgements about the informal sector that Lipton's (1977) notion of 'urban bias' took hold in the African literature.

Bates (1981) used the existence of high rates of urban migration, the burgeoning payroll of governments and parastatals in urban capitals, and the low performance of protected industries, as the empirical basis for making a simple, attention-grabbing critique of African government policies. In the name of development, which was taken as synonymous with industrialisation, African states were overcontrolling their economies, skewing incentives and infrastructural investment towards urban areas and generally undermining rural production which was the real material base of African economies. In Bates's eyes, such 'urban bias' was exploitative rent-seeking on the part of bureaucratic elites who had ceased to represent the interests of the broad masses of the agrarian peasantry. The outcome was a decline in peasant incentives and national production.

Perhaps because of the simplicity of the analysis - its portrayal of a single category of agents as perpetrators of the predicament - subsequent debate was polarised into defenders and critics of African government policies. Underlying premises about the agrarian nature of the continent were taken for granted by both sides. As critics gained in strength, the way was cleared for the introduction of IMF and World Bank reforms of African economies. Structural adjustment packages were deemed to strike at the enemy, i.e. the African state and its maligned policies. Currency devaluation and the dismantling of state marketing agencies were intended to enable the market to determine the 'right prices'. Peasant agricultural producers, it was anticipated, would find their rightful niche in the world market, unfettered by state controls. Yet, structural adjustment has been a period of heightened peasant involvement in NARE and accelerating urban migration in many countries. The reforms have not as yet brought about the intended invigoration of the peasant agrarian sector. Even countries like Ghana and Tanzania which were hailed as World Bank (1994) success stories in the early phases of structural adjustment, have so far, along with the majority of African countries, failed to achieve 'economic take-off' (Engberg-Pedersen, Gibbon, Raikes and Udshort 1996; Sowa 1996). Is it necessary to return to the old debate about peasant rationality or is it time to question western development models' applicability to Sub-Saharan Africa?

Declining Utility of the Informal Sector Concept

As evidence mounts against the wisdom of the neo-liberal experiment in Africa, the informal sector has been a refuge not only for economically disenchanted peasants but also for theoretically disoriented social scientists. The original emphasis of informal sector work was on urban areas (e.g. Hart 1973), but rural informal sector studies have gained currency.

Curiously, over the past two decades the 'informal sector' has remained an amorphous concept defined more by what it is not rather than what it is. Most authors refer to it as the converse of the formal sector, a residual status that encompasses people working outside the formal wage sector and outside established fiscal procedures. Informal employment is characterised by unregulated markets, easy entry conditions related to a lack of formally acquired skills, low investment, and the use of local materials. Since it is generally assumed that informal sector participants are not engaged in 'traditional' peasant agriculture, the sector denotes a realm wedged between the non-agrarian formal sector and the agrarian subsistence sector.

Definitional fuzziness has made the measurement of informal sector activities problematic. The vast range of activities pursued in the informal sector cut across industrial and service sectors and all shades of legality and illegality are included rendering data collection difficult. Even when legality is not at stake, the sector encompasses such a vast spectrum of incomes and skills that it is virtually impossible to distinguish formal from informal. The lack of accurate statistics not only precludes precise awareness of the extent of informal sector activities, but also prevents rigorous comparisons of productivity between formal and informal sectors.

The absence of accurate comparative data has left the door open for a polarised policy debate between those who see the informal sector as the embryo of economic development and those who see it as a sponge of low productivity and poverty. Structural adjustment has brought this debate to the fore again. The SAP-inspired dismantling of parastatals and government places new expectations on the informal sector's economic potential. While some view SAP as a golden opportunity for the full development of the formal sector, others view it as an abuse of the sector, off-loading social welfare provisioning, formerly the responsibility of government, onto an ill-prepared sector (Grey-Johnson 1992).

The circularity of this debate has been continuing now for over twenty years. Meanwhile, through drastic SAP cutbacks in government productive and social services, the dismantling of marketing boards and parastatal and civil service retrenchment, massive numbers of people have left formal employment and large numbers of government-provided services have been erased. The 'informal sector' has filled this vacuum. Whether or not it has done so with greater competence and efficiency is debatable. There are however two very clear and far-reaching implications for both categorisation and policy-making. The first is that the formal sector rather than the informal sector is now the residual. For example in van Dijk's

Accra household survey (Chapter 6), only 11 per cent of the people interviewed worked in the formal sector compared with 75 per cent who participated in the informal sector. Similarly, labour statistics cited in Bagachwa's Chapter 8 record 7 per cent of the total working population in Tanzania in the formal sector relative to 21 per cent in the informal sector. So too, value added in the informal sector exceeded that of the formal sector. Gaidzanwa in Chapter 9 notes that the Zimbabwean formal sector generates 7,000 jobs per year which pales in comparison with the 100,000 school-leavers entering the labour market annually. It hardly makes sense to refer to an informal sector, vis-à-vis the hollow shell that the formal sector of most African national economies now constitutes.

Under market liberalisation, the road from black to parallel to open markets has rendered the informal sector concept largely meaningless. The legitimacy of informal sector activities is no longer in question, thereby undermining a key feature distinguishing it from the formal sector. On the other hand, the fiscal character of the informal sector has moved to the fore, becoming one of the central dilemmas of African national economies. Tax-dodging is all pervasive. A vicious cycle sets in whereby the African state relinquishes its capability to tax at source and must rely on individual citizens and firms who have no tradition of tax accountability and may in fact harbour a historical aversion to direct forms of taxation from the colonial period. The state is unable to exercise its fiscal functions effectively and becomes even more under-resourced. Tax evasion tendencies in the economy also undermine attempts at measuring productivity and output, since most economic agencies are reluctant to let the full extent of their economic activities be known.

Thus, the 'informal sector', which has always been an amorphous concept, is now even more imprecise and non-descript, and, it could be argued, no longer empirically relevant. However, given the enormous intellectual energy that has gone into it over the last 25 years, there is bound to be inertia in dropping it. Furthermore, many foreign aid programmes have centred on assistance to informal sector agents. There is thus considerable material momentum, even vested interest, in 'informal sector development'. In other words, the concept will have its own motivating force for a considerable time to come, regardless of whether it corresponds with empirical reality. It would be unrealistic therefore to advocate its abandonment. However, its deficiencies militate for a rethinking of the developmental processes currently existing in Sub-Saharan Africa before new more relevant categories can be defined and measured. The 'informal sector' concept tends to mask the linkages that individuals and households in Sub-Saharan Africa are effecting between urban and rural areas, and between different occupations, income sources and social identities. It is in this regard that tracing the process of de-agrarianisation becomes a useful endeavour.

Towards an Understanding of African De-agrarianisation

The following chapters of this book consist of recent research findings on de-agrarianisation from a wide range of countries throughout Sub-Saharan Africa. The authors represent the disciplines of economics, geography, anthropology, sociology and political science. Focusing on the unfolding de-agrarianisation process, the multi-disciplinary nature of the contributions affords coverage of a number of different aspects including: income diversification, rural and urban employment patterns, labour markets, food security, migration, rural-urban interaction, landlessness, structural adjustment, the informal sector, rural industries, small-scale enterprise growth, entrepreneurship, gender, class formation, and public works programmes. Similarly, the variety of disciplinary perspectives offers levels of analysis ranging from that of the individual to the nation-state.

Not surprisingly, the research methodologies that underpin the chapters also vary. However, most of them combine synchronic and diachronic data. Recent quantitative survey results and qualitative interview material are related to the historical development of land and labour relations. What is clearly apparent is that there is no uniformity or linearity in the way de-agrarianisation unfolds. Divided into five geographical sections, the chapters which follow provide vital case study material needed to discern the different tendencies of de-agrarianisation for comparison both within Africa and with other continents.

This introduction has deliberately stopped short of summarising the authors' arguments in the belief that readers are better served by first-hand contact with the case study material chapter by chapter. The author best conveys the significance of his/her findings in its local setting. Furthermore, no attempt has been make to standardise terminology throughout the book. Each author has employed concepts adapted to his/her country context. The final chapter of this book, however, juxtaposes the case study findings to evaluate the concept of de-agrarianisation continentally, in the hopes of gaining a deeper understanding of the proliferating forms of economic livelihood and occupational identity in Sub-Saharan Africa.

Notes

* Parts of this introduction draw on my previously published article entitled 'De-agrarianisation and Rural Employment in Sub-Saharan Africa: A Sectoral Perspective', *World Development*, Vol. 24, No. 1, (1996), 97-111. The concept of 'de-agrarianisation' was first discussed at a workshop held at the Afrika-Studiecentrum, Leiden in May 1994. I am grateful to those in attendance whose case study material and theoretical criticism helped revise the concept. See Bryceson and van der Laan (1994) for a summary of the workshop papers and discussions.

1. Besides enumeration difficulties which influence the accuracy of total counts, there is a proliferation of definitions of African urban areas between countries and even within countries from census to census which affects the calculation of population growth rates.

2. Tanzania's unfolding patterns and rates of urbanisation are typical of the continent as a whole. The country's African urbanisation dates back to World War II, gaining strength during the 1950s, fuelled by the emergence of an educated African elite. The migration floodgates opened in the 1960s as job expectations rose following the establishment of state-financed primary schools and minimum wage legislation. The latter effectively established a 'family wage' for urban employees facilitating the reunification of families in towns (Bryceson 1985). Urban growth rates rose to a high of 10 per cent during the 1970s, then slackened in the 1980s as the urban family wage vanished under the duress of a national economic crisis (ILO/JASPA 1978 and 1982; Jamal and Weeks 1993). Interestingly, during this period, urban migration veered towards the smaller towns with populations of between 20,000 to 50,000 and away from the primate and larger cities, a reflection of the fact that the former were areas where urban household self-provisioning of food was more feasible (Bryceson 1993). Municipal estimates suggest that the pattern of urbanisation has reverted to rapid primate city growth in the 1990s as the reinstatement of foreign aid flows and the effects of market liberalisation concentrate wealth and centralise economic activity in 'profitable' centres of demand. Market liberalisation and the decontrol of trade have provided the impetus for recent increased migration because education credentials are no longer such a barrier to attaining an economic foothold, however tenuous, in urban areas. Youth in large numbers, particularly from agriculturally depressed and educationally deprived regions, descend on Dar es Salaam in search of a better life as petty traders. The Minister of State in the Prime Minister's Office estimated that there is an influx of about 300,000 hawkers, popularly known as *machingas*, to Dar es Salaam every year ('Remove Corrupt Officials from City Council', Guardian (DSM) 13/4/96; 'City Brewing Trouble, Traders Tell Govt', Guardian (DSM) 13/4/96. This number is exceptionally large and would have to infer considerable circular migration. In any case, it testifies to policy makers' perceptions of the problem.

3. For example: Burkina Faso: Reardon, Delgado and Matlon 1992; Cameroon: Baumann 1984; Cote d'Ivoire: Vijverberg 1989-90; Kenya: Carlsen 1980, Evans and Ngau 1991; Malawi: Centre for Social Research 1983; Nigeria; Oyebanji 1980; Rwanda: von Braun, de Haen and Blanken (1991); Tanzania: Havnevik 1993; Zaire: Tshibaka 1992; Zambia: Milimo and Fisseha 1986; and general: Byerlee and Eicher 1972; Liedholm 1973; Kilby and Liedholm 1986, Haggblade, Hazell and Brown 1989.

4. Urban households' agricultural activities tend to be of a small-scale subsistence nature or, in wealthier urban households, significant agricultural enterprises are sometimes pursued, but in those cases they do so usually by way of capital export to rural areas. Thus the labour performed is of a rural nature, although its contractual form, usually waged labour, may mark a departure from preceeding patterns (Bryceson 1993).
5. Along similar lines, it has been noted in social science surveys that many African women tend to identify themselves first and foremost as 'mothers', despite their important role in providing material needs for their families through farming and cash-earning non-agrarian activities. This is a reflection of the social recognition they receive for bearing and rearing children in contrast to the lack of recognition their food-provisioning and cash-earning work receives in the male-biased communities in which they live (e.g. Caplan 1995; Dupré 1995).
6. In this chapter, 'industry' refers to mass production of consumer and producer goods by occupationally specialised labour in factory organisations producing on the basis of science and technological advances spurred by the competitive forces of the world market. The 'tertiary' sector, otherwise known as the service sector, is in most classifications a residual category consisting of anything that is not designated as agricultural or industrial. To avoid this method of categorisation, 'services' are defined restrictively as the value-added production of goods and activities provisioned by either public or private economic agents. In the private sector this refers to goods and services which meet an individualised (as opposed to industrial mass product) demand involving customised supply, largely contingent on specific delivery locations and timing. Public sector services embrace adminstration, transport and energy provisioning for goods and service exchange flows. Thus, the service sector is generally two-tiered with a private domain of activities functioning in the infrastructural context of the public-operated domain. Above all, the distinguishing feature of the service sector is not any disassociation from agriculture or industry per se, but its delivery characteristic, i.e. ready accessibility of goods and services tailored to the mobility and time constraints of clients.

References

BATES, R.H. 1981, *Markets and States in Tropical Africa*, Berkeley, University of California Press

BAUMANN, E. 1984, *Activités Informelles en Milieu Rural Véhicule de Transformations Socio-Economique: Le Cas du Centre Rural de SSA, Centre-Sud Cameroun*, Université de Bordeaux, Institute d'Etude Politique

BERKVENS, R. 1996, *A Choice for Farm and Nonfarm Work? Household Income Diversification and Development in Mutoko Communal Area, Zimbabwe*, Catholic University of Nijmegen, the Netherlands, Third World Centre, Master's Thesis

BLACKABY, F. (ed.) 1987, *De-Industrialisation*, Hampshire, U.K., Avebury

BRAUN, J. von, H. de HAEN & J. BLANKEN 1991, *Commercialization of Agriculture under Population Pressure: Effects on Production, Consumption and Nutrition in Rwanda*, IFPRI Research Report 85, Washington DC, IFPRI

BRYCESON, D.F. 1996, 'De-agrarianisation and Rural Employment in Sub-Saharan Africa: A Sectoral Perspective', *World Development*, vol. 24, no. 1, 97-111

____, 1993, *Liberalizing Tanzania's Food Trade: Public and Private Faces of Urban Marketing Policy*, London, James Currey

____, 1985, 'Women's Proletarianization and the Family Wage in Tanzania', in Afshar, H. (ed.), *Women, Work, and Ideology in the Third World*, London, Tavistock Publications, 128-152

BRYCESON, D.F. & C. van der LAAN 1994, *Proceedings of the 'De-agrarianization and Rural Employment' Workshop held at the Afrika-Studiecentrum, Leiden, May 1994*, Leiden, Afrika-Studiecentrum Working Paper vol. 20

BYERLEE, D. & C. EICHER 1972, *Rural Employment, Migration and Economic Development: Theoretical Issues and Empirical Evidence from Africa*, Michigan State University, Department of Agricultural Economics Working Paper no. 20

CAPLAN, P. 1995, 'Children are Our Wealth and We Want Them: A Difficult Pregnancy on Northern Mafia Island, Tanzania', in D.F. Bryceson (ed.), *Women Wielding the Hoe: Lessons from Rural Africa for Feminist Theory and Development Practice*, Oxford, Berg Publishers

CARLSEN, J. 1980, *Economic and Social Transformation in Rural Kenya*, Uppsala, Scandinavian Institute of Africa Studies

CENTRE for SOCIAL RESEARCH 1983, *A Note on the Nature and Extent of the Small-Scale Enterprises in Malawi*, Zomba, Malawi

COHEN, A. 1969, *Custom and Politics in Urban Africa: A Study of Hausa Migrants in Yoruba Towns*, London, Routledge & Kegan Paul

DUPRE, M-C. 1995, 'Mothers, Healers and Farmers in Congo', in D.F. Bryceson (ed.), *Women Wielding the Hoe: Lessons from Rural Africa for Feminist Theory and Development Practice*, Oxford, Berg Publishers

ELKAN, W. 1960, *Migrants and Proletarians: Urban Labour in the Economic Development of Uganda*, London, Oxford University Press

ENGBERG-PEDERSEN, P., P. GIBBON, P. RAIKES & L. UDSHORT (eds) 1996, *Limits of Adjustment in Africa: The Effects of Economic Liberalization 1986-95*, London, James Currey

EVANS, H.E. & P. NGAU 1991, 'Rural-Urban Relations, Household Income Diversification and Agricultural Productivity', *Development and Change*, vol. 22

GREY-JOHNSON, C. 1992, 'The African Informal Sector at the Crossroads: Emerging Policy Options', *Africa Development*, vol. 17, no. 1, 65-91

GULLIVER, P. 1955, *Labour Migration in a Rural Economy: A Study of the Ngoni and Ndendeuli of Southern Tanganyika*, Nairobi, East African Literature Bureau

HAGGBLADE, S., P. HAZELL & J. BROWN 1989, 'Non-Farm Linkages in Rural Sub-Saharan Africa', *World Development*, vol. 17, no. 8, 1173-1201

HART, K. 1973, 'Informal Income Opportunities and Urban Employment in Ghana', *Journal of Modern Afican Studies*, no. 11, 61-89

HAVNEVIK, K.J. 1993, *Tanzania: The Limits to Development from Above*, Sweden, Nordiska Africainstitutet

ILO 1972, *Employment, Incomes and Equality: A Strategy for Increasing Productive Employment in Kenya*, Geneva, ILO

ILO/JASPA 1978, *Tanzania: Towards Self-Reliance*, Addis Ababa, Jobs and Skills Program for Africa (JASPA)

____ 1982, *Tanzania: Basic Needs in Danger*, Addis Ababa, JASPA

JAMAL, V. & J. WEEKS 1993, *Africa Misunderstood or Whatever Happened to the Rural-Urban Gap?*, Basingstoke, Macmillan

KILBY, P. & C. LIEDHOLM 1986, *The Role of Non-Farm Activities in the Rural Economy: Employment and Enterprise Development Policy Analysis*, Cambridge MA, Harvard Institute for International Development Discussion Paper no. 7

LEWIS, W.A. 1954, 'Economic Development with Unlimited Supplies of Labour', *Manchester School of Economic and Social Studies*, vol. 22

LIEDHOLM, C. 1973, *Research on Employment in the Rural Non-Farm Sector in Africa*, East Lansing, Michigan State University

LIPTON, M. 1977, *Why Poor People Stay Poor: Urban Bias in World Development*, London, Temple Smith

MILIMO, M. & Y. FISSEHA 1986, *Rural Small-Scale Enterprises in Zambia: Results of a 1985 Country Wide Survey*, Michigan, Michigan State University Working Paper no. 28

MITCHELL, J. C. 1957, 'Africans in Industrial Towns in Northern Rhodesia', Report of the Duke of Edinburgh's Study Conference, vol. 2, London

OBBO, C. 1982, *African Women: Their Struggle for Economic Independence*, London, Zed Press

OYEBANJI, J.O. 1980, 'Small-Scale Industries in Nigeria: Their Spatial and Structural Characteristics', *Nigerian Geographical Journal*, vol 23, no. 1/2, 99-111

REARDON, T., C. DELGADO & P. MATLON 1992, 'Determinants and Effects of Income Diversification amongst Farm Households in Burkina Faso', *Journal of Development Studies*, vol. 28, no. 2, 264-96

SEPPÄLLÄ, P. 1996, 'The Paradoxes of Accumulation: The Complex Strategies of Diversification and Sharing in Rural Tanzania', Paper presented at the Local Economy Seminar, Scandinavian Africa Institute, Helsinki, May 1996

SINGH, A. 1977, 'UK Industry and the World Economy: A Case of De-industrialization', *Cambridge Journal of Economics*, vol. 1, 113-136

SOWA, N.K. 1996, 'Adjustment in Africa: Lessons from Ghana', *Overseas Development Institute Briefing Paper*, no. 3, July 1996

TELLEGEN, N. 1997 forthcoming, *Rural Entrepreneurs and Economic Stagnation: Development of African Non-Agricultural Activities in Mchinji and Salima Districts, Malawi*, University of Amsterdam, Ph.D. Thesis

TELLEGEN, N. 1993, *Rural Employment in Sub-Saharan Africa: A Bibliography*, Leiden, Afrika-Studiecentrum Working Paper, vol. 18

TSHIBAKA, T. 1992, *Labor in the Rural Household Economy of the Zairian Basin*, Research Report 90, Washington, DC, International Food Policy Research Institute

VIJVERBERG, W.P.M. 1989-90, 'Non-Farm Self-Employment and the Informal Sector in Cote d'Ivoire: A Test of Categorical Identity', *Journal of Developing Areas*, vol. 24, no. 4, 1989-90, 523-42

WORLD BANK 1994, *Adjustment in Africa: Reform, Results and the Road Ahead*, New York, Oxford University Press

II

HORN OF AFRICA

2

Coping with Famine and Poverty: The Dynamics of Non-Agricultural Rural Employment in Darfur, Sudan

Hamid el Bashir Ibrahim

The history of famine in Darfur during the twentieth century is inextricably linked to recurrent drought and war. At least eleven major famines have occurred over the last ninety years, four prior to the formation of the modern nation-state, three during colonial rule, and four since independence.[1] Food shortages have been almost continuous during the last ten years.

Darfur state covers an area of roughly 500,000 square kilometres in the western-most part of Sudan. The climate is arid or semi-arid, with rainfall ranging from almost zero in the north to 800 mm per annum in the south. In 1993 the total population of Darfur was about 3.9 million people of which 71 per cent were farmers, 15 per cent townspeople and 14 per cent nomadic pastoralists. The region's economy is predominantly agricultural, involving peasant subsistence farming and keeping of cattle, camels and sheep. Millet and sorghum are the major subsistence crops in the north and south respectively. Groundnuts, watermelons, sesame and chickpeas are the main cash crops.

The cumulative effect of the famines has engendered diverse coping strategies in the form of a reorientation of rural activities away from agriculture into rural and urban service sectors. This chapter investigates this evolution based on surveys conducted in sixteen villages during the famine of 1992-3. Thirty households were interviewed in each village which, depending on the locality, accounted for between 30-60 per cent of the village population. The sample communities were selected to represent different geographical locations in terms of distance from urban centres, ethnic groups, and modes of production. Villagers were asked questions about their involvement in the major forms of livelihood, namely: agriculture, pastoralism, migration, petty trade, and small-scale enterprises. Various data collection techniques were employed including rapid rural appraisal questionnaires, informal interviews, life histories, and participant and non-participant observation.[2]

The chapter attempts to elicit the contrasting coping strategies of rural dwellers during the famines of 1984-5 and 1992-3 and the nature of socio-economic changes in the interim period. The first section reviews signs of the declining capacity of the agricultural sector to provide viable livelihoods. Villagers' strategies against this decline are described before moving on to a consideration of traditional off-farm means of coping with famine, i.e. labour migration and wage employment. The emergence and significance of the rural service sector is examined and conclusions are drawn about the results of trends over the past decade.

Agricultural Decline

Northern Darfur is primarily agrarian with a majority of its population classified as farmers, but several indicators show the declining capacity of the agricultural sector to sustain the populace, the most telling being that of food deficit experienced by the population. As Table 1 demonstrates in every year between 1984 and 1993 the deficit exceeded 50 per cent of food requirements, with five out of the eight years in fact experiencing a deficit of more than 75 per cent.

Table 1: Food Deficits in Northern Darfur, 1984-92

Year	Shortfall from estimated requirements (%)
1984-5	95
1986-7	73
1987-8	79
1988-9	77
1989-90	54
1990-1	89
1991-2	71
1992-3	80

Source: Save the Children Fund UK Report, 1993

Harvests of the main traditional cash crops - groundnuts and sesame - have fluctuated around a low average. Amongst richer peasants, there has been a shift towards a new horticultural subsector, especially in the oasis and *wadi* areas (i.e. seasonal stream beds of clay soils) of northern Darfur. *Wadi* land is inherently more fertile and has the ability to preserve moisture for longer periods than the dominant sandy *goz* soils. Oranges, mangoes, limes, onions, okra and tomatoes are grown. Increasing emphasis on these crops implies a change in orientation from food to cash crops, wider use of agricultural inputs and animal traction, year-round production rather than sole reliance on seasonal rainfall, and most importantly a growing redundancy of agricultural labour. Due to the small size of the *wadi* gardens, known locally as *geneina*, some members of the *wadi*-farming households are released from agricultural work and can become involved in income-generating ventures or wage employment in or nearby the village. The most common form of employment is on large holdings owned by village merchants and wealthy farmers. The new cropping patterns have thus availed the large landowners of year-round labour for gardening, watering and local transportation.

However, not all households have access to *wadi* land and it in itself does not necessarily translate into riches. Only 34 per cent of farmers were involved in *wadi* production and they face marketing and transportation constraints which force them to sell their produce *in situ* at prices considerably below those prevailing in the towns. Furthermore, although *wadi* cultivation is a drought-coping strategy it has not escaped the effects of drought. Water shortages are widespread. The gum Arabic *hashab* tree, which was traditionally used for soil fertility regeneration, has disappeared as a result of persistent drought. The continuous farming of the *wadi* without fertilisation and soil regeneration from running water has resulted in declining soil fertility. During the 1990-1 drought, water wells used for irrigation dried out to the extent that 8 per cent of the Gaghna village population had to sell their *wadi* gardens to secure food and medicine or the cost of migration to South Darfur, nearby urban centres, or Libya.

The limited supply of *wadi* land and the fragile economics and ecology of household agriculture are contributing to a process of land concentration at the expense of the poor. The indigenous land tenure system in rural Darfur has been historically based on the *hakura,* where land is owned by three or four *sheikhs* (i.e. tribal chiefs or landed gentry), a reward in the seventeenth century for loyalty to the Sultan of Darfur. Thus land has been unequally distributed historically and the economics of famine has accentuated the maldistribution. The landless have to pay land rent, usually in kind and locally known as *futra*, *tuaundi* or *khashm el fas* to the *sheikhs*.

The long-held notion of *goz* land abundance is no longer valid. Desert encroachment has taken its toll and peasant farmers have to cultivate larger acreages to offset the steadily declining productivity of the soil. One old man commented: 'Now we cultivate ten times more land than we used to when life was intact. Before the drought, land productivity was ten times higher'.

With meagre and falling returns from agriculture, only half of the labour effort of most farmers is devoted to the production of food or cash crops and less than 30 per cent of household food supplies are derived from own production (Table 2). These dynamics within agriculture have, among other things, resulted in a continuous food gap for the vast majority as illustrated in Table 1. The proportion of farmers who produced less than 50 per cent of their annual grain requirements (i.e. *muna* translated as 'annual means of subsistence') was 40 per cent in 1989, 100 per cent in 1990, and 82 per cent in 1992.

Table 2: Household Food Sources in Darfur, 1992-3

Sources	Percentage of households
Market	29
Own farm	27
Relief	20
Borrowing	17
Wild foods	7

Source: Author's fieldwork, Darfur 1992-3

Farming households face the difficulty of allocating household labour between employment on their own farm with its low and uncertain returns and working for cash income to meet the pressing need for food. A phrase used to describe this choice is: *'el eid mamsuka'* ('our hands are tied because they are dispersed').

Depleting Resources and Coping Strategies

Since the late 1960s and the beginning of the Sahelian drought, rural Darfurians have been through different sets of forced survival strategies which with the prolongation of drought have become inefficient, ultimately exacerbating rural poverty. More and more, they involve withdrawing resources from household agricultural production to ensure basic survival. De Waal (1987) argues that most households tried to refrain from such measures during the 1984-5 famine to preserve their agricultural livelihood. That they increasingly resorted to them during the 1991-2 famine suggests the eventual end of an agrarian livelihood for large numbers in rural Darfur.

Distress Sales of Agricultural Assets

The sale of productive assets, particularly livestock, has been a key coping mechanism during famine in Darfur. The estimated livestock loss during the 1984-5 famine due to death and distress sales was 31 per cent for camels and sheep, 47 per cent for goats, and 80 per cent for cattle. Due to persistent food shortages since then, with the exception of the 1988-9 agricultural season, livestock loss by 1993 was dramatic: 80 per cent for camels, 91 per cent for cattle, 44 per cent for sheep, 75 per cent for goats, 29 per cent for donkeys and 51 per cent for poultry (SCF-UK 1993). Average household livestock ownership declined sharply (Table 3). Moreover, rural impoverishment has been accentuated by continuously declining terms of trade between livestock and millet during the same period (SCF-UK Reports 1993; Oxfam Khartoum 1993).

Table 3: Average Livestock Ownership per Household in Rural Darfur during Two Famine Periods, 1983-4 and 1992-3

Livestock	1983-4	1992-3
Camels	2.37	0.5
Cows	9.5	0.9
Sheep	13.7	7.7
Goats	27.0	6.8
Donkeys	1.7	1.2
Poultry	4.8	2.4

Source: SCF-UK Reports 1993; De Waal 1987; Holy 1987

The sale of household belongings and assets during the 1985 famine is a well-documented survival strategy (De Waal 1987, Diab and Pyle 1987). By 1990 most valuable assets (e.g. gold, silver and beads) had been depleted and by 1993 only durable assets like agricultural lands, especially in the *wadi,* and fruit trees remained. The case of one female household head in Fetta Barno village is not untypical. Her husband had emigrated to Libya. The remittances he managed to send were not enough to obviate the need to sell most of her household assets. Before the arrival of relief food in the village, she had gradually had to sell household utensils, mattresses, beds, clothes, their two donkeys, agricultural tools and finally their three-quarters of a hectare of *wadi* land. 'For two years we haven't received any remittances from my husband', she explained. By the summer of 1993 she and her children, two of whom had dropped out of school, were relying completely on relief food, meagre donations from relatives and neighbours, and rural wage labour.

Many families in the surveyed villages were reporting the sale of trees and land. In 1990-1 in Barno village, 23 per cent of the households sold palm trees and agricultural lands. Between 1984 and 1993, 60 per cent of the households had sold their agricultural lands and fruit trees in addition to their other livestock. In 1984-5, a palm tree fetched S£50 (i.e. the equivalent of 40lb. sack of millet), but these terms also deteriorated in the 1990s. Distress sales of trees usually take place before the arrival of relief food by NGOs. 'Trees offer us a good annual income, we don't sell them unless the food situation is really difficult.'

Table 4: Average Annual Peasant Income by Source in Gaghna Village, North Darfur, 1991-2

Income Source	S£/Year
Petty trade	25,000
Fruit sales	22,000
Rainfed agriculture	18,000
Vegetable sales	10,000
Remittances	5,000

Source: Author's field notes

With fruit and vegetable sales constituting 40 per cent of household income, the sale of trees and *wadi* land implies serious impoverishment and vulnerability. It also means loss of collateral in case of credit and dowry for marriage. Relinquishing land puts the household in a position of economic distress and social restriction. Ownership of agricultural assets, already skewed prior to 1985, became even more imbalanced during the famine of 1992. The increasing centralisation of assets in the hands of a rural agro-mercantile elite has made the remaining peasant lands increasingly unviable and has fuelled a process of proletarianisation in the countryside.

Local Agricultural Wage Labour

Seasonal agricultural wage labour within rural Darfur, while placing a drain on household labour, nonetheless meets immediate cash needs. There are distinct gender patterns in the implied labour flows.

Seasonal labour migration for the millet harvest is usually undertaken by women from the far northern parts of Darfur to the central and southern regions. The period that migrant women are away, staying either with their employers' households or in the fields, ranges from two to four months during October to February. The women carry out the full range of harvest operations, including cutting, threshing and cleaning. Wages are paid in kind and amount to 8-10 per cent of the produce. Such work should enable migrant women to bring home two or three sacks of millet, i.e. just sufficient supplies to maintain a family during the summer season (March to June).

Table 5: Individual Daily Working Capacity by Agricultural Operation in Sayyah Village, North Darfur, 1993 (all figures in *mukhamas* [0.76 ha] per workday)

Agricultural operation/ Land type		Adult male or female	Elderly male or female	Youngster up to 15 years
Sowing:	dry land	1	1/4	1/2
	wet land	1	1/4	1/2
Ploughing:	virgin land	1/2	1/8	1/8
	not ploughed for 3 years	3/4	1/6	1/6
	second ploughing	1/3	1/8	1/8

Source: Author's fieldwork

Whether women resort to this form of migration depends on their domestic responsibilities, the outcome of the previous harvest, their ability to afford transportation to the workplace and their stamina. Working conditions are known to be difficult and there are obvious health hazards in this type of work over long periods (Table 5).

Another form of seasonal agricultural employment, *khareef*, is usually carried out during the rainy season from June to September when poor villagers work as much as 60 per cent of their time on others' farms. This strategy is clearly to the detriment of household food production and its long-term sustainability. Moreover, rural agricultural wages have fallen in real terms. During 1984-5, an adult's daily income was equivalent to one *kora* (1.8 kg) of millet and only one quarter as much during the 1990-1 famine (Table 6).

Table 6: Comparison of Rural Agricultural Labour Wages and Food Prices 1984-5 to 1990-1

Year	Millet price (S£ /*kora*)[1]	Sowing wage (S£/*mukhamas*)[2]	Ploughing wage (S£/*mukhamas*)[2]
1984-5	5	4	9
1988-9	2	10	15
1990-1	55	15	20

Source: Author's field data

1. *kora* = 1.8 kilogrammes
2. *mukhamas* = 0.76 hectares

Counting household daily food requirements on the basis of six members and daily food requirements of 1400gms per person, the 1984-5 wage could purchase only 22 per cent of the daily requirements of food. By 1990-1, this ratio had declined to an impossible 5 per cent. The vulnerable groups in society, namely children under fifteen and the elderly, are at an even greater disadvantage in the rural labour market. The declining terms of trade between labour and wage food benefited the agro-mercantile elite who capitalised on the famine situation in Darfur.

The coping strategy of seasonal agricultural wage labour is increasingly counter-productive even compared to the urban informal sector; rural wages equal half or even less than the urban informal sector income. The reason why anyone engages in rural wage labour is simply that other choices even if *prima facie* more attractive are not available in unrestricted supply. Moreover there is the locational advantage of rural wage labour and its flexibility in terms of the division of time between their own farm and wage employment on someone else's farm, especially during *khareef*.

In summary, during the inter-famine period between 1984 and 1990 many of the coping strategies, especially that of local agricultural wage labour, were exhausted and rendered counter-productive. Rural merchants manipulated the 'economics of famine' and fixed wages at low levels without suffering any decline in labour supply. The squeeze caused by rising basic food prices and falling cash earnings resulted in a group of increasingly dispossessed and impoverished rural wage labourers. Most were likely to be landless victims of the dynamics of rural agriculture - precarious land tenure, soil fertility decline, *wadi* land sale, and *goz* land shortage. This category represents the poorest and the most de-agrarianised class and constitutes roughly 20 per cent of the rural population.

Labour Migration and Non-Agricultural Employment

The rate of rural-urban migration in Darfur was the second highest in Sudan during 1973-83 and the highest in northern Sudan during 1983-93 (Government of Sudan preliminary census report 1993). Labour migration is not a new phenomenon, nor necessarily related to famine and food shortage. In the early 1930s Darfur was designated as a labour reserve for the plantations of the Gezira Scheme in central Sudan. This instituted an economic dualism whereby adult males migrated, delegating food production to women, children and the elderly. The labour shortages that ensued rendered the production system more vulnerable to famine. On the other hand, labour migration was bolstered by the need for alternative forms of livelihood in the face of the irregularities of the household developmental cycle, land shortage and declining soil fertility, lack of viable cash crops, and increasing demands for cash due to the increasing rate of monetisation of rural life. Presently, the migrating tradition lives on and is no longer restricted to men. Under the duress of the chronic food shortages and famine conditions of the last decade, migration has become even more deeply entrenched.

In Search of Cash and Livelihood in Regional Towns

There are various forms and patterns of migration based on gender and age with distinct geographical destinations and durations. Seasonal migration to nearby urban centres is quite prevalent and takes place during the agricultural slack season from March to June. Destinations include the regional urban centres of Mellit, El Fasher, Nyala, Kutum, Geneina and others. Jobs such as construction, water peddling and domestic services in wealthy urban households are available.

Most migrant women prefer domestic service because this allows them to reside in the employer's household, thus avoiding food and housing costs. Employers prefer unaccompanied women. In addition to food and accommodation, a monthly salary of S£1,000 is paid in Mellit and Kutum and slightly more in El Fashir. In comparison to this, the daily wage in the construction sector would be around S£100-150 without accommodation, while in small enterprises such as water peddling with a donkey cart, women could expect to make S£170-250 on a fifty-fifty income-share basis after subtracting the cost of donkey feed.

Adult male seasonal migration to urban centres within Darfur is common and usually carried out during the slack season. The only jobs available are in the urban informal sector. With the increasing costs of accommodation, savings are minimal and remittances insignificant. Not surprisingly, this form of migration is the least preferred and only resorted to by those unable to meet the costs of more rewarding forms of migration.

Seasonal labour migration of entire families to nearby regional urban centres is only undertaken by destitute families without livestock. Such migration involves initially staying in urban squatter neighbourhoods where housing is free but living conditions squalid. When opportunities arise, such families may become permanent residents in the urban centre and attempt to extract a living in the informal sector.

Searching for a Better Life in the City

Migration to central Sudanese cities, notably Khartoum, Wad Medani, Sennar, and Port Sudan, is limited by the high cost of transportation (S£5,000 by lorry) and the uncertainty of employment prospects. This option is mainly confined to the 'unencumbered poor' - youth and school drop-outs - who are not constrained by immediate social obligations.

People in rural Darfur believe that long-distance migration is more beneficial than labour migration within Darfur. Wage rates are higher - sometimes double or triple - and migrants are able to save money and make remittances on a regular basis. Often this form of migration develops into permanent settlement especially if the migrant is able to secure a good job in the urban informal sector. Sometimes it is a transitional jumping-off point for migration to Iraq or Saudi Arabia.

The benefits of this type of migration should be evaluated against its costs and difficulties, among which strenuous work, difficult living conditions, disease, and psychological distress figure prominently. Many migrants interviewed in Khartoum reported having eaten 'half of their bellies' in order to save money to send home. Those who fail to make ends meet end up as criminals and their children as street children in the cities. Up to 30 per cent of the street children in Khartoum are from Darfur.

The Libyan Connection

Migration to Libya dates back to the late 1960s and early 1970s which corresponds to the oil boom in Libya and drought in Darfur. Historical links through inter-boundary population mobility were always there and often took the form of camel trading and smuggling across the Sahara desert. The migration is demographically selective with mostly young adult males between the ages of 13 and 45 being involved. Currently, the number of migrants to Libya from Darfur is higher than from any other region in Sudan. For example, in Angabo village in South Darfur in 1993, about 60 per cent of the village population in the age group 13 to 45 had migrated to Libya at least once, while in the far northern villages this percentage reached 70-80. Local villagers have coined a term 'Libyan fever' in recognition of the powerful spread-effect of this phenomenon.

The economic contribution of remittances from Libyan migrants was significant until 1990, after which restrictions were imposed by the Libyan authorities due to the deterioration of the oil economy and the international embargo. The decline in remittances from Libya is also attributed to the prevailing loan system that migrants use to cover transportation costs (S£10,000). Migrants borrow money at an exhorbitant interest rate and it takes them more than a year to repay this debt. Falling monetary transfers have been partially compensated by food remittances, e.g. rice, wheat flour and sugar, which were facilitated by improvements in road transportation with the introduction of heavy-duty trans-Saharan trucks. The phenomenon is particularly noticeable in dar Zaghawa, the village with the best links to Libya. Zaghawa migrants in Libya have formed associations in the *emiare* which send food donations back to their kin.

Migration to Libya has played a significant role in the transformation of the rural economies of northern Darfur to the extent that petty trade now is dominated by returned migrants. This is even true of many central Sudanese towns. Thirty per cent of the merchants interviewed in El Malha village in dar Meidoub said they had acquired their starting commercial capital through migration to Libya. However, in response to the Libyan economic recession and reduction of real wages, female tribal singers, who usually play a catalyst role in village public opinion, have been encouraging young people to migrate to Saudi Arabia instead of 'the now poor Libya'.

Migrant wives reported economic hardships with the decline and irregularity of remittances from husbands and sons. Family breakup is quite common. Moreover, because home production suffers from the absence of males, all migrant families have become indebted to village merchants and it is not unusual that savings brought back by returning migrants are expended for debt repayment.

Migration to Libya has become an endemic feature of the local economy - one further manifestation of deepening rural poverty. The circular migration pattern is reflected in the diminished agricultural performance of the returned migrants in their home villages. Interviews with 60 returned migrants in 1993 in North and South Darfur revealed the following:

- only 10 per cent were able to produce enough millet for their annual household consumption during the 1992-3 agricultural season,
- only 10 per cent were able to produce sufficient cash crops, i.e. groundnuts, to meet their households' annual cash needs,
- 20 per cent were indebted, and
- 20 per cent had acquired credit through *shaile* (a rural credit system with a 400 per cent rate of interest).

'It seems like migrants to Libya have been caught in the middle of a zero option. Neither circular migration to Libya nor staying at home can resolve the riddle of poverty', one returned migrant commented. Nonetheless, for the young who are not encumbered with household obligations connected with marriage, migration to Libya is preferred to staying in their home villages. This advantage is often expressed by the saying: 'to cough is better than keeping your mouth shut'. Interestingly, the local villagers, especially the elders or those who cannot migrate, often ridicule the migrants saying that: 'if you want to know whether the returned migrant from Libya achieved any gain from migration, wait and see how long before he starts selling the assets he brought, e.g. radios, cassette recorders, carpets, fancy jeans'.

Growing Regional Service Sector

In spite of the severity of the 1990-1 famine compared to the 1984-5 famine, the migration of *entire* families was not common. This was related to the growing incidence of non-agricultural employment. Labour migration and remittances play a key role in providing capital for such non-agricultural activities.

Darfur region's service sector is composed of urban and rural parts. While the former comprises small-scale enterprises and construction services, the latter includes handicraft production, petty trading, and grass and firewood sales. It is interesting that the latter are on the increase despite the critical absence of adults, especially men, in the economically active age group of 13 to 45. This has to be explained in terms of changes in labour supply, particularly the increase of cash-earning children who do not attend school.

Rising School Drop-Out Rate

A number of factors have had a detrimental effect on primary school attendance in Darfur. Schools closed during the famines of 1985 and 1991 and the removal of subsidies from boarding schools, a measure taken under the country's structural adjustment programme, forced many children to discontinue their education. The growing number of school-leavers usually find refuge in either the rural or the urban service sector, but rarely if at all in the agricultural sector. Table 7 shows the school drop-out rates in Malha village. In the same village, 40 per cent of school-leavers migrated to Libya, 18 per cent to central Sudanese cities, 32 per cent to regional urban centres and the remaining 10 per cent joined the village service sector, primarily as petty traders and animal brokers.

Table 7: School Drop-outs as a Percentage of Total Enrolment in Malha Village Primary School, 1985, 1988, 1991

Grade	1985	1988	1991
First	79	54	50
Second	44	58	43
Third	34	54	46
Fourth	35	45	40
Fifth	32	22	31
Sixth	18	23	20

Source: Author's field data

Even without recent policy setbacks to educational investment, the restricted nature of the educational system in rural Darfur would allow only 10 per cent or so of those enrolled in primary education to proceed further. Moreover, the school curriculum is largely irrelevant to the needs and culture of rural life, being primarily a product of the colonial era designed to train lower- and middle-level administrative and clerical cadres. Thus, a basically anti-rural and anti-peasant outlook is inculcated in the children.

There is a two-way push and pull process involved in declining school attendance. The lack of schooling facilities is one part of the picture but equally important is the pressure exerted by famine and economic impoverishment which increases the attraction of the earnings possible from the rural and urban service sectors.

The diminishing possibilities for children to complete their primary education is part and parcel of the de-agrarianisation process in Darfur. In some senses, the loss is softened by the fact that the always remote prospects of clerical employment are even further reduced as a result of the shrinkage of state-employing organisations under structural adjustment. The decline in formal education is bound to perpetuate the economic and political marginalisation of rural areas.

Petty Trade

Every item in Darfur is now potentially marketable and everyone is a trader. As a coping strategy petty trade has become a common feature of both the rural and urban economies. As one elderly informant observed: 'Thirty years ago we used to think that petty trade brought shame to the individual and his family'. *Um dawarwar*, a circulatory marketing system with a specific timetable, is now established among groups of villages. Thus everyday is a marketing day somewhere. Furthermore, camels are now assuming a new marketing role through inter-village peddling.

Petty trade is believed to contribute as much as 20 per cent to household annual cash income in dar Zaghawa, 15 per cent in dar Berti, and 10 per cent in Malha. The magnitude of the contribution depends on the presence of other income sources, the size of the working capital, and the availability of means of transportation, notably camels and donkeys, to travel greater distances to remote villages where prices and profit margins are higher. Yet, about 90 per cent of the rural population of northern Darfur do not have donkeys or camels.

The main constraint to petty trade is the lack of effective demand. There are too many sellers dealing in the same commodity - a classic case of perfect competition under free entry conditions where chances for cartel or monopolistic arrangements are impossible. Some petty traders borrow money from their more successful counterparts on the basis of an equal sharing of profits, which further decreases their income from this trade.

Firewood and Grass Collection

Villagers who are not too distant from small urban centres collect grass and wood to sell to petty traders in small village markets. In 1993 it was estimated that about 1,000 camels and donkeys per day brought grass to Mellit urban centre from 23 neighbouring villages. On average it took the grass traders two to four days to collect a camel-load and up to two days to reach the town market. The collection sites can be between three and ten hours away from the village. A camel-load fetches S£700-1,000 in Mellit and a donkey-load S£250-500. The recent boom in the grass market in Mellit is attributed to the newly flourishing livestock trade and smuggling across the Sahara to Libya. Local merchants and rich farmers have the advantage of being able to lend their donkeys and camels to poor rural labourers on the basis of an equal distribution of returns, after the deduction of animal feed and water costs.

Given the semi-desert nature of northern Darfur, the environmental cost of firewood and grass collection is inescapable. Thus this specific coping strategy is not sustainable; if anything, it accelerates the deterioration of the area's overall natural resource base.

Handicraft Production

Darfur is now acquiring nationwide fame for its distinctively styled leather work, pottery, blacksmithery, mats and baskets, and carpets. The crafts have developed among the Zaghawa tribal groups despite the stigmitisation of potters and blacksmiths who are isolated in separate villages. The crafts could be considered 'caste'-specific in a similar way to those of the untouchables in India. The position of the artisans is maintained by strong ideological formulations and cultural taboos. Pottery, mat making and wild food processing, i.e. *kawal*, are prohibited, especially during the rainy season because it is believed that they stop the rains and adversely affect crop harvests. Fines from local *sheikh* courts may be imposed on violators. Artisans have to rely on agricultural employment from wealthy farmers as a source of income during the rainy season.

Other constraints on the enterprise are the low local demand at village level, a lack of transportation to urban centres, and the time-consuming nature of the industry especially for women with busy daily routines due to the absence of their menfolk. Urban wages and the income of urban artisans are usually at least three times higher than rural wages (Table 8). Thus de-agrarianisation in rural Darfur implies expansion of the urban service sector as well as that of its rural counterpart.

Table 8: Average Daily Income for Different Occupations in Rural and Urban Service Sectors, Darfur, 1993 (S£)

Enterprise	Rural	Urban
Carpet weaving	21	33
Pot making	23	60
Grass sales (camel)	n.a.	200
Grass sales (donkey)	n.a.	100
Firewood (camel)	n.a.	300
Firewood (donkey)	n.a.	125
Tabag making	10	50
Water peddling	75	300
Construction work	180	450
Tea selling	60	200
Food selling	80	250
Blacksmithery	150	330
Shoemaking	150	500

Source: Author's field data

Conclusion

The economy of Darfur is one of the least developed in Sudan, manifested in its low per capita income and lack of infrastructure. Over the last five decades, the region has experienced the rise and fall of agrarian commoditisation. Implementation of colonial policies - the monetisation of the subsistence economies, the introduction of cash crops and the siphoning off of the labour force to plantations in central Sudan - took place under the influence of cyclical famine and environmental collapse. The coping strategies adopted within local agricultural and livestock systems have become increasingly acts of short-term exigency resulting in the accelerated depletion of agricultural assets and proletarianisation of the population.

Under such circumstances, a shift into rural and urban service employment has been the main option left for an independent livelihood. While the appearance of a rural service sector is notable, it is primarily based on economic and environmental resource depletion. The relative lack of economically sustainable rural employment opportunities compared to those prevailing in urban areas has led to persistent migration from rural areas and deepening rural poverty. Youth are most prone to migrate, leaving responsibility for food production in the hands of women, young children and the elderly. In so doing, rural food shortfalls are likely to be exacerbated. The rural service sector in Darfur is continuously losing its artisans and able-bodied persons to urban areas due to higher wages and the availability of social amenities and welfare measures such as relief food. These and other similar advantages accrue from proximity to power corridors in the urban centres which is in line with the Darfurian saying: 'If you are far from somebody's sight, then you are far from his heart'.

Poverty and famine in Darfur lie in a continuum and are intimately linked to the process of de-agrarianisation. De-agrarianisation as a process of occupational reorientation and population realignment has contributed to economic polarisation by class and gender. Amidst a dwindling resource base, women make up the bulk of the rural dispossessed in Darfur. Perhaps the local saying just cited might be more accurately worded: 'When a woman is far from somebody's sight, she is also far from his heart'. Survival not romance is at stake here.

Notes

1. Famines have been recorded in Sudan during the following years: 1905, 1906, 1907, 1913-5, 1919, 1927, 1948-50, 1970-3, 1984-5, 1991-2 and 1994.
2. Data collection took place between August 1992 and July 1993 as part of a research project entitled 'Coping Strategies and Wild Foods Use in Darfur during the period 1985-93' funded by the Ford Foundation. Surveyed households were visited in three seasons: the rainy season (July-October), winter (November-February) and summer (March-June). To secure a longitudinal perspective, some village communities were selected from among those covered by a similar study in 1985-6 carried out by Alex De Waal. The villages were Barno, Dar Berti, Dar Meidoub, Dar Zaghawa, Gaghna, Fetta Barno, Furawiya, and Halha.

References

DE WAAL, A. 1987, *Famine That Kills. Darfur, Sudan (1984-85)*, Oxford, Clarendon Press

DIAB, M. & A. PYLE 1987, *The Impact of Household Survival Strategies on Future Vulnerability to Famine: Darfur, Sudan (1984-85)*, Khartoum, Social and Economic Research Council

HOLY, L. 1987, 'Economic Strategy and Household Variability in a Dry Savannah Agricultural Society: Berti of Darfur', in M. Salih (ed.), *Agrarian Change in the Central Rainlands: Sudan*, Uppsala, Scandinavian Institute of African Studies

OXFAM 1990-93, *Nutritional and Annual Reports*, Darfur and Khartoum

SAVE THE CHILDREN FUND UK 1990-93, *Annual and Assessment Reports*, Darfur, Sudan

SUDAN, GOVERNMENT of, *Census Reports 1973, 1983 and 1993 (Preliminary Report) of Sudan*, Khartoum, Department of Statistics

3

Farmers without Land: The Return of Landlessness to Rural Ethiopia

Yohannes Habtu

Ethiopia's historic land reform proclamation of 1975 aspired to transform the prevailing quasi-feudal agrarian production and replace it with socialist agriculture and industrialisation. The reform was followed by the establishment of a number of socialist rural institutions, including peasant associations, service cooperatives and producer cooperatives. These measures were backed by the imposition on farmers of forced delivery quotas for agricultural products and resettlement into villages.

The architects of the land reform aimed at redistributing land and increasing rural income as a basis for industrialisation and lasting equality. No person could transfer his holding to another through sale, exchange, succession, mortgage, or leasing; transfer was only allowed through inheritance to the families of deceased holders (Ethiopia 1975). The land reform was popular among the peasantry at its outset. Its implementation succeeded in fundamentally altering agrarian relations. Land was distributed as promised. A uniformity of rural land tenure was attained on a level never before witnessed by the country.

The 1975 land reform, with only amendments in 1990, remains the legal foundation for land entitlement in rural Ethiopia. However, in the intervening two decades land scarcity has reappeared due to population increase coupled with the over-fragmentation of land holdings arising from official efforts to equalise the shares of different types of land (Fasil Gebre Kiros 1980). Such redistribution has exacerbated security of tenure as landed households face not only a decline in the size of their total landholdings but also the physical relocation involved in receiving redistributed portions of land. Disinvestment in land has followed with disastrous environmental effects. Ironically, efforts to equalise land holdings have increased landlessness. Bruce, Hoben and Rahmato (1993) observe that in a few peasant associations as many as 50 per cent of household adult males are functionally landless. The incidence of landlessness is further accentuated by the return of disbanded ex-soldiers to rural areas following the collapse of the Mengistu regime in 1991.

Thus a substantial landless and land-deficit population coexists in Ethiopia today with a majority of farmers controlling small fragmented holdings. Despite this, mass migrations of the rural poor to urban areas and the growth of squatter quarters which plague the metropoli of other African and Latin American countries, have not, to any large extent, materialised. During the Derg's period of government from 1971 to 1991, this situation could be explained by strict restrictions on labour mobility, a vehement campaign of forced conscription into the army which blocked access to the formal labour market of urban areas, and rural dwellers' lack of capital to bridge the gap between arrival at urban centres and securing employment. Currently, despite the waning of the aforementioned policy constraints, continuing high expectations of imminent rural land redistributions have contained the movement of the rural poor to urban areas.

In the absence of any significant large-scale governmental or non-governmental intervention, the most prominent role in tackling the problem of landlessness is played by rural communities themselves. Participation in interlocking land and labour markets is central to rural dwellers' coping strategies. The working of factor markets is evident in both the agricultural and non-agricultural sectors of the rural economy. In the agricultural sector, it is most often manifested in entry of rural households into cash rental of land, sharecropping and labour markets. For the non-agricultural activities, land plays a less strategic role in determining household welfare, whereas the availability and skill of labour as well as capital are more important.

Little is known about the incidence and nature of landlessness in rural Ethiopia and even less about how rural households cope with its consequences. This chapter uses recent survey evidence to examine the participation of the landless population in the land and labour markets of Ethiopia's rural economy.[1] It attempts to construct a tentative picture of smallholder access to land. After providing some background information on the survey site, the characteristics of the landless - their numbers, employment sources, wealth and other economic characteristics - are reviewed. The sections that follow discuss various alleviation strategies, notably cash rental of land, sharecropping and rural labour market participation, in the light of their importance to the landless.

Figure 1: Map of Selale, Ethiopia (Scale 1:250,000)

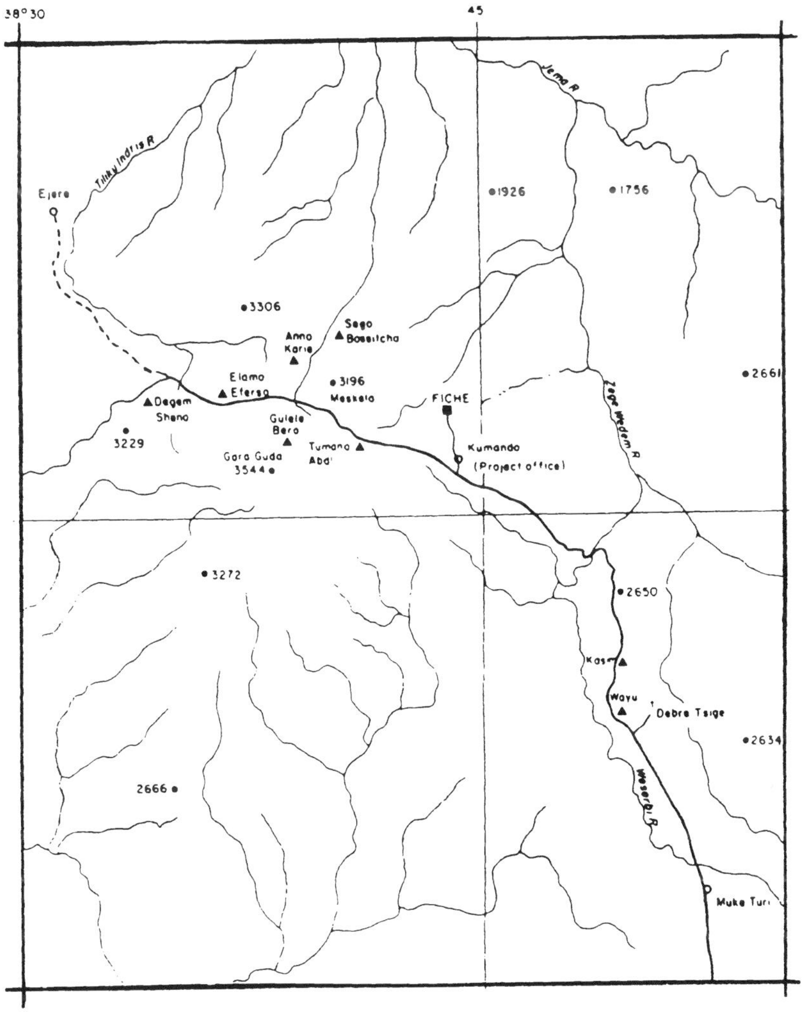

—— All weather road
- - - - Dry weather road
• Elevation
▪ *Awraja* capital
• Towns
▲ Settlement

The Survey Site

The site selected for the study was Selale *awraja*[2] of Northern Shewa region (see Figure 1). At a high elevation of 2,600 metres above sea level, the area is typical of highland mixed crop/livestock farming systems in Ethiopia, with bimodal rain-fed crop production seasons and a strong livestock component in farming. Barley, oats, and horse beans are the most common crops produced on rain-fed fields but some *teff* (an indigenous staple grain) is also grown in pockets of land protected from waterlogging and frost. Horticultural production, mostly onions and garlic, on traditionally irrigated fields is practiced in one of the surveyed peasant associations (PAs). This proved to be the most important venue for agricultural wage labour and cash contracting employment. The survey area is in close proximity to the Jema River Gorge and interaction with farmers from the lowlands, usually in product markets but sometimes also in labour exchange and migration, was common.

The average household size was six persons. Estimated average landholdings were 4.7 hectares, of which 2.4 ha were arable crop land and 1.5 ha natural pasture. Since farming is functionally tied to livestock as well as land holdings, it is pertinent to record that mean herd sizes were 6 local cattle, 5 sheep and 0.04 goats. The population is predominantly Oromo intermingled with Amhara, both followers of the Ethiopian Orthodox Church. Polygamy is therefore the exception rather than the rule and households are composed of monogamous male-headed units with a husband, one wife and their offspring.

Landlessness Defined and Estimated

The 1975 land reform established the principle that land was distributed according to family size. Any newborn in a rural household was technically entitled to land. Any household which did not gain a corresponding increase in landholding with the growth of its family size was eligible for inclusion in the category of land-deficit households harbouring landless offspring, although peasants' rightful claims to land in accordance with this principle were seldom rigorously adhered to.

The incidence of landlessness will necessarily vary depending on how it is defined. A first step was to collect information on the number of people petitioning for land. A review of peasant association records and interviews with the village leadership and applications for land, both written and verbal were used to construct a picture of officially recognised levels of landlessness shown in Table 1.

Table 1: Reported Incidence of Landlessness in Six Peasant Associations

Awraja	Peasant Association	Total No. Households	*Landed Households* Male	Female	*Applications for Land* Male	Female
Debre Libanos	Wayuu	424	361	63	15	0
	Kassim	394	331	63	73	3
Selale	Anno Karie	404	323	12	65	4
	Elamo Eferso	425	295	68	40	0
	Gende Sheno	370	330	40	50	31
	Tumano Abdi	317	267	50	40	0
Total		2,334	1,897	296	283	38

Source: Peasant Association records

The level of documentation was in fact very poor. Most PAs did not have records worthy of rigorous scrutiny. Many records were lost during the short power vacuum that existed in the transition between the government of the People's Democratic Republic of Ethiopia (PDRE) and that of the current Transitional Government of Ethiopia (TGE). Members of the communities tended to view the loss of these records as the basis for legalisation of the skewed land distribution inherited from the Derg era and perpetuated by the current freeze on legal transfers of rural land.

Landless and land-deficit households were clearly more prevalent than the incomplete statistics suggest. It was therefore necessary to construct a definition of landlessness in conformity with peasants' own perceptions and assess its incidence on the basis of survey data. The landless were defined as married family units, residing in the PAs but without direct access to land, and adult young men aged 24 and over who may or may not have been married and had no direct access to land. Twenty-four was determined as the ideal upper age limit for males to marry, from a number of informal interviews. Any marriages above that age being viewed as possible but unusual by the community.

The demographic delimitations of this definition of landlessness have several implications for estimating the incidence of landlessness. In particular the use of 24 years of age as the cut-off is somewhat problematic since it is relatively high compared with the estimated life expectancy of adult Ethiopian males (47 years) (IBRD 1993). It also begs the question of what proportion of the landless under the described age limit have failed to marry because they have no land and are therefore contributing to the deflation of numbers of the landless reported here. No upper age limit was imposed on the sample, and this may somewhat balance the numbers but inflate the mean age of the landless categories. It should be noted that there were some cases of premature inter-generational transfers of land, i.e. the transfer of land to offspring before the death of aged parents or relatives. The exclusion of females in the qualifying age group was enforced in the interests of focusing the study, despite the fact that 13.5 per cent of the landed households were female-headed and 11.8 per cent of the total number of applicants for land in both study *awrajas* were women. This omission should not be interpreted as minimising the importance of the problem of gender issues in rural land access.

The survey was conducted in peasant associations in Wayuu in Debre Libanos and Anno Karie in Selale *awrajas*. The site selection was based more on the diversity of coping or employment options open to landless households than on the reported incidence of landlessness. Both PAs offer peasant participatory public employment programmes in the form of food for work. Wayuu PA, in Debre Libanos boasts a well-kept gravel road joining the centre of the PA to the main Addis Abeba-Gojjam highway. Wayuu is also the site of traditional irrigated farming of onions and garlic which are cash crops. Thus it was expected that these areas would have more buoyant labour and factor markets.

Results of the hut-to-hut survey in the PA revealed the level of landlessness, according to the definition adopted for this study, to be 17.4 per cent. Table 2 distinguishes landed and landless households on the basis of their engagement in land-related transactions or other forms of employment.

Amongst the landless households, 5.1 per cent had sharecropping members, whereas 9.5 per cent had not entered any land transactions which would have afforded them indirect land access in the form of shared or rented land. The rest engaged in fixed contractual agricultural employment, as resident farm labourers are categorically eliminated from indirect access to land, since the terms of their employment bind them to working only on their employer's land.

The landed were even more likely than the landless to access extra land. More than one in five had members engaged in sharecropping or land rental. This involvement in land exchange shows that landed households harbour landless members, i.e. young unmarried males 24 or above who do not have land of their own. On the supply side, 15.4 per cent of households had members who acted as landlords, sharing their land resources to overcome other production resource constraints.

Table 2: Incidence of Landlessness, Land Transactions and Employment

Landholding and Labour Status	Number of Households	Percentage
Landless	75	17.4
No Land Transaction	41	9.5
Land Transaction	22	5.1
Share 'Tenant' Only	22	5.1
Employment	12	2.8
Fixed Agricultural Employee	10	2.3
Non-Agricultural Employee	2	0.5
Landed	356	82.6
No Land Transaction	195	45.2
Land Transaction	161	37.4
Share 'Tenant' Only	88	20.4
Share 'Landlord' Only	63	14.6
Cash 'Tenant'	1	0.2
Cash 'Landlord'	4	0.9
Both Share and Cash 'Tenant'	5	1.2
Total	431	100.0

Source: Author's survey data

Overall, the survey evidence presented in Table 2 suggests that land transfers are common affecting over two-fifths of rural households.

Land Transactions

The 1990 proclamation on a mixed economic policy which amended the Land Reform legalised smallholders' rental of farmland, although with limitations on the duration of contracts. In fact, cash rentals do not play a significant role in enhancing the access of land by the landless. One young landless farmer who still lived in his parents' home admitted to renting land. Subsequent investigation revealed that the land was actually rented by his father who happened to be a relatively affluent farmer with four oxen and sharecropping agreements on three other farmers' land.

The landless face numerous constraints to renting land on a cash basis. Land rental involves making a down payment of most, if not all of the agreed price before the start of the production season. This condition is difficult to meet by cash-constrained landless farmers. In any case, households renting out land prefer to do so with better-off farmers because of their greater credit-worthiness. In other words, cash contractors opt for greater credit-worthiness in terms of collateral assets and the income-generating potential of their contractees.

In the context of landlessness, the most remarkable observation on sharecropping is that its occurrence is only marginally lower than the incidence of landlessness as a whole and exceeds the number of landless households engaged in agriculture. This would imply that enough land exists in the PAs under study for all agriculturally-oriented landless households to access at least one plot of land through some form of share tenancy. The leading obstruction to realising such equity is embodied in the lack of complementarity between the resource constraints of households offering land for sharecropping and the resource endowments of the landless household.

On the supply side, farming households offering land for sharecropping are constrained by a variety of factors, including access to oxen, labour, seed, and modern farm inputs. On the demand side the only surplus factor endowment of the landless household appears to be labour. This effectively narrows the proportion of sharecropping land available to the landless or unwillingly coerces them into other factor markets or sharing arrangements, especially with oxen.

Contrary to expectations, members from landed households are just as likely as members of landless households to engage in shared land arrangements. Over 80 per cent of shared arrangements involve households which already have land whereas less than 20 per cent involve the landless. This skewed distribution of sharecropped land closely resembles the distributional split between landed and landless households shown in Table 2. Even though more than a quarter of the PA households had members engaged as tenants in some sharecropping or cash rental transactions, less than 20 per cent of these were from landless households while 76.5 per cent were from landed households exclusively involved in sharecropping and an additional 5.1 per cent were members of landed households engaged in both shared and cash rentals of land.

The reasons for this seeming anomaly extend beyond the fact that landed households are harbouring landless members. In Table 3, a close look at the socio-economic characteristics of sharecropping 'tenants' and 'landlords' by landless and landed household categories reveals that the landless households are deficient not only in land but also in labour relative to landed households. Thus, they are at a disadvantage in a sharecropping arrangement involving the exchange of labour for land. The landed 'tenant' groups controlling over 80 per cent of sharecropped land are older, better established families with superiority in oxen and labour endowments relative to the landless.

Table 3: Attributes of Sharecropping Tenant and Landlord Households

	Household Socio-Economic Attributes					
Land Access Status	Age of HH Head	Years Married	No. of Oxen	Males < 15	Females >15	Tax (Birr)
Landless: Share 'Tenant'	25.6	4.2	0.7	1.5	1.6	0.0
Landed: Share 'Tenant'	44.6	23.4	1.9	3.4	3.1	29.5
Cash 'Tenant'	53.8	28.5	3.3	4.6	3.5	32.5
Landed: Share & Cash 'Landlord'	56.2	32.8	0.5	1.8	2.1	28.0

Source: Author's Survey Data

The landless lack a competitive edge in any factor markets. Their disadvantage with respect to labour, the one factor that they should be expected to have an advantage in, is striking. Taking household male labour as a proxy for labour availability, landed sharecroppers had a mean of 3.4 males, landed cash tenants 4.6, but the landless only 1.5. Even 'landlords' had a comparative advantage in labour over the landless and their resource constraint was oxen rather than labour. But complementary exchange is even less likely in this regard, since the landless are ill-equipped to exchange oxen for land.

It is not known how many of the advantages derived from sharecropping which accrue to landed households are used to lessen the exigency of their own landless offspring or kin, but the available evidence infers a strong connection between the two. Furthermore, it seems more than coincidental that the distribution of sharecropped land within the landless groups is skewed in favour of landless household members who remain within their parents' home. This gives the sub-group, comprising 77 per cent of the landless tenant group, closer access to family capital for penetration of the inter-locked markets. It can hence be concluded that the role of sharecropping in land access enhancement of the landless is limited to mainly reinforcing the efforts of a slightly better-off group of landless young men who maintain strong ties with their parental households and benefit from access to family resources.

In summary, the survey evidence suggests that the effect of cash rental of land and sharecropping on alleviating the plight of landless households is limited. Only 29 per cent of landless households achieved indirect access to land through these means. Against this background and given the low levels of rural/urban migration that prevail, rural labour markets and/or participation in the non-agricultural sector become crucial sources of livelihood for landless households.

Rural Employment Opportunities

There are two general sources of employment in rural areas, that of agriculture and non-agriculture. The former can be divided into three subsectors listed in ascending order of importance: 1) the private commercial sector, 2) the state farm sector, and 3) the smallholder sector. The first category always small before the Derg was totally suppressed during the twenty years of the Derg's socialist programmes. Although now permitted, its contribution still remains minimal.

The state farm sector, which was the recipient of vast capital infusions from the Derg, never attained the status in agricultural production and employment that had been envisaged for it at its inception. Following the undoing of the Derg, a number of disputes arose over the sector's land rights and production was disrupted. Given its high capital-intensity, the sector is in any case not a significant employer of unskilled labour, except seasonally during the peak cotton harvest season in the Awash valley and in new tea plantations. In the survey area, the state farm sector generated negligible employment, amounting to a couple of guards, some barn hands and a clerk at one dairy farm.

By contrast, the smallholder sector plays a leading role in employment, but the average farm size combined with the growing use of improved inputs ensures that its capacity to generate additional employment is restricted. The demand for hired labour in the smallholder sector was observed to emanate from two main categories of households: 1) fully labour-deficit households, and 2) partially labour-deficit households. The former were characterised by the absence of sufficient quantities of family labour for adequate utilisation of agricultural production resources all year round. The second and broader category constitutes households facing seasonal shortfalls in the supply of farm labour who seek specific skills at specific times of the year. The nature of the smallholder sector's demand for labour coupled with the seasonal attributes of agricultural production generated marked labour market segmentation into: 1) a fixed annual contractual labour market, satisfying the needs of fully labour-deficit households, and 2) a shorter-term agricultural labour market.

The two categories are distinguished on the basis of the duration of employment, rates and forms of payment and degree of fluctuating labour demand.

Fixed Contractual Labour

The contribution of fixed contractual labour in alleviating the dilemma faced by the landless is reported in Table 2. At the PA level, households with members engaged in this form of labour constitute 2.3 per cent of total households and 13.3 per cent of all landless households.

The two main occupational forms of fixed contractual labour are employment as a resident farm labourer or a resident shepherd. Shepherds are usually young men. The duration of fixed contractual labour employment is at least a year, often several years. As a result of its long duration, the contract is characterised by less vulnerability to seasonal fluctuations. Invariably, employment of resident farm labourers and shepherds emanates from landed households.

The supply of labour in this market is a monopoly of the landless. There were no members of landed households that competed to attain full-time annual employment in the homes of other landed households. Entry into such employment is effected through negotiation on wage rate and form of payment. The employer is bound to providing food and lodging in addition to an annual wage. The upper limits on the timing of payment is initially agreed upon and any advance payments are left to the discretion of the employer or subsequent negotiations. The employee is tied to one employer thereby precluding other sources of cash income.

Amongst the small sample of fifteen respondents in this category, mean annual wages were reported to be very low at Birr 204 (US$41). Consequently, while the landless in this category became more food secure - in fact as secure as their employers - residual non-food incomes were extremely low by any standards. This situation is partially explained by the prevailing low levels of income in the Ethiopian smallholder sector and hence in the capacity of employers to remunerate hired labour. However, at the micro-level, the form of payment and duration of contracts were observed to be important determinants of the real remuneration level.

A difference in net payment of Birr 172 (US$31) was found between employees who agreed to payments in cash only and employees who negotiated payments in both cash and kind, the advantage falling to those being paid in cash and kind. Because employees can sell their in-kind payments which come in the form of agricultural produce, this considerable difference accrues only in as far as employees have the capacity to exploit seasonal prices in agricultural product markets and is therefore a function of not only the size of their in-kind payment but also its timing.

One important feature of fixed contractual labour is the age of the labourer. The mean age of participants in this labour category is very low, standing at an average 21.8 years, with an average of 4.7 years of contract work already behind them.

A long contract duration reflects occupational security, shielding the landless employed in this segment of the labour market from the seasonality that prevails in the rural wage and casual labour markets more generally. This protection lasts for a considerable period of time. The difference in the mean current age and contract duration yields a low age of 17.2 years for entry into this market. A major proportion of landless employees in this labour market (41.7 per cent) entered the market at or below fifteen years of age, while 33.3 per cent entered between 15 and 20 years, and 25 per cent between 20 and 25 years.

Data are not available for determining the number in the remaining age classes (above fifteen years at start of employment) who may have entered at or below fifteen years of age because initial investigations focused on the duration of current contracts. Most of the landless engaged in fixed labour contracts and particularly those in the fifteen years or below age class entered the market on shepherd-hiring arrangements which matured into farm labour contracts as the employee grew older.

Shepherd-hiring agreements normally arise from negotiations between the employer and the parents or guardian of the employee. Consequently entry into the market is not always a matter of choice for the employee. On the other hand, there is no evidence that workers in this category are eager to leave the market. This is curious given the fact that only 16.6 per cent of respondents in this market category were found to be married which would make them 'settled' with a wife to support. Questions were put to respondents on their motives for remaining employed as fixed contract labourers in the hope of attaining some measure of understanding about their reluctance to leave the market (Table 4).

Table 4: Motives for Remaining in a Fixed Agricultural Labour Contract

Motive	Percentage of Respondents
To gain professional experience in the absence of other skills	41.7
No work in other sectors or town	25.0
To assist family who also live off farming	16.7
To improve farming skills	8.3
Agriculture is more profitable	8.3

Source: Author's survey data.

Though a substantial 25 per cent of those responding cited awareness of constraints in non-agricultural and non-rural employment markets, the majority maintain their participation in the fixed labour contract markets because of a desire to build careers in the farming profession and their lack of marketable skills outside agriculture.

Short-term Agricultural Labour Markets

Outside of the fixed contract agricultural labour markets, the participation of the landless in other labour markets functions to meet the needs of partial labour-deficit households. As discussed earlier the demand for hired labour from these households is seasonal, manifested in demand for labour to assist in or conduct specific agricultural activities like sowing, weeding or harvesting activities for an agreed duration of time. Consequently labour supply in this market category is not a strict monopoly of the landless. Some landed, labour-surplus households enter the market for short durations.

The market share of the landless is further diminished by practices of traditional reciprocal labour exchange arrangements such as *debo*, whereby labour-deficit households pool their labour for work on each other's fields at critical points in the year. The payment arrangement is restricted to the provision of food and drink to the participants during the days worked.

Under these conditions, the workings of the agricultural wage labour markets are temporally and spatially scattered and therefore very difficult to treat exhaustively in a study of this scope. In particular the spontaneity of employment leads to very subjective arrangements in the context of terms of reference and remuneration agreed upon by employer and employee. One can however distinguish two main types of short-term agricultural labour markets: task-based labour-contracting and daily labourer markets.

Labour-contracting arrangements are characterised by the prevalence of piece-rate payments. This occurred most frequently in subcontracting of labour-intensive tasks such as watering cash crops like onions and garlic with water from irrigation canals, land preparation for *teff*, etc. For the landless, entry into these arrangements was observed to be the most lucrative given the relatively high wage rates and the comparatively extended duration of employment. The labour contracts tended to entail the labourer undertaking a specific range of tasks for part of the production season in exchange for one or two lump-sum payments. Remuneration varied according to the size of plots and type of activities. The benefits accruing to the landless fortunate enough to get such contracts were twofold. First, there was an element of credit manifested in advance payment of part of the lump-sum at the start of the season. Second, the use of irrigation technology combined with the extended duration of employment allowed the labourer some flexibility in the distribution of his time. He could fulfil his labour contract and still have time to pursue other labour opportunities.

In contrast with the task-based contractual labour markets, the casual agricultural labour market is characterised by the prevalence of a daily wage rate. These rates were sensitive to seasonal swings in the demand for labour, ranging from a minimum rate of Birr 2 per day for cutting grass to Birr 8 per day for late ploughing of land.

Table 5: Frequency Distribution of Landless Labourers' Employment (Percentage)[1]

Type of Employment	Jan	Feb	Mar	Apr	May	Jun	Jul	Aug	Sep	Oct	Nov	Dec	Mean
Agricultural													*59.6*
Land preparation								27.8			16.7		3.7
Cutting grass		5.6							11.1	44.4			5.1
Weeding grain							22.2	33.3	44.4	5.6			8.8
Sharecropping	5.6		5.6	5.6	5.6	5.6			5.6				2.8
Harvesting grain	22.2						5.6			27.8	33.3	44.4	11.1
Harvest transport											5.6	5.6	0.9
Threshing and winnowing											11.1		0.9
First ploughing			5.6			5.6							0.9
Second ploughing			5.6	11.1	16.7	22.2	22.2						6.5
Planting onions	11.1	27.8	5.6										3.7
Weeding onions		11.1	33.3	38.9	16.7								8.3
Harvesting onions					22.2	38.9	22.2						6.9
Non-Agricultural													*15.9*
Weaving cloth	16.7	16.7	11.1	11.1	5.6	5.6			5.6			11.1	7.0
Preparing/selling beverages	5.6	5.6	5.6	5.6	5.6	5.6	5.6	5.6	5.6			5.6	4.7
Trading			5.6	5.6	5.6	5.6	5.6	5.6					2.8
Collecting/selling firewood	5.6	5.6										5.6	1.4
Other Categories													*24.6*
Food for Work programmes	11.1	11.1	11.1	11.1	11.1	11.1	11.1	5.6	11.1	22.2	22.2	16.7	13.0
No work	22.1	11.1	11.1	11.1	11.1		5.6	22.2	16.7		5.6	5.6	10.2
Migrated other area		5.6									5.6	5.6	1.4
Total	100	100	100	100	100	100	100	100	100	100	101	100	100

Source: Author's survey data

1. The table is based on data from sixteen landless labourers selected in the labour contracting and the daily labourer category, as well as one landless sharecropper who also participated in this labour market. The latter was included to give some indication of the temporal variation in his labour activities. Also one of two landless labourers who migrated outside the *awraja* in search of agricultural employment was included to demonstrate the seasonality of migration.

The occurrence of casual labour opportunities is even more scattered temporally than that of contractual agricultural jobs and is therefore difficult to report on at the aggregated level of the market. Entry into this market is unrestricted and the supply of labour is comprised of both landed and landless groups. Despite the lack of formal entry restrictions, this market seemed to compete for its labour supply with the demand for family labour in the agricultural activities of landed households, self-employment in the non-agricultural sector and non-agricultural labour markets. The temporal overlap of various types of work is illustrated in Table 5.

Table 5 gives an indication of landless labourers' allocation of time to different types of employment. It is useful to note that agricultural wage labour accounted for roughly 60 per cent of the time, approximately 40 per cent arising from work connected with staple food crops and 20 per cent from horticultural cash crops. Non-agricultural work time, primarily that of cloth weaving and petty trade, accounts for a very low 16 per cent. The residual time, constituting 24 per cent of the total, represents 'surplus labour' devoted to government food-for-work programmes, migration or 'no work'.

The evidence in Table 5 suggests that there are no special market niches for the landless. Their wage opportunities cover the full gamut of the task-based and daily markets. However, what is most notable is the existence of sustained unemployment suggested by the category 'no work' as well as heavy year-round participation in 'food for work' programmes. Persistent unemployment implies the market's failure to clear as well as a shortfall of public works coverage. Landless labourers are left to rely on family and kin.

Conclusion

The findings of this research suggest that landless households have very limited access to land from interlocking land and labour markets. This is demonstrated by their small share in sharecropping (19.1 per cent of total sharecropped land) and their total absence from the cash rental market. A lack of labour endowments when compared with landed households, even those which employ outside labour is a contributing factor. A slight comparative advantage in oxen access was insufficient to offset the even greater advantage of landed households competing in the same markets. In the face of such a stiff competitive environment, most landless households that manage to penetrate the interlocking markets (77 per cent of landless sharecroppers) only do so with the help of parental resources.

Those who do not have access to parental resources have to resort to rural labour markets for their livelihood. Demand for them is restricted by the limited capacity of smallholder landed households to afford hiring labour. Weak labour demand induces segmentation of labour markets into fixed contractual labour markets and short-term agricultural labour markets. Though it provides a considerable level of employment security, the former is characterised by extremely low levels of remuneration. Entry into the fixed contract markets is most often effected before the landless attain adulthood. Upon reaching adulthood, many of these employees remain in the market as an investment for a career in agriculture.

The short-term agricultural labour market was divided into task-based labour contracting and daily labour markets. The former mostly involved work in traditional agricultural operations connected with field irrigation that was available only to a limited numbers of labourers who enjoyed better employment security and flexibility. The daily labour market was characterised by severe seasonality resulting in a high level of employment insecurity and labour mobility.

Parallel to the year-round existence of labour-intensive public works schemes, there was a sustained level of unemployment. This implies a reliance by the landless on free transfers and remittances from already resource-poor households. Given the limitations in the prevalence of full-time employment in non-agricultural activities and the predisposition of young landless households to seek a future in agriculture coupled with their tendency to lean on already resource-poor family and kin in times of market failure, the overall picture that emerges is one of deepening duress and poverty not only in terms of land deprivation but also poor access to local labour markets. The incidence and intensity of impoverished landless groups are bound to worsen until such time as a mechanism for sustainable accommodation of rural demographic dynamics is attained.

The adoption of Employment Based Safety Nets by the Transitional Government of Ethiopia in its Disaster Prevention Strategy is a step in the right direction but can only serve as a short-run palliative. There are insurmountable constraints in securing and sustaining the level of resource and institutional requirements necessary for maintaining all of the landless on food-for-work or cash-for-work programmes year round. It appears that there is no single solution to the present state of affairs. Nonetheless, this should not be met with apathy on the part of government and donors. Various measures to stimulate agricultural growth and more serious investment in the non-agricultural rural economy could provide viable means of livelihood for the landless. In view of Ethiopia's tumultuous rural history, one need not over-emphasise how important such measures are.

Notes

1. This study was part of the International Livestock Center for Africa (ILCA) household survey on 'The Role of Credit in the Uptake of Smallholder Livestock Technology' which took place from December 1992 to March 1994. At the time of data collection the author was employed as a research assistant for the Role of Credit Project.
The sample for this research was based on an examination of records of six peasant associations selected for the Credit Study (see Map). Surveys were carried out at two levels. The first was a single visit hut-to-hut census of two PAs covering a total of 843 households. This was necessitated by the poor state of PA records and by the exclusion of landless families from available lists. The purpose of the PA survey was to record the incidence of landlessness, land-related transactions, labour hiring and non-agricultural employment at the PA level.
Based on the results of the PA wide survey which revealed the strategies used by households to surmount their lack of access to land, the second level of enquiry involved a more detailed study of 48 landless households engaged in land related transactions or marketing of labour. Their strategies were broadly identified as: 1) cash rentals, 2) sharecropping, 3) agricultural fixed contractual labour, 4) agricultural wage/casual labour and 5) employment in non-agriculture.
The sample of the subsequent household survey aimed at stratification by participation in the above variables. Cash rentals were discarded as stratifiers because of their lack of occurrence among landless households while employment in non-agriculture was not used because, while significant at the PA level, the diversity of employment activities in the sector caused them to be too fragmentary for incorporation in a meaningful single visit household survey.
2. At the time of the study an *awraja* was the third level of government administration in Ethiopia after the national and regional levels.

References

BRUCE, J.W., W. HOBEN & D. RAHMATO 1993, *After The Derg: An Assessment of Rural Land Tenure Issues in Ethiopia*, Draft submitted for discussion at the Workshop on Rural Land Tenure Issues in Ethiopia, 27-29 August 1993, Addis Ababa

ETHIOPIA, GOVERNMENT of 1975, 'Proclamation on Public Ownership of Land', *Negarit Gazetta*, 34th year, no. 26

FASIL GEBRE KIROS 1980, 'Agricultural Land Fragmentation: A Problem of Land Distribution Observed in Some Ethiopian Peasant Associations', *Ethiopian Journal of Development Research* , vol. 4, no. 2, 1-14

IBRD (International Bank for Reconstruction and Development) 1993, *World Development Report*, New York, Oxford University Press

III

WEST AFRICA

4

Not by Farming Alone: The Role of Non-Farm Incomes in Rural Hausaland

Kate Meagher and Abdul Raufu Mustapha

Economic development has historically been associated with a declining share of agriculture in GDP and a shift of population to towns. There is a corresponding decline in the proportion of agricultural to non-agricultural incomes. The current context of structural adjustment and environmental stress in Africa has called into question this basic tendency. With an adjustment-induced shift in the terms of trade in favour of agriculture, it is by no means clear that growth should be associated with a relative decline in agricultural incomes. At the same time, increasing environmental stress may reduce the contribution of agriculture to incomes in ways which are not dysfunctional on the receiving side.

Sources of employment that are supposed to absorb labour out of agriculture have declined because of the economic crisis. The failure of the import substitution model of industrialisation and pressures for privatisation and the development of small-scale industry in rural as well as urban areas have redefined the framework of industrial development. The trends however are ambiguous. The growing importance of small-scale informal activities may be an indicator of a new pattern of economic development in unstable market conditions, or may simply represent a diversification into marginal survival activities in the context of economic and environmental decline.

An understanding of the current direction of agrarian change thus requires a careful empirical examination of the relationship between agricultural and non-agricultural incomes within wider historical, environmental and economic contexts. This chapter attempts such an analysis for rural Hausaland in northern Nigeria. It begins with a consideration of some of the major theoretical issues involved in African agrarian change and proceeds to trace the historical evolution of de-agrarianisation in northern Nigeria from the pre-colonial period to the beginning of the structural adjustment era. A subsequent section analyses the impact of adjustment on this process, drawing on field studies carried out in the Kano village of Rogo between 1974-5 and 1992-3, and in two other villages. This is followed by a brief look at the impact of ecological pressures.

The analysis concentrates on the role of non-farm rather than strictly non-agricultural incomes, since agricultural wage labour is included in the non-farm income category. Agricultural wage labour plays a role similar to that of non-agricultural activities in absorbing labour which can no longer be effectively contained within the household farming unit.

Theoretical Considerations

Two theoretical debates are relevant to the issues at hand. The first relates to the role of non-farm activities in agrarian development in Africa. The second centres on the developmental potential of small-scale informal activities in the context of the global economic crisis and restructuring.

Three broad positions can be identified with respect to the former debate in Nigerian literature. The first is that increasing non-farm activities facilitate rural development (Hill 1972; Byerlee et al. 1977; Matlon 1977; Williams 1988). Non-farm activities and agricultural production are essentially complementary in that they absorb surplus labour, particularly in the off-season and among marginal farmers, and generate resources for agricultural intensification. A second position argues that increasing involvement in non-farm activities contributes to a breakdown of rural society. Non-farm activities draw labour out of agriculture and intensify rural labour shortages (Watts 1983; Wallace 1978; Beckman 1987). The third position is that the impact of non-farm activities varies according to class, agricultural systems and economic context (Berry 1993; von Braun and Pandya-Lorch 1991). In periods of economic expansion, or in agricultural systems based heavily on food crops, non-farm activities may facilitate agricultural investment and accumulation; in agricultural systems based on tree crops or in periods of economic decline, diversification into non-farm activities is more likely to represent the struggle for survival.

The second debate directs attention more specifically to the impact of major shifts in the wider economy on the process of de-agrarianisation. The question is whether small-scale informal activities can serve as an engine of growth for rural society in periods of economic crisis and whether they can generate more positive linkages with agriculture and local industry than the previous state-led model of industrialisation.

These questions are taken up in the debate between flexible specialisation and informalisation perspectives. According to advocates of flexible specialisation, small-scale informal activities are uniquely well-suited to leading the process of economic development in Third World countries, especially in times of crisis. They are better able to adapt to disturbed circumstances and segmented markets. The source of this vital flexibility is seen to lie in the ease of combining several enterprises, including farming, and the ability to draw on informal networks of kinship, community and ethnicity for the mobilisation of labour and capital (Rasmussen 1992; Hansohm 1992).

The informalisation perspective calls into question the developmental potential of informal sector expansion under conditions of crisis (Portes et al. 1989). It argues that the proliferation of small-scale activities represents a shift by fiscally-troubled states and large-scale capital towards cheaper and more flexible social arrangements of production and reproduction which involve the exploitation of family, community and ethnic structures of support and labour control. In industrialised countries this process has involved a relocation of production processes and services into the rural areas where there is greater access to unprotected forms of labour (Summers 1991; Marsden 1992; Baxter and Mann 1992). In less-developed countries, the process appears to centre on the informalisation of reproduction, in which the working population is cut loose from state-funded services and economic assistance, and thrown back on informal forms of income generation (Lanzetta de Pardo 1989; Grey-Johnson 1992; Jamal and Weeks 1993).

Several issues raised in these debates are central to evaluating the extent and economic implications of de-agrarianisation in rural Hausaland. The impact on traditional institutions of access to labour, land and capital must be viewed in the light of new opportunities and pressures created by economic crisis and structural adjustment. Does de-agrarianisation represent an increased flexibility in income generation or a response to state neglect and economic or ecological adversity?

Non-Farm Activities in Rural Hausaland

Ecological and Socio-Political Factors

Hausaland lies in the north of Nigeria, stretching from guinea savannah to sahelian ecological zones. The climate is characterised by a short rainy season of three to five months and a long dry season during which agricultural producers are often compelled to pursue other income-earning activities. Maize, sorghum and millet are the major staples and major cash crops. Owing to the predominance of Islam-induced female seclusion, women have little direct participation in agricultural production but income-earning activities from within the family compound are pursued.

A variety of cultural, political and historical factors have also combined to reinforce the importance of non-farm activities in rural Hausaland. The influence of Islamic inheritance practices, the pre-colonial state system, and the development of food-crop agriculture have made access to land and labour more vulnerable to commercialisation and in turn increased the importance of non-farm incomes (McDowell 1969; Beckman 1987; Mustapha and Meagher 1992). This is in contrast to the situation of the cocoa-growing Yoruba peasantry in the south-west of Nigeria. Here, the more clan-based social structure and the peculiarities of tree crop production have tended to limit the commercialisation of land and labour (Berry 1985; Mustapha 1991).

History

In pre-colonial Hausaland a well-developed array of non-farm activities, particularly trade and craft production, constituted a central component of rural livelihoods as well as an important link with the wider political economy (Baier 1980; Hill 1972; Watts 1983). The early years of the colonial period witnessed the destruction of many of the more specialised crafts through taxation, competition from cheap imported goods, and the diversion of raw materials to serve the needs of the metropole (Mustapha 1990; Bello 1982; Baier 1980). While narrowing the scope for traditional non-farm activities, colonial taxation and the general commoditisation of rural life increased the need of the peasantry for cash. This was met in part by the development of groundnut and cotton exports, the colonial demand for labour, and new opportunities for investment in trade and transport. The bulk of the rural population, however, diversified into a variety of petty craft and service activities which were increasingly reoriented to the use of imported raw materials (Jaggar 1973; Mustapha 1990).

After independence, the internal terms of trade began to turn against agriculture in the context of import-substitution industrialisation, falling commodity prices, and later the import euphoria of the Nigerian oil boom. The introduction of fertilisers and other improved inputs under the green revolution strategies of the 1970s intensified the need for non-farm incomes to fund input purchases. In northern Nigeria, the pressures on agricultural livelihoods were exacerbated by the intensification of cycles of drought from the late 1960s onward, which increased the importance of non-farm incomes and circulatory migration in bad years.

The oil boom economy intensified the role of non-farm activities in rural differentiation since access to them became increasingly dependent on access to imported goods and urban incomes (Norman 1970; Matlon 1977). The low returns available from more traditional activities frequently failed to finance adequate levels of agricultural production for the household, weakening control over family labour and increasing the dependence on low-income non-farm sources of income to hire labour or make up for shortfalls in food production (Wallace 1978; Watts 1983; Beckman 1987).

The structure of non-farm activities that emerged was highly vulnerable to crisis in the urban economy. With the onset of economic crisis in 1982 these weaknesses became evident. Urban jobs dried up, access to inputs and capital for informal activities became more difficult and cut-backs in state expenditure and inflationary pressures unleashed by the crisis increasingly turned both consumer and producer terms of trade against small-scale grain farmers (Meagher 1991; Meagher and Yunusa 1991; Swindell and Iliya 1992).

Structural Adjustment and De-agrarianisation

The history of non-farm activities in rural Hausaland up to the introduction of Nigeria's structural adjustment programme in 1986 is one of import-led and urban-dependent expansion. The trend towards de-agrarianisation proceeded in the context of severe pressure on agricultural and non-agricultural income sources, or in response to the policy distortions of the oil boom, rather than from the development of stable income opportunities outside agriculture. Structural adjustment represented an attempt to address these distorting influences. Policies of devaluation, liberalisation of producer prices and input distribution, and the unconventional move of banning imports of rice, maize, wheat and barley, aimed to shift the terms of trade in favour of agriculture and against urban and import-based activities. Theorists predicted a trend towards 'reverse migration', i.e. a population shift back to rural areas in response to increased agricultural production incentives and depressed urban livelihoods (Addison and Demery 1989; Pinstrup-Andersen 1989, but also Jamal and Weeks 1993 in contradiction).

The reality, however, has been less compliant. For one, the dependence of northern Nigerian agriculture on food crops rather than export crops has made it less responsive to devaluation. For another, the widespread use of purchased inputs makes northern Nigerian farmers more vulnerable to market forces. This is particularly striking in the case of fertiliser, the bulk of which is procured on the open market. In the face of devaluation and the progressive removal of input subsidies, sky-rocketing production and living costs have tended to outstrip the increase in grain and other crop prices (Table 1). The implications of these trends for the process of de-agrarianisation require a closer look at the complex social dynamics of access to productive resources in rural Hausaland, and the way they have adapted to the pressures and opportunities created by structural adjustment.

Table 1: Index of Fertiliser, Grain and Rural Consumer Prices in Nigeria (1985 = 100)

Year	Fertiliser price index (official)	Fertiliser price index (market)	Grain price index	Rural consumer price index
1986	112.2	127.8	53.4	-
1987	112.2	-	60.6	-
1988	112.2	194.4	173.0	182
1989	164.6	305.6	179.2	273
1990	225.6	255.6	174.0	293
1991	225.6	-	329.9	328
1992	426.8	766.7	535.8	471

Source: FASCOM Price List 1985-90; KTARDA Quarterly and Annual Reports 1985-92

Trends in De-agrarianisation

Evidence from village studies suggests that patterns of de-agrarianisation vary according to class, location and economic conditions. Data from Rogo village (Table 2), in the grain surplus region of Hausaland, show the proportion of total cash income derived from non-farm activities in three different years: 1974-5 which corresponds to the early oil boom; 1989-90, the year following the first major SAP-induced price rises; and 1992-3, which shows the state of affairs under continually rising input and crop prices. As a large fairly commercialised village, Rogo has a generally high level of non-farm incomes, on average just over one-half of total cash income. The figures presented do not include women's incomes, which, in rural Hausaland, are largely non-agricultural. This will tend to underrepresent the extent of de-agrarianisation in poorer households, where women's incomes represent a larger share of total income (Matlon 1978; Peutz and von Braun 1991).

Table 2: Share of Non-Farm Activities in Total Cash Income in Rogo Village, Nigeria, 1974-5, 1989-90 and 1992-3 (percentage)

	1974-5[1]	1989-90[2]	1992-3[3]
Small-scale	53.2	60.4	67.0
Medium-scale	49.0	67.7	57.4
Large-scale	84.4	58.3	46.6
Average	55.7	59.7	53.0

Source: Fieldwork

1. Sample from Matlon (1977). Small-scale farmers represent the first two quintiles of Matlon's sample, medium-scale the third and fourth quintiles, and large-scale the fifth.
2. Sample from Meagher (1991). Data from this study and the resurvey in 1992-3 do not include incomes from livestock, which is a fairly insignificant proportion of agricultural income in Rogo.
3. Sample from Meagher (1991), resurveyed in Meagher and Ogunwale (1994).

On average, the data indicate the rising importance of non-farm incomes between 1974-5 and 1989-90, followed by a decline between 1989-90 and 1992-93. However, this aggregate trend masks divergent patterns of de-agrarianisation among different economic strata of farmers. Large-scale farmers show a continuous decline in the proportion of income derived from non-farm activities, falling from 84 per cent to 47 per cent of total cash income. Medium-scale farmers, who had less access to non-farm activities prior to the oil boom, show an increase in their role between 1974-5 and 1989-90, and a decline under structural adjustment. Small-scale farmers, however, show a continuous trend toward de-agrarianisation, with non-farm activities rising from 53 per cent to 67 per cent of total cash income.

Patterns of de-agrarianisation in other parts of rural Hausaland vary. Table 3 compares the share of non-farm incomes from a different stratification of the 1992-93 Rogo sample with two other villages represented by a 1992-3 survey of Unguwan Dinya which is located within the Funtua-Bakori agricultural development and irrigation projects, and a 1989-90 survey of Danyashe, a village a few kilometres from the border with the Niger Republic in the arid northern region of Nigerian Hausaland. The importance of non-farm incomes is significantly lower in Unguwan Dinya at 42 per cent of total cash income, and higher in Danyashe, where they constitute more than two-thirds of total cash income. In Unguwan Dinya, subsidies for irrigated farming introduced under the structural adjustment programme have encouraged a greater reliance on agriculture than on non-farm activities. In Danyashe, which is in a grain-deficit region, high grain prices and declining rainfall have made non-farm incomes crucial to food security.

Table 3: Share of Non-Farm Income in Three Hausa Villages during the SAP Period (percentage)

	Danyashe	Rogo	Unguwan Dinya
Lower Stratum	65.3	74.1	39.7
Upper Stratum	72.8	49.5	44.0
Average	67.3	53.0	42.1

Source: Fieldwork

It is necessary to look at the ways in which access to productive resources and markets have been affected both in agriculture and in non-farm activities in order to understand more precisely how structural adjustment measures have produced these various patterns of de-agrarianisation and re-agrarianisation. These in turn have affected the distribution of resources within the household and between households, with significant implications for the process of de-agrarianisation.

Structural Adjustment and Agricultural Production

Rising prices of agricultural inputs and food rather than a shift of urban investment and manpower into rural areas are the driving forces behind the growth of non-farm activities. Rising prices have resulted in a declining use of fertiliser and other inputs among small-scale farmers (Wedderburn 1988; Institute of Agricultural Research 1990). This has had a negative effect on agricultural production, particularly in the case of maize and cowpeas, two of the major cash crops in the region (Institute of Agricultural Research 1990; NAERLS 1989; KTARDA 1991; Mustapha and Meagher 1992). Better-off farmers are not equally affected by rising input costs because of their ability to delay crop sales until later in the season and to sell in urban, industrial and border markets (Swindell and Iliya 1992; Meagher and Ogunwale 1994). This is confirmed by time series data from Rogo (Table 4). Small-scale and medium-scale farmers show declining use of fertiliser and pesticides, and declining levels of agricultural production, while large-scale farmers show an increase on all counts.

Table 4: Changes in Input Use, Production Levels and Proportion of Grain Deficit Households in Rogo Village, Nigeria, 1989-90 and 1992-3 (percentage change)

Farming category	Fertiliser use	Pesticide use	Crop production	% Increase in grain deficit households
Small-scale	-25	-45	-28	17
Medium-scale	-26	-69	56	16
Large-scale	255	250	257	0
Average	68	-49	75	15

Source: Fieldwork

Medium-scale farmers show a decline in both fertiliser and pesticide use, but still register an aggregate increase in crop production, possibly due to their continued ability to control family labour and the intensified exploitation of that labour in the face of other resource constraints. Equally significant is the fact that households in this category are differentially affected. Increasing production is accompanied by an increase in the percentage of grain deficit households, indicating that the productive and self-provisioning capacity of some medium-scale farmers is being eroded. As the table shows, the proportion of small-scale and medium-scale farmers suffering from grain deficits has increased by 17 per cent and 16 per cent respectively between 1989-90 and 1992-3. The pressure of grain deficits is much more severe in the northern part of Nigerian Hausaland where the majority of farmers only produce enough foodgrain for six to seven months of the year (Meagher 1991).

Within this context, small-scale farmers are increasingly dependent on non-farm sources of income to fund inputs and purchase food and other household necessities. Nearly three-quarters of Rogo smallholders fund input purchases from non-farm activities and remittances, compared to 63 per cent of better-off farmers. Rising input costs only serve to increase the need for non-farm incomes. Large-scale farmers on the other hand, at least those in the grain surplus region, have found crop prices sufficiently remunerative, despite rising input costs, to increase their dependence on agriculture.

De-agrarianisation and Access to Land and Labour

The way in which changing conditions of access to land and labour has affected the role of non-farm incomes is less clear than the case of inputs and grain prices. Berry (1993) argues that in the context of the increasing commercialisation of agriculture, membership in social networks has remained the central means of access to land, while access to labour is increasingly dependent on the ability to earn cash through crop sales or non-farm incomes. This view, however, is influenced by Berry's work on the cocoa-growing peasantries of Ghana and Nigerian Yorubaland. In Hausaland, trends in access to both land and labour appear to be more mixed.

In the case of land, there is evidence of growing commercialisation and concentration. During the 1970s, a process of diffusion of land ownership vied with pressures toward concentration, owing to the increasing commercialisation of food crop farming and the desire of women and non-resident others to maintain their legal entitlement to land (Ross 1987; Mustapha and Meagher 1992). The pressures of structural adjustment, however, appear to be tilting the balance in favour of increasing concentration of land ownership in the hands of large- and medium-scale farmers. Among poorer farmers, there is an increasing incidence of mortgaging and sale of land, either for production capital or because of the inability to fund cultivation (Meagher 1991; Swindell and Iliya 1992; Mustapha and Meagher 1992). In addition, abuses of the 1978 Land Use Decree and state incentives and pressures for agro-industrial local sourcing have resulted in the appropriation of large tracts of land for private and industrial farms (Andrae and Beckman 1987).

On the other hand, rising food costs are encouraging urban dwellers to turn to farming. Access to land is less through purchase than through rental in the peri-urban areas or the reassertion of deferred or dormant claims to land within home communities. This trend limits the extent to which the return of urban dwellers to farming is capable of injecting capital into the rural areas.

Trends in access to labour are similarly mixed. Farmers of all strata find themselves hard hit by increasing commercialisation and the cost of labour. Among small-scale farmers, this has reinforced the recourse to non-farm activities to fund agricultural production. It is also leading to cut-backs on ridging and weeding because of the inability to afford the necessary labour (Meagher 1991; KTARDA 1989). The resulting declines in production further reinforce the dependence of small-scale farmers on non-farm income.

The ability of small-scale farmers to benefit from rising agricultural wages is blunted by the fact that the increases have lagged behind the cost of living, as well as the fact that they take labour away from their own farms during critical periods (Egg and Igue 1993; Berry 1993; Meagher and Ogunwale 1994). Increasing dependence on non-farm incomes for input funding, combined with declining real agricultural wages, has resulted in increasing labour shortages, despite talk of a reversal in rural-urban migration. Indications from some studies are that the predominant direction of migration is still from rural to urban areas (CBN/NISER 1992; Gibbon 1993; Meagher and Yunusa 1993).

The rising cost and scarcity of labour has motivated an increase in the use of female wage labour, particularly in harvesting and threshing. There has been some suggestion that this involves the weakening of female seclusion practices (Swindell and Iliya 1992), but evidence from Rogo suggests that most female labour is drawn from women beyond child-bearing age and pastoral Fulani women, neither of whom is subject to seclusion.

In contrast to the general trend of increased commercialisation of labour, the high cost of labour and labour shortages have motivated a return to the mobilisation of labour through social networks. Young children are increasingly pressed into service by their families, especially for planting. Among poorer farmers, there has been a resurgence of the traditional practice of communal work parties known as *gayya* (Meagher 1991; Mustapha and Meagher 1992). However, although cheaper than hired labour, *gayya* is inefficient in responding to the requirements of timeliness in many operations.

Under economic pressure though, social networks do not play a uniformly positive role in facilitating access to labour. Access to resources through membership in kinship and other social networks is not an automatic feature of rural life since such membership requires the investment of time and resources (Ross 1987; Berry 1993). The rising cost of gifts, assistance, food and transport is constraining rural dwellers, especially poorer households, from maintaining network links with their rural and urban relatives. With the continuing crisis, the previously symbiotic exchange of food and economic assistance between rural and urban relatives has begun to break down. Thus, farmers with the option prefer using labour over which they have more direct control. Koranic scholars and local school teachers use their students on their farms, and wealthier farmers who provide hostels for migrant labour use that service to mobilise labour for their own farms.

In fact, economic hardship is forcing poorer households to resort to social networks in ways that actually decrease their access to labour. Sending children out to relatives or for Koranic training continues to be an important coping strategy. This serves to relieve the household of mouths to feed and gains them access to the urban-earned remittances that Koranic students can generate through employment in the urban informal sector, usually in itinerant activities such as hawking or petty load carrying (Mortimore 1989; Meagher and Yunusa 1993). Such migration is usually off-season, but rising transport costs often restrain the timely return of urban migrants.

Impact of SAP on Non-Farm Activities

At the same time as structural adjustment is forcing small-scale farmers to diversify into non-farm activities, it is also eroding the profitability of many of the same activities. Better-off farmers, on the other hand, are not only better placed to benefit from the shift in agricultural fortunes, they also have the capital to seize promising new opportunities in the non-farm sector. However, the pressures of current economic conditions on both the supply and the demand side of non-farm activities are restricting rather than expanding the range of profitable options.

Supply-side Pressures

Structural adjustment has resulted in a decline of employment opportunities in the urban formal sector and an over-saturation in the urban informal sector (Meagher 1991). This has in turn limited non-farm opportunities among medium- and large-scale farmers (Swindell and Iliya 1992; Peutz and von Braun 1991). Moreover, the impact of devaluation on the cost of imported inputs and urban supply networks has also adversely affected rural-based activities, decisively exploding the myth that the dependence of rural non-farm activities on local sources would insulate them from the pressures of SAP (Bagachwa and Stewart 1989). 'Modern' informal activities, which are presented as the cutting edge of rural income diversification, have been among the worst hit. Rural transporters, grain grinders, mechanics, welders and photographers have suffered from the high cost of equipment and materials (Meagher 1991; Meagher and Yunusa 1991 and 1993).

The myth of local sourcing has been further discredited by the impact of SAP on access to locally produced tools and raw materials. Many such inputs have some import content, e.g. scrap metal for blacksmiths' tools and materials, fertiliser for agricultural commodities, chemicals and dyes for leather or textiles. In addition,

SAP-induced incentives for exports and local sourcing force small-scale producers to compete with exporters, urban consumers and local industry for access to local raw materials. Local hides for leather are increasingly exported, while scrap metal is exported or recycled by urban industry, making these materials scarce in rural areas (Meagher 1991).

While the costs of engaging in non-farm activities are rising, the business capital of most farmers is being eroded by the rising cost of agricultural production and household survival. In Rogo, 60 per cent of the lower stratum of farmers and 26 per cent of the upper stratum complained that high grain prices decreased their business capital (Meagher and Ogunwale 1994). The result is an increasing concentration of rural dwellers in low-income non-farm activities, where capital requirements are small but competition is correspondingly great and profits meagre (Meagher 1991).

Demand-Side Developments

Bagachwa and Stewart (1989) point out that demand is a major constraint on the development of non-farm activities. The hope has been expressed that, under structural adjustment, rising agricultural incomes would boost demand while declining urban incomes would create further demand by reorienting demand towards rural goods and services (Bagachwa and Stewart 1989). Things have not worked out quite that way in rural Hausaland. Agricultural incomes have fallen among the lower strata of farmers, the group most likely to provide an expanding market for rural goods and services. Hardship in the urban areas has generated an over-saturated urban informal sector, which not only caters to the demand generated by urban dwellers, but is increasingly penetrating rural areas to compete with the rural informal sector. In Rogo, 52 per cent of small-scale farmers claimed their non-farm activities suffered from declining returns, and an additional 16 per cent claimed real returns were worse.

Areas of expanding demand in the Rogo non-farm sector were limited to local inferior goods and 'hardship' markets. These include tailoring and repair of basic household items such as shoes, bicycles and plastic goods. These activities cannot operate as engines of growth since demand for them is bound to decline as incomes rise, even among the lower strata of the rural population. Activities that have a better scope and have done well under SAP are those with skill- or capital-based barriers to entry. These include plastic and scrap metal recycling in the urban centres, and large-scale trade in agricultural commodities. However, long-distance grain trade, once the mainstay of agrarian accumulation in rural Hausaland (Clough

1981; Williams 1988), has not escaped unscathed. Most small- and medium-scale traders interviewed in Rogo in 1990-1 had been forced to stop or reduce their trade by 1993. Large-scale traders, who had access to expanding urban, industrial and border markets, were benefiting until the unbanning of wheat and the devaluation of the CFA Franc induced a collapse in grain prices.

De-agrarianisation and the Household

Ideological Issues

Under economic pressure there is a tendency for the burden of household survival to shift to women (Beneria 1991; Meagher and Yunusa 1993). In rural Hausaland, this process involves an inversion of the traditional structure of financial responsibilities. According to Islamic ideology, which defines male and female obligations among the bulk of the rural Hausa, the provisioning of the household is a male responsibility. Although women have traditionally engaged in income-generating activities, their incomes are reserved for 'personal' use, meaning expenditure on their own relatives, gifts for ceremonies and extra expenditures for their children.

Women's incomes are now increasingly devoted to the purchase of basic household necessities that are theoretically the responsibility of their husbands, including soup ingredients, soap and clothing (Meagher 1991). This process is masked through a gradual extension of the meaning of 'personal' expenditure, and by the rise of an ideology of 'pitching in', which presents as intermittent and temporary something that is increasingly becoming the pervading norm in poorer households. In better-off households, women's incomes have even become an important source of credit for agricultural inputs and labour.

Women's Incomes and Household Reproduction

The rising importance of women's incomes in household production and reproduction constitutes a *de facto* process of de-agrarianisation, since women are generally restricted from engaging in agriculture. Women who do farm, principally women from better-off households or from the far north, find their productive capacity increasingly disabled in the current economic environment since they are even more susceptible than men to high labour and input costs. Not only is their level of production capital usually lower but they are required to farm largely by means of hired labour, or the labour of husbands and children, which is less available as labour constraints increase.

In non-farm as well as agricultural pursuits, the profitability of women's activities has been undermined by the climate of rising input costs and weakened markets. The majority of women in the villages studied were involved in processing agricultural commodities, largely grain, groundnuts and rice, all of which have experienced 300 to 400 per cent price rises since 1985. In Rogo, over two-thirds of the women interviewed had been forced to cut down production because of the high cost of raw materials. The high capital costs of the more lucrative activities were tending to concentrate women in the petty snack trade, where increased competition and weak markets were further squeezing profits. Significantly, a number of women reported reduced ceremony attendance and other forms of investment in social networks (Meagher 1991).

In the face of declining subsidies and institutional support and the threat these pressures are posing to rural livelihoods, the state is now attempting to institutionalise the increasing reliance on female incomes. The formation of women's groups for increased income generation, and the devotion of research and extension resources to these activities have become dominant themes in Nigerian rural development strategies (Institute of Agricultural Research 1992). While the official ideology speaks of the 'empowerment of women', the reality is that of a shifting of the burden of reproduction from the state to women. As Geisler points out: 'The "empowerment" that is supposed to spring from such activities has thus far conferred on women the doubtful "power" of supplying the services and the labour that states are not willing or able to finance any longer' (Geisler 1993).

De-agrarianisation and the Environment

Much of Nigerian Hausaland lies within the semi-arid zone which is characterised by average annual rainfall of less than 1,000 mm, a short growing season and periodic drought (Mortimore 1989). The central role of non-farm activities in rural Hausa society has evolved not only in response to the short duration of the farming season, but as a means of coping with unreliable rainfall and the constant threat of drought.

It has generally been accepted that the semi-arid zone has experienced declining rainfall in the past 20 years. In the semi arid part of rural Hausaland, the decline since the 1970s has been of the order of 33 per cent of the long-term mean (Mortimore 1989). Further south, in the area around Rogo, there is no evidence of declining rainfall, but increased variability. A late start or early cessation of rain and prolonged dry spells during the growing season have become more frequent. This exerts a negative effect on yields and tends to lead to an increase in insect infestation with consequent increasing stress on cropping patterns (Mustapha and Meagher 1992).

Increased rainfall uncertainty has intensified the reliance on non-farm activities, both out of necessity and as an insurance measure. In the far north of rural Hausaland, where local income-earning opportunities are few and relatively unremunerative, circulatory migration has traditionally been used to fill in the gaps in household income (Mortimore 1989). Among slightly better-off farmers the relationship between environmental stress and de-agrarianisation has been mitigated in the past 10 years by the rise of small-scale irrigated farming during the dry season (Meagher 1991; Kore 1993). In Rogo, circulatory migration occurs particularly in times of stress such as during a drought or in periods of severe economic pressure (Mustapha and Meagher 1992).

Debate exists as to whether the increasing unreliability of rainfall and the resulting dependence on non-farm activities represent a temporary trend in a larger cycle or the advance of a more permanent process of desertification and a dissolution of the peasantry. Mortimore (1989) believes that increasing dependence on non-farm incomes represents a process of adaptive response in the context of a harsh and unstable natural environment. This process of de-agrarianisation, particularly as realised through seasonal or other forms of temporary migration, is neither disruptive of agricultural systems nor necessarily permanent. Rather, it is one means of enhancing the flexibility of the system and hence its capacity to withstand stress.

Other environmental commentators focus on the fragility of semi-arid agriculture and the vulnerability of traditional adaptive mechanisms to economic pressures within the wider economy (Meagher and Mustapha 1992; Watts 1983). Diversification strategies oriented towards maximising flexibility in an environment of uncertainty may contribute to the process of environmental degradation and undermine rather than enhance the sustainability of agricultural systems:

> ...crops and techniques of production which provide flexibility in the short run do not necessarily serve to enhance the sustainability of agricultural production in the long run. Under unstable economic and political conditions, farmers are reluctant to tie up land, labour, and capital in long-term projects, such as soil conservation, water control, or fixed capital formation, which may sustain soil fertility or

> augment the availability of land and labour. Instead, they are likely to spend more time in off-farm employment or out-migration... (Berry 1993).

This debate cannot be resolved here. A great deal more research would be needed before it can be established whether and how increased non-farm activities cripple agrarian livelihoods or undermine environmental management practices. What is clear is that in the context of structural adjustment, new stresses have been added to an already sensitive balance. Notions of the resilience and flexibility of semi-arid agrarian systems rely heavily on the persistence of traditional social welfare mechanisms and the continued absorptive capacity of the urban informal sector (Mortimore 1989). Earlier discussion has indicated that these stress-absorbing mechanisms can no longer be taken for granted. Without them, environmental pressures are likely to entail the degradation of both rural livelihoods and their natural resource base.

Conclusions

The experience of rural Hausaland serves to illustrate that the trend towards de-agrarianisation is not unstoppable nor is it necessarily developmental. It is a process that is taking place within a context of specific policy measures and socio-economic and environmental factors. The liberalisation of goods and foreign exchange prices under SAP and other measures to encourage the local sourcing of grain for industrial and consumer uses have shifted the terms of trade in favour of agriculture for those with access to high-value urban and border markets. The result has been to increase the share of agricultural incomes among large-scale farmers. Among poorer farmers, the increasing commercialisation and rising costs of agricultural production are resulting in a degenerative process of de-agrarianisation, exacerbated by the intensification of environmental stress. Poorer households are forced to diversify into a variety of marginal non-farm activities in order to make ends meet.

Despite the prevailing context of a triumph of market forces, social networks have remained an important source of access to land and labour. This does not diminish the role of non-farm activities however, since these activities can provide a context for the mobilisation of non-wage labour, as well as contributing resources to invest in maintaining membership in kinship, community and ethnic networks. In the face of growing economic pressures, however, active membership in social networks is increasingly restricted to better-off farmers. The rising cost of farming leaves weaker rural households less able to invest in social networks, gradually eliminating their function as a rural safety net (Reardon 1991; Berry 1993). This reinforces the dependence of poorer households on commercial forms of access to resources for production and for the reproduction of the household.

In the process, rural-urban ties and attendant patterns of migration and resource flows have not been reversed so much as disrupted. The contention that shifting terms of trade against urban centres would channel resources and labour into the rural areas rests on the assumption that the greater reliance on market forces would not affect the persistence of ties between rural and urban relatives. In rural Hausaland, the evidence suggests that, on average, these ties have been weakened by adjustment, forcing a large proportion of rural households to increase their reliance on non-farm avenues of access to resources, including an intensification of seasonal patterns of rural-urban migration.

The result has been a trend towards greater fragility rather than flexibility of rural livelihood strategies and towards diversification rather than specialisation. Rural non-farm activities are plagued by the increasing saturation of the rural and urban informal sectors and an intensifying cost-price squeeze, which limits their scope for flexibility or innovation. These pressures also tend to undermine the development of the levels of quality and skill that would be necessary to attract linkages with industry or other formal sector institutions (Bagachwa and Stewart 1989; Liedholm 1990). Activities that are benefiting from the shift of demand away from urban or imported goods are doing so in the context of pressures which encourage a decline in quality and variety in order to reduce costs (Meagher and Yunusa 1993).

These trends make it unlikely that the growing importance of non-farm incomes in rural Hausaland will encourage the emergence of decentralised production strategies and industrial subcontracting. What appears to be happening is an informalisation, not of production, but reproduction. As the state withdraws from the provision of social services and subsidised access to inputs and credit, diversification into a variety of survival activities is necessary to fill the gap in rural incomes. The burden of this process is falling increasingly heavily on women, despite their general lack of participation in agricultural production. If the example of rural Hausaland is anything to go by, inadvertent de-agrarianisation engendered by SAP will prove as unsustainable as the import-substitution industrialisation it has replaced.

References

ADDISON, T. & L. DEMERY 1989, 'The Economics of Rural Poverty Alleviation', in S. Commander (ed.), *Structural Adjustment and Agriculture*, London, ODI and James Currey

ANDRAE, G. & B. BECKMAN 1987, *Industry Goes Farming: The Nigerian Raw Material Crisis and the Case of Textiles and Cotton*, Uppsala, Scandinavian Institute of African Studies

BAGACHWA, M. & F. STEWART 1989, *Rural Industries and Rural Linkages in Sub-Saharan Africa: A Survey*, mimeo

BAIER, S. 1980, *An Economic History of Central Niger*, Oxford, Clarendon

BAXTER, V. & S. MANN 1992, 'The Survival and Revival of Non-Wage Labor in a Global Economy', *Sociologia Ruralis*, vol. 32, no. 2-3, 231-47

BECKMAN, B. 1987, 'Public Investment and Agrarian Transformation in Northern Nigeria', in M. Watts (ed.), *State, Oil and Agriculture in Nigeria*, Berkeley, Institute of International Studies, University of California Press

BELLO, S. 1982, *State and Economy in Kano 1894-1960: A Study of Colonial Domination*, Zaria, Ahmadu Bello University Ph.D. Thesis

BENERIA, L. 1991, 'Structural Adjustment, the Labour Market and the Household: The Case of Mexico', in G. Standing & V. Tokman (eds), *Towards Social Adjustment*, Geneva, ILO

BERRY, S. 1985, *Fathers Work for Their Sons: Accumulation, Mobility, and Class Formation in an Extended Yoruba Community*, Berkeley, University of California Press

____, 1993, *No Condition is Permanent: The Social Dynamics of Agrarian Change in Sub-Saharan Africa*, Madison, University of Wisconsin Press

BRAUN, J. von & R. PANDYA-LORCH (eds) 1991, *Income Sources of Malnourished People in Rural Areas: Microlevel Information and Policy Implications*, IFPRI Working Papers on Commercialization of Agriculture and Nutrition no. 5

BYERLEE, D. et al. 1977, *Rural Employment in Tropical Africa: Summary of Findings*, Michigan, Michigan State University Working Paper no. 20

CBN/NISER 1992, *The Impact of SAP on Nigerian Agriculture and Rural Life*, National Report vol. 1, Ibadan

CLOUGH, P. 1981, 'Farmers and Traders in Hausaland', *Development and Change*, vol. 12, 273-92

EGG, J. & J. IGUE 1993, *Market-Driven Integration in the Eastern Subregion: Nigeria's Impact on its Immediate Neighbours*, INRA/IRAM/UNB Synthesis Report

FASCOM 1985-1992, *Price List*

GEISLER, G. 1993, 'Silences Speak Louder Than Claims: Gender, Household, and Agricultural Development in Southern Africa', *World Development*, vol. 21, no. 12, 1965-80

GIBBON, P. (ed.) 1993, *Social Change and Economic Reform in Africa*, Uppsala, Scandinavian Institute of African Studies

GODDARD, A.D. 1973, 'Industry in Zaria', *Samaru Research Bulletin*, no. 181

GREY-JOHNSON, C. 1992, 'The African Informal Sector at the Crossroads: Emerging Policy Options', *Africa Development*, vol. 17, no. 1, 65-91

HANSOHM, D. 1992, 'Small Enterprise Flexibility in Sudan', *IDS Bulletin*, vol. 23, no. 3

HILL, P. 1972, *Rural Hausa: A Village and a Setting*, Cambridge, Cambridge University Press

INSTITUTE OF AGRICULTURAL RESEARCH 1990, *Agricultural Extension Services,* Cropping Scheme Meeting, Zaria

____, 1992, *Technology For Women: Terminal Report*, Zaria, Institute of Agricultural Research, Ford Foundation Project

JAGGAR, P. 1973, 'Kano City Blacksmiths: Precolonial Distribution, Structure and Organisation', *Savannah*, vol. 2, no. 1, 11-25

JAMAL, V. & J. WEEKS 1993, *Africa Misunderstood or Whatever Happened to the Rural-Urban Gap?*, London, Macmillan

KORE, H. 1993, 'L'Impact des Echanges Frontaliers sur la Dynamique des Systèmes de Production et la Securite Alimentaire: Le Cas de la Region Deficitaire de Diffa', in J. Egg (ed.), *L'Economie Agricole et Alimentaire du Niger: Vers une Integration au Marche du Nigeria?*, INRA/UNB/IRAM

KTARDA 1985-1992, *Crop and Weather Reports,* Katsina

____, 1991, *On-Farm Adaptive Research,* Katsina

LANZETTA DE PARDO, M. et al. 1989, 'The Articulation of Formal and Informal Sectors in the Economy of Bogota, Columbia', in A. Portes et al. (eds.), *The Informal Economy*, Baltimore, Johns Hopkins University Press

LIEDHOLM, C. 1990, *The Dynamics of Small-Scale Industry in Africa and the Role of Policy,* Washington, D.C., GEMINI

MARSDEN, T. 1992, 'Exploring a Rural Sociology for the Fordist Transition', *Sociologia Ruralis*, vol. 32, no. 2-3, 209-30

MATLON, P.J. 1977, *The Size Distribution, Structure, and Determinants of Personal Incomes among Farmers in the North of Nigeria*, Cornell University Ph.D. Thesis

____, 1978, *Income Distribution and Patterns of Expenditure, Savings, and Credit among Farmers in the North of Nigeria*, Department of Agricultural Economics Occasional Paper 96, Cornell University

McDOWELL, C. 1969, 'The Breakdown of Traditional Land Tenure in Northern Nigeria', in M. Gluckman (ed.), *Ideas and Procedures in African Customary Law*, Oxford, Oxford University Press

MEAGHER, K. 1991, *Priced Out of the Market: The Effect of Market Liberalization and Parallel Trade on Smallholder Incomes in Northern Nigeria*, McNamara Fellowship Report

MEAGHER, K. & M.B. YUNUSA 1991, *Limits to Labour Absorption: Conceptual and Historical Background to Adjustment in Nigeria's Informal Sector,* UNRISD Discussion Paper 28

____, 1993, *Informalization and Its Discontents: Coping with Structural Adjustment in the Nigerian Urban Informal Sector,* Geneva, UNRISD Research Report

MEAGHER, K. & S. OGUNWALE 1994, *The Grain Drain: The Impact of Cross-Border Grain Trade on Agricultural Production in Northern Nigeria,* Research Report for IRAM/INRA/LARES Project on the Eastern Sub-Market (Nigeria and neighbouring countries)

MORTIMORE, M. 1989, *Adapting to Drought: Farmers, Famines and Desertification in West Africa*, Cambridge, Cambridge University Press

MUSTAPHA, A.R. 1990, *Peasant Differentiation and Politics in Rural Kano: 1900-1987*, University of Oxford D.Phil. Thesis

____, 1991, *Structural Adjustment and Multiple Modes of Social Livelihood in Nigeria*, UNRISD Discussion Paper 26

____ & K. MEAGHER 1992, 'Stress, Adaptation and Resilience in Rural Kano', *CNS*, vol. 5, no. 2

NAERLS 1989, 1990 & 1991, *The Performance of the 1989 Cropping Season in Nigeria*, Summary of a Compilation of Field Evaluation Reports

NIGERIA NATIONAL ARCHIVES, *Taki Assessment and Revenue Survey, Kano Province*, Kaduna, Kanprof. 1708A

NORMAN, D.W. 1970, 'Labour Inputs of Farmers: A Case Study of Zaria Province of the North Central State of Nigeria', *Samaru Research Bulletin*, no. 116, Zaria, Institute of Agricultural Research

PEUTZ, D. & J. von BRAUN 1991, 'Sources and Instability of Income of the Malnourished Rural Poor in the Gambia', in J. von Braun and R. Pandya-Lorch (eds), *Income Sources of Malnourished People in Rural Areas: Microlevel Information and Policy Implications*, IFPRI Working Papers on Commercialization of Agriculture and Nutrition no. 5

PINSTRUP-ANDERSEN, P. 1989, 'The Impact of Macroeconomic Adjustment: Food Security and Nutrition', in S. Commander (ed.), *Structural Adjustment and Agriculture*, London, ODI and James Currey

PORTES, A., M. CASTELLS & L. BENTON (eds) 1989, *The Informal Economy*, Baltimore, Johns Hopkins University Press

RASMUSSEN, J. et al. (eds), 1992, 'Introduction: Exploring a New Approach to Small-Scale Industry', *IDS Bulletin*, vol. 23, no. 3

REARDON, T. 1991, 'Income Sources of the Malnourished Rural Poor in a Drought Year in Burkina Faso', in J. von Braun & R. Pandya-Lorch (eds), *Income Sources of Malnourished People in Rural Areas: Microlevel Information and Policy Implications*, IFPRI Working Papers on Commercialization of Agriculture and Nutrition no. 5

ROSS, P. 1987, 'Land as a Right to Membership: Land Tenure Dynamics in a Peripheral Area of the Kano Close-Settled Zone', in M. Watts (ed.), *State, Oil and Agriculture in Nigeria*, Berkeley, Institute of International Studies, University of California Press

SUMMERS, G. 1991, 'Minorities in Rural Society', *Rural Sociology*, vol. 56, no. 2, 177-88

SWINDELL, K. & M.A. ILIYA 1992, *Accumulation, Consolidation and Survival: Non Farm Incomes and Agrarian Change in Northwest Nigeria*, Project on African Agriculture Working Paper no. 6, New York, Social Science Research Council

WALLACE, T. 1978, 'The Concept of Gandu: How Useful Is It in Understanding Labour Relations in Rural Hausa Society?', *Savannah*, vol. 7, no. 2, 137-50

WATTS, M. 1983, *Silent Violence*, Berkeley, University of California Press

——, 1987, 'Agriculture and Oil-Based Accumulation: Stagnation or Transformation?', in M. Watts (ed.), *State, Oil and Agriculture in Nigeria*, Berkeley, Institute of International Studies, University of California

WEDDERBURN, S. 1988, *Key Issues in Formulating Fertilizer Price Policy: An Evaluation of Multiple Impact of Alternative Price Levels*, Kaduna, Annexes, APMEU

WILLIAMS, G. 1988, 'Why is there No Agrarian Capitalism in Nigeria?', *Journal of Historical Sociology*, vol. 1, no. 4, 345-98

5

Winners and Losers: Household Fortunes in the Urban Peripheries of Northern Nigeria

Mohammed A. Iliya and Ken Swindell

De-agrarianisation needs to be understood in terms of location, time and class of people, in recognition of the fact that the processes of change in Africa are produced by the refraction of external forces through prisms of local experience, while locally generated changes are constructed within particular cultures and environments. Therefore, the following analysis is location- and time-specific, dealing with urban hinterlands in north-west Nigeria and spanning the period from 1976 to 1990, when the Nigerian political economy underwent significant changes associated with the oil boom and its aftermath.

During this period towns expanded and new urban-based job opportunities attracted rural dwellers from the hinterlands, either as permanent migrants, or as daily commuters. Many rural households became increasingly dependent on non-farm jobs and sold land, others used off-farm income to improve and extend their farms and take advantage of rising food prices in the towns. The urban food market also stimulated large-scale farming in the peripheries, while the expropriation of land by the state for institutional uses fed into the de-agrarianisation process. The downturn in the Nigerian economy at the beginning of the 1980s, however, led to a contraction of employment, especially in service and construction industries. Some households which were over-dependent on non-farm incomes became vulnerable, while others benefited at their expense. The social and economic differentiation of households increased, and there were conspicuous 'winners and losers'.

The role of towns in shaping social and economic change in Africa has been the subject of extensive discussions, as urban product and job markets have had an important impact on surrounding areas. In the 1960s, urban-rural interactions became part of development planning, whereby cities were seen as growth-poles and a means of development from above. However, from the 1970s onwards such development scenarios were attacked from diametrically opposed camps of populists and Marxists, principally on the grounds of urban-bias. More recently in the 1980s the attack on urban-bias has been taken up by the New Economics and Counter Revolution in development economics espoused by the World Bank and the IMF.

Clearly urban-rural relations are of continuing concern and importance, both on theoretical and practical grounds. But is the concept of a rural-urban divide necessarily the most appropriate one? Perhaps there is a case for emphasising the urban region and the changing interactions between town and countryside, together with an analysis of the multiplicity of production and exchange relations within towns and urban hinterlands. For example, the provisioning of cities links producers and consumers, food supply bridges the conditions of production, ecology and conditions of exchange which reveal the exercise of power by different groups and classes. Another important bridge, and one particularly relevant to this chapter, is the town as a source of employment for rural people, many of whom combine farm and non-farm work, either sequentially or contemporaneously. Also there are urban dwellers who have rights to land and farms within rural areas. Many households and individuals 'straddle' town and countryside, and there is a double participation in the wage sector and domestic-based agriculture. Rural communities and households frequently comprise a heterogeneity of production and exchange relations, where none is fully interpretable without reference to the other.

Such situations are symptomatic of partially transformed economies and the juxtaposition of different production systems, which engender periodic, seasonal, and daily flows of people, goods, services and capital. Many extended households are bi-local or multi-local, as they preserve varying levels of social and economic cohesion although they are geographically divided. Therefore, it is necessary to be wary of simplistic dichotomies such as urban versus rural and avoid separating urban and rural development issues. Terms such as urban and rural are useful in identifying physical entities and directional flows, but there are dangers of conflating people with places, which is one weakness of the urban-bias model. It is people rather than places which are exploited, and the poor and the well-off are found in both towns and villages. Neither can it be assumed that differences between towns and villages are greater within either of these categories.

Urban-rural relationships are particularly important in Nigeria, which is the most populous country in Africa and where some of the continent's largest towns and most extensive areas of urbanisation are to be found. During successive military regimes and periods of turbulence which have marked post-independence Nigeria, the creation of new states with their attendant state capitals has been used to dampen down inter-regional conflicts, as well as rewarding political allies and clients. Such derived urbanisation was a prominent feature of the 1970s and 1980s, inflating modest provincial towns and expanding historic urban nuclei.

North-west and north-central Nigeria are predominantly Muslim, inhabited by the Hausa and Fulani who have a long history of centralised urban-based states extracting tribute and taxation from allegiant populations in densely populated hinterlands. There is a corresponding history of trading and a well-developed social division of labour, evidenced by a wide spectrum of small-scale service and manufacturing entities. The long dry season was traditionally the time when rural people found off-farm work. This phenomenon expanded during the colonial period as new systems of taxation and monetisation stimulated seasonal circulatory migration. For example, in the 1950s some 250,000 men left both rural and urban areas of Sokoto Province to become dry season labour migrants principally in southern Nigeria and the Gold Coast (Prothero 1957; Swindell 1984). Thus traditionally, there was both occupational specialisation and household diversification in the north-west, with the former more characteristic of urban areas and the latter of rural ones.

The situation changed with the oil boom, and arguably at this point de-agrarianisation accelerated as the proportion of rural household incomes derived from non-farm work began to rise, and dependence on them strengthened as jobs became more numerous and accessible through cheap transport. Traditional dry season non-farm employment was replaced by permanent employment, with some rural households, or some household members, having more specialised non-farm jobs. People in urban peripheries and hinterlands lost interest in farming, and some sold land. During the 1980s, however, the collapse of the oil boom combined with structural adjustment caused retrenchment and cut-backs in the private and public sectors, with subsequent job losses, while the ban on food imports raised food prices. The economic crisis has deepened in the 1990s, precipitated by economic mismanagement and further financial deregulation, coupled with anxieties about the governance of Nigeria. Urban food prices have continued to rise, and capital is being shifted into commercial farming using hired farm labour, which is an important source of income for many households. In addition to these changes in the Nigerian political economy, increasing population densities, land fragmentation and periods of climatic uncertainty have added to the impetus to find off-farm work as a means of survival.

It is against this background that the following analysis looks at households principally in the hinterland of two towns in Sokoto State - Gusau and Sokoto - using 1989-90 survey findings. The former developed as the railhead town of the north-west and now comprises some 80,000 to 100,000 people. The latter is the state capital and historic centre of the Sokoto caliphate and has a population of some 250,000 people.

Rural Households and Non-Farm Work in the Gusau Periphery

The survey examined extended or composite households in three villages located between two and fifty kilometres around Gusau. One-quarter of these households could be described as co-residential, that is where the head and his married and unmarried sons lived in the same compound. Another quarter comprised heads who had one or more sons living in the village, and one or more living in town. But the majority were households where the head lived with his wives and younger children, while sons and their families resided in towns. In general, households were best described as composite families characterised by a variety of fluid relationships and obligations displaying both centripetal and centrifugal tendencies. They were arenas of cooperation and conflict, of bargaining and negotiation, which bound them into social groups in addition to the ties of descent and kinship. The social and economic 'glue' which held a number of separated households together appeared to be the continued rights to land, especially in the face of rising land prices. In addition, rising urban food prices not only made farming of certain crops such as beans more attractive, but strengthened food transfers between urban- and rural-based household members.

Non-farm and off-farm jobs were a source of both internal and external differentiation, and the incomes derived from them influenced levels of well-being. Non-farm jobs were crucial to the physical reproduction and survival of some households, but they also allowed some to have moderate prosperity, and for a few the possibility of sustained accumulation. In 1989-90, households could be differentiated according to the nature and array of their non-farm jobs, together with the strength of linkages and transfers between heads and their sons, and the degree of dependence on non-farm incomes.

The data collected in our study villages showed that both individuals and households frequently combined several jobs which spanned formal and informal occupations, rural and urban-based employment, and self-employment and hired labour. But despite such variations there were three discernible groups of households according to their occupational characteristics.

Wealthy Farming Households with Jobs and Business Connections

One conspicuously wealthier group comprised those families whose head had a permanent job within the state sector or who had businesses such as trading and contracting, or who possibly combined all of these occupations. In addition the heads of households in this group had non-resident sons who also had permanent salaried jobs in banking, teaching, nursing or accountancy and who were making remittances of N1,000 or more. Some indication of the relative value of the naira at this time can be given in terms of the price of food in the local market where a 25 kg bundle of millet cost N30. All of the families in this wealthier group had a firm foothold within the state sector and were well-versed in the workings of its bureaucracy, as well as having had formal western education or training.

This group of families were representative of those members of rural society who were incorporated into the 'modern sector' especially after the Nigerian oil boom of the late 1970s and who were still enjoying the benefits of the recirculation of oil rents via the state wages bill, or through trading with state agencies. While salaries from teaching or nursing may not be substantial, these were permanent jobs which, taken together with the produce of their farms and inputs provided by other family members, allowed household heads to generate relatively good incomes, as well as the possibility of accumulation and farm improvement. Also, as previously noted, some of those interviewed were combining these jobs with private sector activities as traders and local contractors. The wealthiest head interviewed was a full-time trader and contractor, while one former teacher had moved into full-time grain trading. Within this group of relatively well-off families there was also a Koranic teacher whose status within the village allowed him access to group labour, as well as labour from his students and a substantial income from consultations.[1]

Wealthier household heads and their families were either undertaking salaried employment in the modern formal sector with other occupations rooted in the traditional Hausa social division of labour, or they were fully committed to trading. All were involved in farming, primarily as commodity producers. For some households the route to salaried employment has been via western education, but for others, access to better jobs and business opportunities has been through their membership of, or clientage with the local Muslim aristocracy and related political parties. Furthermore the influence of politicians and bureaucrats has been enhanced by 'catchment area politics', which refers to the policy whereby permanent employment in the government sector is reserved for indigenes of that state. As Sokoto state was divided into 37 local government areas in 1989, local politics played an important role in sharing out available jobs. The patronage of village and district heads was actively sought, especially for semi-skilled and unskilled jobs. The power of local governments was also strengthened after 1987 when the military government decided to finance them directly, rather than through subventions to the states.

One example of successful non-farm employment spanning the past 20 years was provided by an informant in Dayau village. This man was currently a nursing superintendent in Gusau, a profession which he combined with grain trading, petty trading and farming. As a young man he had been close to his father, who was the District Head, a title to which he had hoped to succeed but in fact had not done so. After attending the local primary school, he studied at a teachers' training college and his first professional job was not as a nurse, but as a primary school teacher. During this time, largely through his father's influence, he became a licensed buying agent for the United Africa Company. In 1976 he transferred to nursing, but it was his job as a buying agent which formed the springboard for his present activities as a grain buyer and petty trader.

The wealthiest head in the survey, the full-time trader and contractor previously referred to, was the son of the late village head, who in turn had been brought up as a child with the District Head in the household of the late Sultan of Sokoto. His non-farm annual income was N23,000-40,000 depending on the flow of petty contracts and grain deals, together with returns from hiring out his ox-plough, and the business from his petrol-driven grindery.[2] Such petrol-driven food grinders capable of producing N50 per day profit were found in all the villages surveyed, and were run by local well-to-do farmers or by relatives of urban-based entrepreneurs. In addition to non-farm income, the yield from the informant's farms was estimated at N19,170.[3]

It is difficult to assess incomes in many rural situations, especially on a comparative basis. In our survey, incomes have been derived from declared non-farm earnings, transfers of money and gifts, and the value of crops harvested using local market prices at specific dates. This rather crude method enabled us to estimate orders of magnitude for sorting household heads into three categories. Thus the wealthiest head had a potential income of over N50,000 per annum, well in excess of other household heads in the upper echelons who had estimated annual incomes of between N11,700 and N19,169 from farm and non-farm sources. With one exception, all of those in this group enjoyed non-farm incomes which amounted to between 48 and 60 per cent of their total incomes.

Poor Farming Households with Sporadic Supplementary Employment

Turning to the poorest households it becomes apparent that the criteria used for grouping household heads does not simply rest on total income, but also on the continuity and reliability of their off-farm and non-farm employment, and of contributions from their sons. For example, poorer household heads had non-farm jobs which were seasonal or casual, and if they were permanent they were the poorest paid occupations. These households were involved in non-farm jobs as a means of survival in rural areas and were frequently 'land poor'. One head was a watchman at the Gusau flour mills during the dry season. One sold firewood during the wet season and repaired houses in the dry season. Another head was a casual migrant worker in the dry season, while another sold water, and a third sold herbal medicines. Although non-farm incomes are low and come from casual rather than permanent employment, these earnings nonetheless formed a substantial proportion of the total household income. Of the household heads interviewed in this group, the majority derived between 33 and 58 per cent of their incomes from non-farm sources. In this respect the proportion of non-farm earnings of the poor was similar to that of the wealthy, but in total these earnings were many times smaller and were vital to household reproduction.

Total annual household incomes of the poorest group ranged from N2,000 to N7,455, and, unlike the other two groups of household heads, transfers of money and gifts from their non-resident sons were either non-existent or of a very low order. The jobs of non-resident sons matched those of their fathers, and included jobs as watchmen, domestic servants and begging. Even if they did have better clerical jobs, they made no contribution to their fathers' households in their home village. In general the rural poor were not characterised by either their unemployment or underemployment, but by having a lot of work to do with rather low returns.[4] These households showed little specialisation, but considerable income diversification. Their jobs were erratic, seasonal and poorly paid, and were pursued in order to survive. The conditions and hours worked were also less than satisfactory which led some workers to take either traditional Hausa or western type stimulants to enhance their work capacity. Some employers even mixed stimulants into mid-day food to maximise output from their workers.

Intermediate Farming Households with Reliable Non-Farm Employment

As in other investigations of the rural economy, it was not difficult to identify the wealthier and poorest household heads, but the intermediate group was more diverse and variable. In terms of their non-farm jobs, the pattern of this group seemed to be one of modest, permanent jobs for the head such as that of messenger, cleaner, cobbler or blacksmith, but better-paid employment for non-resident sons. The jobs of the sons were more like those of the wealthier household heads, that is they had permanent waged or salaried jobs in the urban formal sector, for example as a driver, soldier, mechanic, telephone operator, teacher, nurse or clerk. This group of household heads with upwardly mobile sons maintained close links with them and consistently received remittances and other transfers, while the sons exerted considerable influence on farming compared with the other two groups. The sums of money remitted varied from N375 to N825, with one exceptional transfer of N1,485. These sums may seem relatively small, but they comprised important inputs into the farms of the recipients. However, the contribution of non-farm incomes and gifts to household heads in this middle group was more variable than for the other two, ranging from N6,000 to N9,000, and comprising from 14 to 60 per cent of total incomes.

It is within this group that one can frequently see the signs of a 'generational progression' in non-farm employment. For example, one elderly household head was a farmer, as well as a barber, a traditional Hausa occupation, who as a young man had gone on dry season migration to look for casual employment. His sons, however, who had completed some primary education, commuted to the town where they worked as carpenters and craftsmen, and farmed in the evenings and at weekends.[5] On the other hand the grandsons were away at secondary school and unlikely to remain in the village household, as they hoped for permanent jobs in the towns.

Investment Potential of Non-Farm Incomes

Non-farm jobs of household heads, together with gifts and transfers from successful children clearly formed an important segment of the incomes of all those interviewed in 1986-9. This invites the question of how these monies and goods were used, to what end and for what purpose. Informants' responses showed that investment in their farms was important. While the purchase of land was often a significant outlay, the recurrent cost of buying fertiliser and using ox-ploughs was closely related to off-farm income. Fertiliser could be obtained from the local agricultural development project at the subsidised price of N10 per 50 kg bag, but unfortunately it was bought up by local big-men, traders and bureaucrats who resold it at N40 per bag. As for ox-ploughs, very few owned them, as the ox-teams costing N2,500 were too expensive to buy, train and keep. The majority of households hired them, often from itinerant plough-teams employed by urban-based entrepreneurs, or wealthier rural farmers.

There was little indication that the increased use of ploughs had created new linkages and advantaged local blacksmiths. Ploughshares were often replaced rather than repaired. They were available at subsidised prices from the local agricultural development project at N650 for a fortunate few, while the majority paid N1,200 to those who had bought up available stocks at the lower price. The introduction of ox-ploughs in general had a negative effect on local industry, as blacksmiths made less ridging and weeding hoes, and only infrequently repaired ploughshares. On the other hand this decline in a traditional industry was offset by the expansion of motor mechanics in the larger villages along the main road who serviced vehicles, especially motor cycles.

Non-farm incomes were also used for education, hiring labour and for investment in grain trading. The latter is a traditional Hausa activity and part of the inter-regional trading patterns of Hausaland which can be an important source of income through manipulating the troughs and peaks in seasonal prices and differences between town and countryside (Clough 1985). Investment in 'politics' which could also include formal political parties, was also important. Since political power is underwritten by status, investment in social position through alms-giving, lavish weddings, and general forms of clientage are of importance. Social position and power can influence access to resources and may be paramount in the settlement of land disputes. The issue of land is important since its loss and gain related to the oil economy have been powerful inputs into the process of de-agrarianisation. While land accumulation, loss and expropriation were apparent around Gusau, the Sokoto periphery provides the best example of the processes at work in the 1970s and 1980s.

Land Expropriation and Accumulation

The process of de-agrarianisation in urban peripheries and hinterlands was stimulated by the state expropriation of land, together with the physical expansion of towns during the oil boom in the 1970s. Land speculation, especially along the main roads, led to the purchase and holding of land in anticipation of urban growth, a process which involved a number of interests, such as urban speculators, village heads, and land brokers, but the largest tracts of land were taken by the state for institutional uses (Swindell and Mamman 1990). The late 1970s saw the growth of schools, universities, government housing, airports, military establishments, and agricultural development schemes. For example the University of Sokoto in the mid-1970s acquired a site of 5,600 ha, some 5 kilometres from Sokoto, which encompassed several villages located on prime agricultural land, a tract equivalent to the built-up area of the town. Not all the farmers affected had moved by the 1990s, as building works slowed with the recession, but since the 1970s this and other projects have dispossessed between 20-30,000 inhabitants of the Sokoto hinterland. To the south-east of Sokoto, north of Gusau, the building of the Bakolori Dam flooded a large area which dispossessed some 14,000 people. Development schemes and the expansion of large towns in northern Nigeria have occurred in densely populated and intensively farmed areas, and they have been an important stimulus for farmers to look for non-farm and off-farm employment (Lubeck 1979).

While land speculation and expropriation have been conspicuous during the past 16 years, land has also been acquired and accumulated within villages, through a developing land market. Thus there has been an increase in the proportion of land acquired through purchase (*saye*), as opposed to inheritance (*gado*), which in some cases has led to the accumulation of land and/or the consolidation of plots to produce larger fields better suited to ox-ploughing.[6]

During the 1970s the expanded job market in Sokoto city and other regional towns provided a much wider scope for non-farm incomes, which encouraged farmers to disengage from agriculture, sell some of their land and to become dependent on non-farm incomes. Some of these new 'semi-proletarians' were created by direct dispossession, but others by the deepening commoditisation of land and labour. The conditions of existence in the Sokoto region include high rural population densities, permanent field cultivation, and very little surplus land. Some informants spoke of complex domestic units being divided as the head could neither provide sufficient land, implements and fertilisers, nor obtain loans from the agricultural development agencies dominated by larger farmers. On division, the farms were individually so small as to be incapable of providing support even for nuclear households. They were consequently sold or kept as weekend allotments and people took casual jobs as agricultural or urban labourers. In the buoyant period of the late 1970s this was not a daunting prospect. The casual labour market in Sokoto was booming, while some used money from land sales to set up as petty traders.

There were also households with members who had become well-entrenched in non-farm employment, with permanent relatively well-paid jobs in the state or local government sectors. Drivers, messengers and carpenters earned a steady income, while others were successful as petty traders and contractors to local governments intent on expanding local infrastructure and schools. In the school sector, even the small-scale contracting of commodities such as washing-powder and blankets became a lucrative proposition. Larger contractors who supplied food to schools made huge profits. During the civilian regime of 1979-83, Sokoto state increased the number of local governments from 19 to 37, creating new opportunities for recirculating oil money, as well as for paying off those who had supported the National Party of Nigeria (NPN), the victor in the 1979 election.

Many prosperous rural households were among those who had established some client relationship with the NPN, or local rulers, and had secured jobs and contracts within the state sector, and were involved in double participation in different economies and social relationships. They had access to national production surpluses, monetised and circulated by the state, as well as production surpluses from their own farms. Numerous examples have been encountered in Sokoto of households whose involvement in non-farm work was matched by their investment of surplus income and profits in buying land to expand their farms, while they employed labour throughout the farming season in contrast to their poorer neighbours who were only casual hirers. In the boom years of the mid and late 1970s local labour within villages was not easy to come by, so migrant workers came in and lodged in villages, or became itinerant labourers. These men from outlying villages up to 20 or 30 kilometres away found agricultural wage rates in the periphery well above what they could earn as labourers back home.

With the fall of the civilian government in 1983 and the return of the military, there followed a period of economic restructuring, leading to the loss of many jobs and contracts within the state and local government sectors. Events turned against many of those who appeared to be consolidating their positions as *petits bourgeois* and as emergent capitalist farmers. As a result of job losses and the economic downturn, those who had a few years previously bought land were now having to sell it. Several informants declared that in 1985 they were selling land at prices less than they had paid for it. These families retreated into a position where their land holdings approximated what they were in the early 1970s. Others who had sold land on entering the job market in the belief that it would last, found themselves if not landless, then land poor, as well as jobless. Other farmers, who had not benefited from the oil boom either through jobs or land accumulation, were selling land to face the stringencies of the new economic climate of the late 1980s. Some, of course, held their ground, but there appears to have been a 'squeezing' of small and medium-sized farmers.

By the 1990s the economic climate had deteriorated further and the polarity between the rich and poor in both town and countryside became more marked. Devaluation occurred in 1986, but in 1993 the government decided to allow the naira to float against other currencies in an attempt to try and achieve convergence between the official and unofficial exchange rates. The outcome was a short-lived convergence, quickly followed by a massive devaluation and further price inflation, especially of foodstuffs. The banks did particularly well out of deregulation, unlike the urban and rural poor. High population densities and the temptation of poorer households to sell land to tide them over the crisis often reduced their farms to mere allotments.

As jobs in both the government and private sectors have contracted, many of the poorer rural and urban households have become part of a floating labour force which provides casual urban labour, and now increasingly waged farm labour within the Sokoto hinterland. Some informants in 1993 said they were taking payment half in wages and half in fertilisers, which could either be used on their farms or sold at a profit since imported fertiliser has become very expensive as a result of devaluation. The acceptance of fertiliser as payment indicates the continuing attachment to farming, especially in an era of high food prices, and although farms may be very small, they are still integral to household reproduction. The absence of widespread dispossession also means there is competition for farm labour among domestic and commercial farmers at critical points in the cultivation cycle. This probably accounts for the relatively high daily wage of N60 (one bundle of millet costs N75). However, the improved purchasing power of farm wages in the last few years should not obscure the casual short-term nature of this kind of employment, nor the possible effects of labourers having to delay attending to their own farms because of their other jobs.

The Expansion of Capitalist Agriculture

For some households, the 1990s have seen a significant shift from a relatively wide array of non-farm jobs to a narrower base of casual day labour. It would appear that casual farmwork has to some extent replaced or supplemented former jobs in the modern sector. But if there has been 're-agrarianisation' it has not necessarily meant a return to household farms. Instead it is a reflection of the strengthening of agrarian capitalist relations of production among medium-sized and larger entrepreneurial farmers. People work for urban-based farmers or for wealthier rural ones who have accumulated land on the periphery. In many households there must now be a distinction between unpaid farm labour on family farms and waged farm labour outside the household. Not only have job options been reduced for poor and some middle-range farmers, but recent information collected from the Gusau households investigated in 1989-90 shows that the transfer of gifts (*taimako*) has been reduced as life becomes harder for sons with town jobs. Also, it is much more difficult to raise the small informal loans important to smaller farmers for the purchase of fertilisers and ox-plough hire.

The late 1980s and early 1990s have seen a new phase of land accumulation around the large towns of the north, associated with the rapid expansion of irrigated wheat farming on the river-bottom lands and the upland cultivation of millet and beans. The former was precipitated by the government's ban on imported wheat in 1986 which contributed to the general rise in food prices, but especially that of wheat as the demand for bread is so entrenched. Wheat prices rose 650 per cent between 1986 and 1988 and another 33 per cent between 1988 and 1989. The wheat boom around Kano almost assumed the proportions of a land scramble as 'overnight farmers' moved into the floodlands (Kimmage 1991). Under the 1978 Land Use Decree, land is vested in the state and can be reallocated at the discretion of the state irrespective of prior entitlements. Using clientage and patronage, the urban and military elites, bureaucrats and managerial classes, together with prosperous rural farmers, have acquired large tracts of land, some of which they rented to kin or clients. Pump irrigation was also expanded around Sokoto not only for wheat but also for vegetable and fruit farming.

The strengthening of capitalist relations of production in the late 1980s was not confined to irrigated lowland farming. It has also spread to the upland cultivation of millet, sorghum and beans. The largest upland farms being developed by capitalist farmers lie on the edges of the close-settled zone especially to the south, south-east and west of Sokoto in the wetter part of the Sokoto-Rima basin. Although it is difficult to get accurate measurements of these farms, estimates suggest continuous cultivation in the wet season of 30 to 200 hectares which are huge areas compared with upland holdings averaging 2 hectares. All these farms have appeared since 1980. The owners include a permanent secretary in the government, a retired army officer and a former state governor. These are the 'new men' who have entered the land market and capitalist farming. On the other hand there are *Sokotawa* such as an eminent Malam from Sokoto and a rich Sokoto merchant. These farms are usually supervised by a member of the owner's family who recruits wage labour from households in local villages, although on one farm, workers were brought daily by lorry from Sokoto. A survey of medium and large farms in 1987 clearly indicates the increase of large capitalist farms in the Sokoto region. Furthermore, of the 150 medium and large farmers invesugated, 23 per cent of them controlled about 80 per cent of the arable land on these farms (Labaran 1987).

Conclusion

The process of de-agrarianisation in northern Nigeria suggests that the rise and fall of the oil economy has been of profound significance, together with the ways in which the state has directly and indirectly channelled resources towards various interests. The processes of social and economic change appear to have been acute in the vicinity of towns as a consequence of the impact of rapid urban growth on the surrounding rural areas. Changes in agriculture have been related to the waxing and waning of non-farm incomes among rural households, the selling and buying of land, access to agricultural inputs, and vulnerability to a fading urban job market. There has also been dispossession and an increase in the 'land poor' through the expropriation of land and the strengthening of agrarian capitalism. Such changes in urban hinterlands have been recorded in many similar areas in Africa, and although the oil boom has been highly significant in Nigeria, economic expansion and urban growth were evident in many countries until the late 1970s (Swindell 1988).

In the urban hinterlands of Nigeria, as well as those elsewhere, the agriculture-led creation of non-farm employment posited by some development theorists seems to have been reversed. It is non-farm work which has changed agriculture and there have been limited developments of forward and backward linkages as agriculture has changed. The lesson appears to be that primitive accumulation in agriculture does not necessarily lead to subsequent investment in the rural industrial sector. One of the best and longest-established prospects for profit and income maximisation in much of West Africa is trading, especially foodstuffs through the manipulation of wet and dry season price fluctuations. Also, the investment of money in education, status, social networks and politics at the local and regional levels is important and allows access to resources. For poorer farmers, the combination of farming on limited holdings, combined with non-farm jobs or waged farm work for big commercial farmers, is a necessary way of survival. In Nigeria as elsewhere, the process of de-agrarianisation in urban hinterlands is socially differentiated among households and must be contextualised within the existence of high population densities, environmental uncertainties and volatile political economies.

Notes

1. *Malami* (sing. *malam*) are Koranic teachers, and their students' (*almajirai*) ages and levels of study reflect the proficiency and accomplishments of the *malam. Malami* dispense cures, foretell futures and offer prayers for their clients, for which they charge fees. These may be substantial if the client is wealthy.
2. Some indication of these income levels may be gained by comparing them with the salary of a Grade 1 University Lecturer which in 1989-90 was N12,000.
3. Based on the December prices for millet and sorghum, and February prices for groundnuts and beans.
4. For similar observations from South Africa see Lowe (1986: Chapter 14).
5. For an exploration of changing work rhythms in Southern Nigeria see Guyer (1992).
6. It is important to distinguish between land used and land owned. For example, land inheritance may be delayed by non-residence and in the interim, it may be used by other family members. Delayed inheritance, as well as future inheritance, serves to maintain links between a migrant and his home village. Land not used by owners may be pledged or rented (Ross 1987). In the present survey, the land holdings referred to are farmed by the head of household, and acquired through inheritance, purchase, or rental. Household land may be bought and sold as circumstances change. Land sales are part of the process of land circulation, rather than of accumulation.

References

CLOUGH, P. 1985, 'The Social Relations of Grain Marketing in Northern Nigeria', *Review of African Political Economy*, vol. 34, 16-34.

GUYER, J. 1992, 'Small Change: Industrial Farmwork and Collective Life in a Western Nigerian Savanna Town', *Africa*, vol. 62, no. 4, 465-89

KIMMAGE, K. 1991, 'From "Wheat Trap" to Wheat Boom in Nigeria', *Africa*, vol. 61, no. 4, 471-501.

LABARAN, A. 1987, 'Land Appropriation for Capitalised Farming in the Sokoto Region', in M. Mortimore et al. (eds), *Perspectives on Land Administration and Development in Northern Nigeria*, Kano, Bayero University, 46-57

LOWE, A. 1986, *Agricultural Development in South Africa*, James Currey, London

LUBECK, P.M. 1979, 'Contrasts and Continuity in a Dependent City: Kano, Nigeria', in J. Abu-Lughod and R. Hay (eds), *Third World Urbanization*, London, Methuen

PROTHERO, R.M. 1957, 'Migrating Labour from North-Western Nigeria', *Africa*, vol. 27, no. 2, 251-61

ROSS, P. 1987, 'Land as a Right of Membership: Land Tenure Dynamics in the Kano Close-Settled Zone' in M. Watts (ed.) *State, Oil and Agriculture in Nigeria*, Berkeley, University of California,

SWINDELL, K. 1984, 'Farmers, Traders and Labourers: Dry Season Migration from North-West Nigeria', *Africa*, vol. 54, no. 1, 3-19

____, 1988, 'Agrarian Change and Peri-Urban Fringes in Tropical Africa', in D. Rimmer (ed.), *Rural Transformation in Tropical Africa*, London, Belhaven, 98-115

SWINDELL, K. & A.B. MAMMAN 1990, 'Land Expropriation and Accumulation in the Sokoto Periphery, North-west Nigeria 1976-96', *Africa*, vol. 60, no. 2, 173-187

6

Economic Activities of the Poor in Accra

Meine Pieter van Dijk

Structural adjustment policies have been implemented in Ghana since 1983 and the World Bank now considers Ghana an African success story. In its view, the country has moved 'from adjustment to development', and scores 'well' with respect to fiscal and exchange rate policies, 'fair' in terms of monetary policies, and 'adequate' on macroeconomic policies (World Bank 1994). This says little about the plight of the poor.

This chapter presents results from a qualitative poverty assessment carried out in a suburb of Accra called Abeka in 1993.[1] Household poverty and urban labour markets were studied in relation to each other. Information was collected on 28 economic activities in which households were involved.[2] Definitions of poverty advanced by the poor themselves and their coping strategies, the functioning of labour markets, rural-urban relations under structural adjustment, labour market flexibility and informal sector growth potential are reviewed and policy implications drawn.

Meaning of Poverty in Abeka

Abeka is a typical suburban neighbourhood in the north-west of Accra located about 20 minutes by bus from the centre of town. It has recently grown rapidly primarily due to migration, with an estimated three-quarters of the heads of households in Abeka being migrants.[3] At the time of the study, there were no precise data on the borders of Abeka, nor on its population, number of plots, houses or social services.

The research focused on the household as the primary unit of analysis and traced the relation between household poverty and the economic activities of members in 50 households, numbering a total of 318 persons of whom 105 (33 per cent) were in the economically active ages of 15 to 55 years and not studying.[4]

Qualitative methods were used to assess the impact of adjustment programmes on the urban poor.[5] Informants were asked the following questions:

- Did they consider themselves poor? If so, why, and how were they coping?
- Did members of poor households operate in different labour markets? How did they find jobs and which factors constrained the proper functioning of these markets?
- In which activities were members of poor households involved and which factors impeded their further development?
- To what extent did the urban poor have a rural background? Were they still maintaining relations with rural areas?

Despite the embarrassment of the question: 'Do you consider your household to be poor?', most people answered straightforwardly.[6] Reactions ranged from giggling to: 'Don't you see my situation', 'Look around you at this environment', and 'Poverty is God-given'. Typically people make a distinction between misfortune as a temporary phenomenon and poverty as a more permanent state of affairs. The local languages have two different words for these two situations, the linkage being provided by the statement that 'misfortune can lead to poverty'.

Notions of poverty went beyond material deprivation to the realm of moral failure: 'A poor person cannot achieve his aspirations'; 'He cannot send his children to school'; 'Poverty is not just material, it is also spiritual'; and 'In hard times everything is allowed'. One group of girls stated: 'If we cannot find employment we are forced to go into prostitution'.

Some of the definitions of poverty mentioned were based on comparison: 'What is given to me is enough and comparing myself with others, I am not poor'. The statement 'Everybody has his own wishes and aspirations' also infers a relative definition of poverty, going further to suggest that the same level of endowments may produce different outcomes. Two households could have identical endowments but use them quite differently, depending on their preferences and habits. Some people gave a definition of what a rich person would look like as a contrast to what they considered as poverty.

Half the households interviewed in Abeka considered that they were poor. Their reasons for thinking so were classified into eight categories, namely: no money for basic needs, no assets, bad appearance, un- or underemployment, incomplete family structure, misfortune, misconduct and vulnerability (Alberts and van Dijk 1994).[7] There are obvious advantages in opting for a multi-faceted definition of poverty which is based on people's own perceptions. It is difficult to obtain an accurate picture of the income of all members of the household and how much they contribute to household expenditures which could provide an objective assessment of a household's overall financial standing. Data about borrowing and lending, pensions, redeployment fees and remittances can be even more elusive and unreliable. The people themselves consider poverty a much broader phenomenon than low earnings. Qualitative poverty assessment goes beyond identifying the poor by bringing out culturally defined dimensions of poverty and linking poverty to what people are doing to overcome poverty through coping strategies.

Poverty and Coping Strategies

Coping strategies can be defined as the patterns of behaviour and activities of poor households which enable them to cope with their resource-poor conditions. The strategies are essentially concerned with the mobilisation and management of scarce resources. A classification of coping strategies was made, distinguishing between consumptive strategies (adjusting expenditures and falling back on other people) and productive strategies (developing economic activities and diversifying activities as a form of risk spreading).

Adjusting expenditures is usually a first reaction. Spending less on food and delaying medical treatment, however, may have adverse effects, especially for children. Less nutritious foods are chosen and cold or cooked food is bought in the street instead of preparing food at home. In one neighbourhood, 90 per cent of the poor declared that they had to adjust their food expenditure and many resorted to buying prepared food in the street because it was cheaper than preparing it at home. These families often cut back on schooling costs. Children were removed from private schools and eventually there was often insufficient finance to send them to public schools. Girls' education was usually the first to go, particularly at secondary or higher levels. A sizeable proportion of households in many neighbourhoods were no longer able to afford school fees.

In an urban context where traditional ties are becoming less important, it may no longer be possible for the poor to always fall back on their family, friends, tribesmen or regional kin. Poor households try to develop additional economic activities. However, starting from a position of low assets makes it difficult to turn these into rewarding activities. Investments are minimal, the location may not be optimal, and the person concerned may not have the appropriate skill and experience when a new activity is started. Female traders often sell very small quantities with low margins. Often too many sell the same product, which makes it hard to make a reasonable living. The tendency to use working capital for the necessary daily household expenditures may lead to what Ghanaians call 'eating into profit'. At the end of the week not enough money is left to buy new stock, to pay unavoidable charges or to cover transport costs.

Poverty leads to more child labour. In one neighbourhood, one in every five school-aged children was involved in economic activities, usually of a trading nature. Child labour is a productive strategy in the short run, but certainly has a long-term negative impact on the child's possibility to develop his/her cognitive skills.

Diversifying existing activities can be seen as a form of risk spreading. Examples are female traders selling additional products or metal workers advancing new models or products. Many resort to buying and selling on credit, or participate in rotating savings and credit associations called *susu* in Ghana. Others sell very small quantities or use different ways of packaging. Additional examples of diversification found during the fieldwork were renting out rooms, encouraging children to take up different kinds of apprenticeship, investing in children's education and training, money-lending and gambling.

Poor People in Segmented Labour Markets

The most important activities of the households interviewed were trade, particularly the food trade, as well as informal manufacturing of all kinds of artisanal products and handicrafts. Seventy-one per cent of the economically active household members were in the informal sector (i.e. 1.5 persons per household). Eleven per cent were involved in the formal sector, 6 per cent in farming, and another 11 per cent unemployed. Women have to rely more than men on the informal sector and usually end up in trade and food processing activities. Men dominate in the metal and wood working trades, and in activities such as tailoring, wholesale trade and personal services.

Labour markets in Ghana are segmented. Segments distinguished in this study are in terms of formal versus informal, different activities within the informal sector, ethnic groups and gender. Interviewees often operated in several labour markets simultaneously. Poor households usually have less education and training and get sifted down into less rewarding economic activities.

The formal sector can be distinguished from the informal using the criteria of size, legal status, and registration. Within the formal sector a distinction is made between working for the government (increasingly less attractive given declining salary levels and the chances of being redeployed) and working for the private sector, where the average income is somewhat higher but the risk of being fired is greater. One out of every five households has a member working for the government or in the private sector.

Within the informal sector different economic activities can be described as different segments if the transition from one to the other is not easy. A distinction is made within the informal sector between those involved in trading, manufacturing of all kinds of artisanal and handicraft activities, and different kinds of services. However, it makes sense to distinguish between different informal sector activities within these subsectors. The argument is that productivity (taking income as an indicator of productivity) within an activity may not vary, but it does vary from one activity to another. Within the informal sector, the self-employed can be distinguished from employees or owners working with employees.

Job Search and Unemployment

When asked what kind of activities they undertook to find a job, interviewees' replies ranged from going from house to house or workshop to workshop; presenting oneself at the job site; writing applications to government or the private sector; going through a period of apprenticeship; asking friends and relatives to help in the search; to praying. In fact, very few write letters or go to employers. Many think that the government announces vacancies for which candidates have already been selected. Young people complain about a lack of 'connections' that they feel are requisite for getting a job. Two suggested that you have to pay to obtain certain jobs. Most people circumvent the problem of job search by opting for self-employment. They initiate economic activities with the attitude of trying their luck.

Households piece together their livelihood on an *ad hoc* basis. For example, in one family the oldest brother made the rounds of car welders in search of a job. One brother, without specific skills kept his eye on job advertisements and accepted casual employment in the meantime. Two other brothers were engaged in football playing and singing respectively, hoping one day they would achieve fame or at least a viable livelihood. The father remained in farming because he possessed no other skills. The female members of the family were involved in food processing and trading.

Some interviewees harboured the feeling that a person is educated for only one job. 'I am in textiles and that is all I know', or 'Once a carpenter, always a carpenter'. However, there were examples to the contrary, people switching from one occupation to another even at the expense of losing their skills, e.g. a car mechanic who wanted to go into second-hand clothes trading. Strange combinations emerged as people switched from one apprenticeship to another, worked in the formal sector during the week and informal sector at the weekend, or pursued different occupations simultaneously, e.g. a religious education teacher who also worked as an electrician.

School drop-outs had great difficulty finding employment, similarly the sick and the weak, the handicapped and women with children. Almost one-quarter of all households had one unemployed person. This goes against the usual interpretation that the poor cannot afford unemployment. Interviewees expressed concern about the lack of employment opportunities. Their main worry was how their children would find jobs, or places to set up business in the future.

Informal Sector Activities

Up to three-quarters of all economic activities in which the poor are involved can be classified as informal. Over half of the members of the households studied were self-employed (56.3 per cent), meaning that they had no employees and were their own boss.

The distinction between the formal and informal sector is not rigid. In the first place, many people previously employed in the formal sector are now working in the informal sector. Secondly, a number of pupils coming out of the official vocational training system still go for a period of apprenticeship in the informal sector to learn practical skills or to explore whether they want to become self-employed.

The informal sector is by no means homogeneous. Hairdressing, for example, is highly prized by most women, while food trading has less status. Remarks reflecting the job stigma of certain occupations are: 'You lose a lot of respect when you do this job' (a woman carrying water at the market for women who are cooking food), and 'Selling second-hand clothing does not befit you'. Feelings of self-worth are sometimes at stake, e.g. 'Not repaying a debt means losing the respect of the community' (a female trader unable to pay back credit from her suppliers).

Apprenticeships and Job Training

In the informal sector, a definite period of apprenticeship is considered necessary to impart skills which are normally not developed at school. Usually three to five years are needed and a few apprentices continue afterwards as workers. By definition, apprenticeship is a short-term labour relation between the master and apprentice. This relationship varies a lot from activity to activity and from master to master. Masters usually hire apprentices from their own kin or rural birthplace. Cooperation between different masters is also based on kinship or rural birthplace.

In some garages large numbers of apprentices worked for very little money and were often idle, while some welders complained of difficulty in finding good apprentices. Apprentices or workers are sometimes in charge of the enterprise while the master is away. However, when asked about the economic aspects of the business, apprentices knew virtually nothing since they were not allowed to deal with customers or delve into accounts.

Apprenticeship fees, which in several occupations have risen recently, regulate the numbers of new entrants in the informal sector. The status of being an independent master makes it attractive to start on one's own account. A number of small units work with family labour and no salary is paid, particularly to girls helping their mothers. Apprentices not only learn skills but are also introduced into supplier networks and learn the mechanics of being self-employed. This infers the need to strengthen ties between formal and informal education and training. The two are complementary and should be considered as such.

Formal vocational training programmes have certain costs and uncertain benefits. It has become more difficult for graduates of vocational training institutes to find jobs, implying that it is even more difficult for drop-outs of these institutes. The drop-outs claimed that their parents were unable to pay their fees. Most change their aspirations after a period of open unemployment.

Overall, the strong link between education and employment prospects, a central premise of the post-independence development era in Ghana, has been called into question. It touches all levels and types of training and even extends to formal schooling. An O level diploma is no longer a sufficient qualification for a government job. Many government services have increased the requirements for employment and public sector employment is not increasing and is now less rewarding. Some interviewees mentioned, however, that certain government services had not been affected by retrenchment, notably the fire brigade, the police and the army.

Rural-Urban Relations under Structural Adjustment

At the time of the study in 1993, structural adjustment had succeeded in making agriculture more profitable. Agricultural production and exports increased and trade between rural and urban areas seemed to have intensified. Meanwhile real wages in urban areas had fallen. Nonetheless some households explicitly said that they did not want to farm since farming was 'very tiring'. A large number of people moved to Accra because they expected a higher wage in the city with the kind of skills, education and training they had. Still, they kept in close touch with their region of origin, or aimed to settle in their home area at a later stage. Ethnic affiliations played a substantial role in labour networks and in establishing different forms of cooperation with other entrepreneurs. Looking for jobs and exploring employment opportunities were hardly feasible without the assistance of fellow tribesmen. Subcontracting was delegated to tribe members.

Since the initiation of the adjustment programme more goods have been available, more activities are taking place, and more buildings are being repaired and new ones erected. Adjustment has created new business opportunities. The urban poor have relied largely on the urban informal sector[8] to survive since adjustment started. Economic liberalisation has brought about a very competitive environment for labour and the informal sector in urban areas. Not all of the poor's informal economic activities will survive, but at least the individuals concerned will have acquired business experience.

Within the informal sector, a differentiation process is occurring, leading to a large number of only marginally profitable enterprises combined with a few very rewarding activities. As one interviewee remarked: 'Structural adjustment has not gone to the ground. The positive effects are not felt by the people'. Or as another person phrased it: 'The goods are plenty, but we do not have the money to buy them'.

Labour Market Flexibility and Returns to Labour

A distinction can be made between five types of labour market flexibility according to wage, working time, space, occupation, and sector. People were highly flexible in their working hours. Spatial mobility was reflected in the number of people who moved to Accra because they expected a higher wage in the city. The evidence with respect to sectoral and occupational flexibility is mixed. The labour market is highly competitive, and as such, relatively efficient. However there is a price to be paid. Wages have adjusted downwards substantially and the people interviewed repeatedly remarked that consumer prices had increased far more rapidly than wages. According to Baah-Nuakaoh (1993) real wages in the manufacturing sector fell by one-third in Ghana between 1987 and 1992, and were not sufficient to support a household. Poor people in particular usually end up in more marginal economic activities and need several sources of income to improve their situation.

Wages earned by the people interviewed varied, but most were at the lower end of the scale. Household viability required combining economic activities of different household members. Better-off households spanned a larger number of activities. As an apprentice, one could survive in Accra on 500 Cedis (around 75 US cents) per day; a family of two adults and two children would need three times as much.

Very little regulation is currently being enforced in the formal sector. Minimum wages do not exist and wages as low as 8,000 Cedis per month are common, well below the legal minimum. There is also no social security. Sickness, accident or a death in the family can change life drastically. Such events are key catalysts of poverty.

A number of interviewees were prepared to do 'anything', sometimes out of desperation. The job histories of many people have been shaped by the drastic changes in Ghanaian economic policies in the preceding decades, creating opportunities and pitfalls for successive groups of people. The Queen Mother of Abeka, for example, used to have a passbook to sell essential commodities. She sold meat from the Cattle Board which was later abolished by Field Lieutenant Rawlings when he came to power. At present she is running a bar, but business is declining because of competition from new bars serving stronger drinks. She would like to go into cloth trading. A woman interviewee trading in textiles also used to benefit from the passbook system. Once it was discarded she lost her monopoly and changed her occupation.

Chhibber and Leechor (1993) assume smoothly functioning labour markets, except for the urban formal sector which is characterised by rigidity and distortions. This seems indeed to be the case as far as wage, time, spatial, occupational, and sectoral flexibility are concerned. It does not mean, however, that the market provides a reasonable wage for those who are willing to be flexible.

According to the World Bank, a continuation of liberal economic policies will enable Ghana to cash in on its favourable location, low-cost labour, and enterprising people. The missing ingredient yet to come forward is foreign capital investment.

Productivity and Growth of Informal Sector Enterprises

The fieldwork confirmed the heterogeneity of microenterprises in the informal sector. At one end of the spectrum are thriving microenterprises with growth potential and at the other end are marginal economic activities. In between is a whole range of more or less productive income-generating activities.[9]

All the economic activities studied displayed differentiation in profitability levels and scale of operations. Food processing activities are predominantly marginal, existing in a vicious cycle of low turnover and low profitability. There are exceptions in this sector though whereby product diversification and efficient management triggered dynamic growth, creating what is popularly referred to as a 'Booming Banku Business' success. There is a tremendous glut in the market for textile-related activities, but here again specialisation and a good location can create opportunities in an overcrowded market. The metal-related activities give a similar picture of constraints and potential for growth when flexible specialisation is pursued (Rasmussen et al. 1993). Construction activities are generally dynamic with many entrepreneurs being able to carve out a share in the booming construction industry in Accra. The most striking difference between the two ends of the spectrum of activities is the level of productivity. These economic activities generally suffer from low productivity as measured by the income of the owner.[10] A comparison of incomes accruing in the economic activities of the poor and non-poor indicates different productivity levels.

Low productivity is the most striking problem of informal sector activities. Monthly incomes do not usually exceed 20,000 Cedis. Low productivity is related to small initial investment arising from limited or no borrowing opportunities, low levels of technology and training, a poorly developed infrastructure and high production costs. Additional factors contributing to low earnings are the seasonality of many activities and an array of taxes, registration and licensing fees.

In summary, informal sector constraints can be classified in terms of: first, the macroeconomic environment, i.e. the negative policy context and the discouraging impact of taxes and regulations; second, the entrepreneur, notably his/her limited education, training, and business skills; third, the enterprise, namely low initial investment, inappropriate technology, location, and finally, the market, i.e. the demand for products and services. The most pressing problems in Accra's informal sector lie at the level of the entrepreneur. Lack of access to capital and a very narrow focus on the neighbourhood are real constraints for most. Most trading activities have a very limited scope, but traders' success stories reveal that the ability to seek and discover niche markets does pay off. Some small entrepreneurs show a remarkable ability to adapt to difficult circumstances and improve their situation.

Policy Implications

The informal sector embraces a wide range of economic activities from those which merely facilitate people's survival to those with high growth potential. Different policies are needed to reach different categories of informal sector businesses. For those serving as a seed-bed for entrepreneurship it is important that the government create the right policy environment. Furthermore, it may be necessary to provide targeted assistance to dynamic enterprises. Finally for those who would not be benefiting from these policies, assistance should be given through safety-net measures.

The World Bank's poverty study on Ghana was aimed at developing a long-term and Ghana-specific poverty alleviation framework (Chhibber and Leechor 1993). To achieve such poverty reduction a labour-intensive development strategy would need to be developed. Policies and programmes can help the poor in three ways: first, by creating a positive macroeconomic environment and stimulating economic growth; second, by directly supporting their economic activities; and third, by providing safety-net constructions necessary for those who are not able to undertake rewarding economic activities.

Economic growth has been very important for poverty alleviation in many countries. The same applies for Ghana, where the agricultural and industrial potential needs to be more fully developed. The government should formulate and implement macroeconomic policies necessary to create conditions for economic growth and try to link rural and urban economic growth. It should take a more positive attitude towards the economic activities of the poor and try to stimulate the necessary increase in the productivity of these activities. Appropriate macroeconomic policies will help the development of micro and small enterprises. Technology policies could be directed towards developing products and improving production methods of micro and small entrepreneurs. Physical planning policies could help to make land and infrastructure available.

At present many rules and regulations make the life of small entrepreneurs complicated and selective deregulation may help the development of this sector. A large number of taxes are exacted and it is not always clear to informal sector agents which taxes need to be paid for what purpose. The government could clarify the system and redesign it to avoid small enterprises being driven into illegality to avoid taxation.

Labour markets would benefit from a good information system. The present employment services do not have feedback mechanisms. Monitoring of labour market development is a necessary foundation for good policy formulation. Most importantly, education and training need to be geared more to the market. Small entrepreneurs need a far more diversified range of marketable skills.

A whole range of projects and policies can contribute to labour-intensive activities. Often the private sector will have to be stimulated to start these activities, to provide access to small entrepreneurs and to subcontract to them. Priorities are:

- Organisations of small entrepreneurs should be encouraged. These already exist in many branches and some are functioning well, e.g. those for hairdressing, garages and women involved in food processing. These organisations can act as a platform for discussion and exchange of new ideas and experiences. They should also be the interlocutor for negotiations with the government.
- Local and municipal governments should reserve space and provide infrastructure for micro and small enterprises.
- The tax system should be clarified and the government should explain how entrepreneurs can benefit from the taxes they pay.
- Subcontracting and other relations between micro and large enterprises should be developed.
- Technology development and innovation diffusion must be stimulated.
- Female entrepreneurs should be specially targeted. Some are already quite successful, but most are restricted to a handful of traditional activities which have limited development horizons.
- The formation of clusters of economic activities should be stimulated to embrace enterprises of different sizes.
- Small enterprises should be helped to gain access to credit, training and marketing channels. Private banks and training institutes could be convinced that this is an important market.

- Innovation diffusion centres should be encouraged to play a role in the development of small and microenterprises. To assure maximum use of these centres, a business and technology support system should be put in place (Pedersen et al. 1994).
- Entrepreneurship development programmes should be organised, particularly for enterprises which are blocked at a certain level and find it difficult to take the next step.

The urban informal sector has shown enormous dynamism in coping with structural adjustment. Nonetheless, research at the household level has demonstrated that many people are not benefiting from the opportunities created. The concern here is not with those who have lost their traditional advantages like government servants or trade monopolists, but old people without family support, female heads of households, and the sick or handicapped. For these groups, safety-net constructions are necessary.[11] People who lack skills or initiative or who are not sufficiently entrepreneurial need help. Refugees and women abandoned by their husbands are also vulnerable. A general improvement in the economic situation will eventually create more possibilities for these people, but in the short term some kind of targeted aid is required.

The policies and interventions suggested here address the productive coping strategies of the urban poor through a variety of means. Most importantly, policy efforts should facilitate the poor's own actions by being sensitive to how the poor define poverty and are endeavouring to propel themselves out of poverty.

Notes

1. Research for this chapter was undertaken with Wim Alberts as consultants for the World Bank financed by the Netherlands Trust Fund. The results do not represent the views of the World Bank. Fieldwork in Abeka was carried out with Dan Inkoom from the Technology University in Kumasi.
2. For comparative reasons data were also collected on 24 other economic activities taking place close to Abeka, mainly along two important roads (van Dijk, 1993b).
3. The criterion used is 'born outside Accra'.
4. The United Nations definition of a household as: 'a group of individuals who have lived and eaten together for a period of at least nine months in the year preceding the interview' was adopted.

5. The choice for a qualitative, more in-depth study in three neighbourhoods was made because several quantitative large-scale household surveys (Ghana Living Standards Surveys) had been carried out recently, although their data analysis was much delayed thereby precluding a comparison with the qualitative results (Alberts and van Dijk 1994).
6. Responses in the neighbourhood survey revealed subjective definitions of poverty which are listed by theme (in bold italics) as follows (frequency of reply is bracketed): ***Lack of money:*** 'Absence of money' (4), 'If one cannot afford to eat enough' (3), 'Someone who cannot afford basic amenities or basic needs' (3), 'Everything is very expensive' (1), 'A poor person has no property' (1), 'A poor man cannot buy food and clothes' (1), 'The poorest of the poor cannot afford any food, clothing or shelter' (1), 'A poor man is someone without savings' (1), and 'Someone who lives from hand to mouth' (1); ***Lack of Livelihood and/or Illness:*** 'A poor person has no means to live on' (2), 'Poverty is when one is sick, cannot work and has no helper' (2), 'Not having anything to sell in difficult times' (1), 'Things are bad, don't you see me crying' (1), and 'Poverty is if a person has no work' (1); ***Adverse Material Circumstances:*** 'A poor person is someone whose children cannot go to school' (2), 'Poverty is bad living conditions' (1), 'Look at the environment and you see it' (1), 'A poor man has nowhere to sleep' (1), 'A poor person does not have what he needs' (1) and 'People living in this neighbourhood are poor' (1); ***Personal Failure or Insufficient Effort***: 'Poverty is the lack of a big push' (2), 'A poor person is someone who cannot achieve his aspirations' (1), 'Poor people do not plan, but only reproduce' (1), 'If you cannot feed your children you are poor' (1), and 'Poverty is when you need a little more to make ends meet' (1); ***Relative Poverty:*** 'If what is given to you is not enough and you compare yourself to others, you can conclude you are poor' (1), 'Everything is not enough' (1), 'Someone who suffers too much before he can eat' (1), and 'Poverty is all the efforts one has to make to get something done' (1); ***Lack of Support from Others:*** 'A person who does not have any help and has to do everything on his own' (2), 'Poverty is not having help in times of crisis' (1), and 'A poor person is someone who does not have anyone to cater for him' (1); ***Dependence on Others:*** 'If you need assistance from someone else' (1), 'If you have to accept odd jobs to make a living' (1), and 'If you need to take your pan to your neighbour's house' (1); ***Divine Will:*** 'Poverty is God's decision. Man cannot decide what he will become' (1) and 'Being poor is to survive by the grace of God' (1).
7. The poor's criteria for defining themselves as impoverished was: 1) ***No money for basic needs*** including food, school fees, medical expenses, rent and starting capital for a business; 2) ***No assets*** namely, a proper house, means of production, employable skills or household appliances; 3) ***Bad appearance*** denoted by dress, posture (gait and movement) and speech; 4) ***Un- or underemployment*** defined as unemployed adults in the household or adults depending on odd or irregular jobs; 5) ***Incomplete family structure*** embracing divorced (sometimes abandoned) women with children, families left behind by migrants who stopped remitting, and old people without family support; 6) ***Misfortune*** including disease, accidents, death in the family and funeral obligations, house eviction or confiscation of possessions, and a refugee status; 7) ***Misconduct*** including dubious moral standards, alcoholism, drug addiction, and prostitution; and 8) ***Vulnerability*** characterised by the

feeling that one is currently poor but could easily fall into poverty, and a marginal ability to cope.

8. The definition of the informal sector is based on the lack of legal status for the enterprise and the absence of a legal wage and social security.

9. The issue of whether the informal sector is a genuinely productive sector or simply an absorptive sector that disguises labour underutilisation, requires the comparison of findings from a number of surveys already carried out and the collection of information from a new random sample of microenterprises.

10. Income is taken as an indicator for productivity as would be true in a competitive market.

11. Ghana has already gained some experience with a kind of socio-economic development fund, PAMSCAD.

References

ALBERTS, W. & M.P. van DIJK 1994, *Urban Poverty and Employment in Ghana: A Qualitative Assessment*, World Bank consultancy draft report, Washington D.C.

BAAH-NUAKAOH, A. 1993, *The Informal Sector in the Social and Economic Development of Ghana*, Frankfurt, GTZ

CHHIBBER, A. & C. LEECHOR 1993, 'Ghana: 2000 and Beyond', *Finance and Development* vol. 30, no.3

DIJK, M.P. van 1993a, *A Qualitative Urban Poverty Assessment in Abeka, Accra*, World Bank consultancy report, Washington D.C.

DIJK, M.P. van 1993b, *Economic Activities in Abeka*, World Bank consultancy report, Washington D.C.

PEDERSEN, P., A. SVERRISSON & M.P. van DIJK (eds) 1994, *Flexible Specialization and Other Approaches to the Dynamics of Small-Scale Industries in the South*, London, Intermediate Technology

RASMUSSEN, J., H. SCHMITZ & M.P. van DIJK (eds) 1993, 'Flexible Specialization: A New Paradigm for Small Enterprises?', *IDS Bulletin*, vol. 23, no. 3

WORLD BANK 1994, *Adjustment in Africa: Reforms, Results and the Road Ahead*, Oxford, Oxford University Press

IV

EAST AFRICA

7

Urban Trajectories in Rural Livelihood Strategies: Household Employment Patterns in Kenya's Coast Province

Dick Foeken

The Kenyan Coast has long been exposed to international influences, serving as a port of call for seafarers for centuries and entrepot of the Arab ivory and slave trades during the nineteenth century. Coast Province is now considered an economically backward area in the Kenyan economy with limited agricultural opportunities. The livelihood strategies of its rural inhabitants reflect this and there is a concomitant blurring of rural and urban boundaries in the residential and occupational patterns of the population.

In this chapter off-farm employment activities of rural household members are viewed as contributions to the diversification of the household's sources of income. The term 'livelihood strategy' is used to refer to the manoeuvring space households have in making a living (Druijven 1990). In the largely uncapitalised economic environment of rural Coast Province the most fundamental asset of households is their labour power. This labour is allocated to a variety of activities: agricultural or non-agricultural, for subsistence or market, local or non-local (Dietz, Druijven and Foeken 1992).

Current research reveals that economic diversification rather than specialisation is crucial to the pursuit of household livelihood (Hoorweg, Foeken and Klaver 1995; Hoorweg et al. 1991; Foeken and Tellegen 1992; Tellegen, Verstrate and Foeken 1992). Furthermore, the pattern of diversification is conditioned by household economic stratification. A distinction is made in this chapter between three household income categories drawing attention to the fact that better-off households practice more diversified livelihood strategies and have 'more manoeuvring space' than poorer households.

The analysis begins with a brief description of the study area and survey design. It then focuses on salient socio-economic features of the persons, i.e. the workers engaged in off-farm activities: who they are and what their main employment characteristics are. These employment characteristics are then related to different patterns of household income diversification, and, ultimately, to different types of livelihood strategies and their relative success in providing household welfare.

Coast Province: Low Economic Performance and Expectations

With a population of 1.8 million in 1989 (Central Bureau of Statistics (CBS) 1994), Coast Province is Kenya's most populous province and one of its poorest. The region has lagged behind central and western Kenya. The province scores comparatively poorly on most accepted development indicators such as infant mortality (129 versus 109 for Kenya as a whole), childhood malnutrition (39 per cent stunted versus 28 per cent; 5 per cent wasted versus 3 per cent), and enrolment of girls in primary education (58 per cent versus 83 per cent). Living conditions are harsh and estimates place the incidence of rural poverty at over 40 per cent, which is higher than for Kenya generally (CBS 1983; CBS/UNICEF 1984; Foeken et al. 1989). The economy is primarily characterised by subsistence agriculture. Industry and services have experienced little development except for tourism.

The coastal strip receives the most rainfall, the highest average annual amount (over 1,300 mm) being in the south-eastern part of Kwale District. Going inland, rainfall quickly diminishes: at a distance of 50 km it falls below 700 mm per annum. As a result, the drier zones in the hinterland offer only limited potential for rain-fed agriculture and are more suitable for livestock rearing whereas the relatively humid zone near the coast has a wider potential for food and cash crops. In general, the low reliability of rainfall severely restricts the scope and intensity of agricultural activities in the whole of the region (Foeken 1994). Although occasional surpluses are realised in good years, the population is regularly confronted with drought conditions (Ministry of Environment and Natural Resources (MENR) 1984a, 1984b).

The data used in this chapter are drawn from a 1985-6 study of Kwale and Kilifi Districts (see Figure 1), the two districts that account for more than two-thirds of the rural population of Coast Province. The study involved a random sample of 300 rural households in six locations, in two different districts and in three different agro-ecological zones.[1]

Figure 1: Kwale and Kilifi Districts

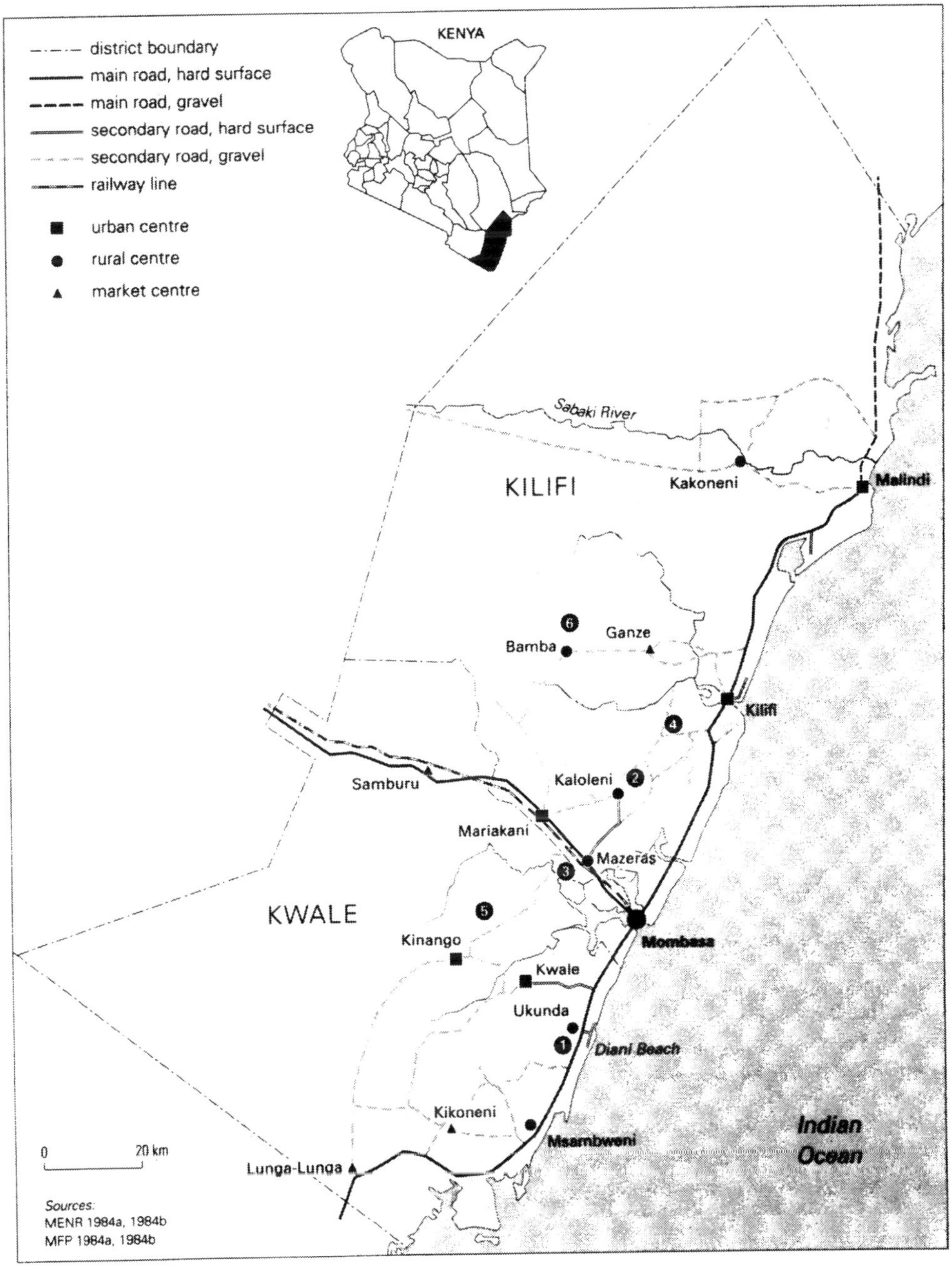

The three agro-ecological zones cover about two-thirds of the land surface of the two districts and according to estimates by Jaetzold and Schmidt (1983) include almost 90 per cent of the farm families.

Fifty households were randomly sampled in each research location, a household being defined as a group of people residing under one roof or under several roofs within a single compound, who are answerable to the same head and share a common source of food (Hoorweg, Kliest and Niemeijer 1988). Each household was visited five times in the period between June 1984 and October 1986, at intervals of three to four months. The data used here derive from the first round and cover the twelve months prior to the interview, i.e. the period from June 1984 to June 1985.

For each household the annual income for 1984-5 was assessed by adding the income from employment, the income from cash crop and livestock production, as well as the value of staple crop production. In order to standardise for household size, incomes are expressed in Kenyan shillings per consumer unit per year. One consumer unit (cu) is an adult equivalent based on energy requirements. Three income classes were distinguished, notably less than KSh.1,000/cu, KSh.1,000-2,999/cu, and KSh.3,000/cu and more.[2] These classes are denoted as 'low' (109 households, or 37 per cent of the study population), 'middle' (123 households, 41 per cent) and 'high' (65 households, 22 per cent). Remarkably, each income category is very evenly distributed over the three agro-ecological zones.

The 'low' category reflects households with an annual income below the so-called 'food poverty line', defined as the income needed to purchase minimum calorie requirements, i.e. nutritional needs at minimal bodily function at minimum body weight (Foeken et al. 1989).These were estimated at 2,115 kilocalories per consumer unit per day costing KSh.990/cu per year (rounded up to KSh.1,000/cu). This is only slightly lower than the food poverty line calculated by Greer and Thorbecke (1986) for Coast Province as a whole.

Employment in Coast Province

The concepts of 'rural employment', 'off-farm employment' and 'non-agricultural employment' must be defined. Of these, the first concept is locational, indicating all income-generating activities in rural areas with the exception of households' own production of primary agricultural products. It includes, for instance, processing and selling of self-produced foodstuffs, like roasted maize, but also a regular job in the formal sector. Strictly speaking, 'off-farm employment' includes all income-generating activities outside one's own farm in rural and urban areas. The work may be of an agricultural or non-agricultural character, whereas 'non-agricultural employment' refers to activities not involving plant or animal husbandry which take place in rural or urban areas.

In the sampled population, off-farm activities form an essential element in earning a living. Opportunities for such work are primarily found in Mombasa, the principal town in the region. According to CBS estimates for the formal sector, more than three-quarters of all wage employment in the districts of Kwale, Kilifi and Mombasa was concentrated in the provincial capital at the time of the survey. A further 14 per cent was in Kilifi District, and 9 per cent in Kwale (CBS 1986).

A total of 403 persons in 297 households - or 1.4 persons per household - were engaged in some type of off-farm activity (Table 1). Four broad categories are distinguished:

> ***Regular employment*** denotes all wage employment on a regular basis. This may be in the formal or informal sector and in the agricultural, industrial or service sector. This type of employment is usually secure. With 41 per cent of workers, it formed the largest category in the study.
>
> ***Temporary employment*** denotes wage labour on a temporary basis, usually for a period of some months.[3] Again, this applies to all sectors. For 14 per cent of the workers this was the main source of off-farm employment.
>
> ***Rural casual labour*** involving primarily farm work on neighbouring farms is the most insecure of the three types of wage labour in terms of regularity and income because the labourer is hired and paid on a daily basis. One-fifth of the workers relied on this type of employment.
>
> ***Self-employment*** denotes all income-generating activities carried out not as an employee and excluding the sale of primary, unprocessed farm products. One-quarter of off-farm workers were in this category.

Table 1 shows where the workers were located. More than 80 per cent were based in either Mombasa or in their own district. The majority (55 per cent) of those with a regular or temporary job were found in the urban area of Mombasa District. Self-employment and, not surprisingly, rural casual labour are more bound to the direct vicinity of the workers' homestead.[4] From the figures in Table 1, it is possible to make a rough distinction between urban and rural employment. Leaving the category 'elsewhere' aside because it is a mixed category in terms of the urban-rural distinction, and defining 'own district' as rural since the towns in Kwale and Kilifi District are small, about 55 per cent of off-farm activities can be categorised as rural employment.

Table 1: Off-Farm Workers by Type and Place of Work*

	Place of Work				
Type of work	Mombasa	Own location[1]	Own district[2]	Else-where[3]	Total
Regular employment	93	33	20	21	167
Temporary employment	32	20	3	3	58
Rural casual labour	20	51	4	4	79
Self-employed	22	65	11	1	99
Total	167	169	38	29	403

Source: Author's data

1. Location refers to the administrative unit.
2. Excluding one's own location.
3. Rural workers but also including 10 persons with a regular job in Nairobi or other Kenyan urban locations.

* The above notes apply to all the subsequent tables.

For each category in Table 1, the average earnings from off-farm employment during the study year were calculated and corrected for residency so that the actual figures are estimates of incomes reaching the households. The results are shown in Table 2. Average earnings come to about KSh.5,100. Rather surprisingly, self-employment in one's own village was at least as rewarding as migration to towns.

At household level, average off-farm income was about KSh.1,260/cu, which compared with a total average household income of KSh.2,000/cu. This implies that more than 60 per cent of household income was derived from off-farm activities. Cash crops and livestock contributed 13 per cent, the remaining 25 per cent being the calculated value of subsistence production (Foeken et al. 1989). Bearing in mind that the study population consisted entirely of *farming* households, these figures clearly indicate the importance of off-farm employment for the rural population of Coast Province.

Table 2: Off-Farm Workers' Average Earnings by Type and Place of Work (KSh/Worker, 1984-85)[1]

	Place of Work				
Type of work[2]	Mombasa	Own location	Own district	Elsewhere	Total
Regular employment	5,135	11,583	4,383	5,323	6,343
Temporary employment	3,456	3,161	-	-	3,512
Rural casual labour	1,073	1,622	-	-	1,405
Self-employed	6,115	6,699	11,103	-	7,012
Total	4,456	5,703	6,000	4,562	5,132

Source: Author's data

1. Income earned by part-time residents was estimated at 75 per cent of full earnings and that earned by non-residents as 25 per cent and refers to the first round of the survey. Where the number of cases is less than ten, no income figures are given.
2. For notes concerning place of work see Table 1.

Income Divisions

Tables 3 and 4 show some characteristics concerning off-farm employment for the three household income categories. The most salient finding is that off-farm employment is a far less important source of income in low-income households compared to others. This is also true when measured in terms of numbers of workers and in terms of their contribution to household income.

For their survival the low-income households primarily depend on their own food production, the value of which comprised almost 60 per cent of their total income (compared with 27 and 16 per cent for the middle- and high-income households).[5] Nevertheless, income from off-farm employment, however small, is of vital importance to these households because it is the major means of buying all kinds of necessary items, including food.[6] Moreover, one-third of their off-farm income is derived from casual labour on nearby farms, a type of labour that is usually only performed in case of urgent cash needs.

Table 3: Off-Farm Numbers Employed and Average Income by Household Income Category

	Household income category		
	Low (N = 109)	Middle (N = 123)	High (N = 65)
Number of workers:			
Absolute	79	196	128
per household	0.7	1.6	2.0
Average Income:			
Off-farm activities (KSh/cu)	152	1,124	3,372
Rural casual labour (KSh/cu)	50	125	53
Off-farm activities as % of household income	30%	61%	71%
Rural casual labour as % of income from off-farm employment	33%	11%	2%

Source: Author's data

Table 4 reveals little variation in the distribution of workers over the four types of off-farm employment. Moreover, the percentage of workers in the low-income class working in Mombasa is higher than in the two other income groups. In other words, contrary to expectations there is no correlation between household income and regular and/or urban employment. Thus the reason why workers in the low-income class earn less than half their middle-income counterparts and about one-fifth of the high-income group cannot be found in different occupational statuses or different work locations, but in the type of activity. A major reason for workers' poverty in the low-income category is that they only have access to low-paid jobs, be it in Mombasa or elsewhere. The question as to how far this relates to such factors as gender, age, and education is dealt with in subsequent sections.

Table 4: Off-Farm Employment by Type and Place of Work, and Household Income Category

	Household income category		
	Low (N = 109)	Middle (N = 123)	High (N = 65)
Type of work (%)			
Regular employment	34.1	41.3	46.1
Temporary employment	7.6	16.8	14.8
Rural casual labour	38.0	20.4	7.0
Self-employed	20.3	21.4	32.0
Total	100.0	100.0	100.0
Place of work (%)[1]			
Mombasa	48.1	42.4	35.9
Own location	27.9	39.8	46.9
Own district	11.4	8.7	9.4
Elsewhere	8.9	5.6	5.5
Total	100.0	100.0	100.0
Average earnings from off-farm employment (KSh/Worker)[2]	1,887	4,480	8,133

Source: Author's data

1. For notes concerning place of work see Table 1.
2. Income earned by part-time residents was estimated at 75 per cent of full earnings and that earned by non-residents as 25 per cent.

Gender

The main differences along gender lines are presented in Table 5. Above all, the absolute numbers are conspicuous: 85 per cent of all workers are men. In particular in the lowest household income category, the ratio between male and female workers is even more skewed at 12:1, against 5:1 in middle- and high-income households. Moreover, almost half of the men had a regular job, against only 15 per cent of women. Over half of the women were self-employed and another 25 per cent performed casual labour on nearby farms. There are some differences concerning the type of work according to household income. In the lowest income category fewer men had a regular job (36 per cent), while an equal number (37 per cent) relied on rural casual labour. This also applied to the women (50 per cent), while the self-employed women were all (except one) from middle- and high-income categories.

Table 5: Main Characteristics of Off-Farm Employment by Gender

	Men	Women
Total number	342	61
Type of work (%):		
Regular employment	46.2	14.8
Temporary employment	15.2	9.8
Rural casual labour	18.7	24.6
Self-employed	19.9	50.8
Total	100.0	100.0
Place of work (%)[1]		
Mombasa	46.2	14.8
Own location	34.8	82.0
Own district	10.8	1.6
Elsewhere	8.2	1.6
Total	100.0	100.0
Average earnings from off-farm employment (KSh/Worker)[2]	5,380	3,739

Source: Author's data

1. For notes concerning place of work see Table 1.
2. Income earned by part-time residents was estimated at 75 per cent of full earnings and that earned by non-residents as 25 per cent.

Most men either found a job in Mombasa (46 per cent)[7] or in the vicinity of their homestead (35 per cent). Moreover, it is evident that as household income increases, the percentage of men working in Mombasa *decreases* from 51 to 40 per cent and working in their own location *increases* from 25 to 43 per cent. This indicates that men in richer households managed to find relatively well-paid local jobs. The same cannot be said of the women. As could be expected, they are predominantly working in or in the direct vicinity of their homesteads and this applies to all income categories.

The average off-farm earnings of men are much higher than those of women, a reflection of the time men are able to devote to these types of activities.[8] For the only type of work at which one may assume that both men and women spend more or less the same amount of time, i.e. regular employment, average earnings were about the same. Only nine women, however, had a regular job. In all other types of employment, including rural casual labour, men earned substantially more than women. Furthermore, the difference between male and female earnings was particularly high (2.5:1) in low-income households. This indicates that few women in these poor households perform some type of off-farm employment, and even that is on a casual basis.

Age Groups

Nearly all off-farm workers belonged to the 20-50 year age group and within this range were fairly equally distributed over three age classes (Table 6). Moreover, the three age groups were themselves also very equally distributed *within* each of the three household income categories. As for the type of work concerned, Table 6 points to an interesting shift from temporary employment to self-employment with age. A similar shift can be observed with respect to place of work, notably from Mombasa to the worker's own location. This indicates that off-farm workers take up temporary jobs in Mombasa and subsequently return to their home areas in order to start business activities there. Such a shift can be seen in all income categories, although it is most noteworthy in the highest income group. This could point to a successful shift in monetary terms.

There is a substantial difference in off-farm earnings between the younger (< 30) and the older (>40) age groups: older workers contributed much more to household income than younger ones, which can partly be explained by the shift in location just mentioned. Again, this occurs in all household income classes, although comparatively less so among the poor.

Table 6: Off-Farm Employment: Main Characteristics by Age Group

	Age group (years)		
	< 30	30 - 39	> 40
Total number	159	128	116
Type of work (%)			
Regular employment	39.6	41.4	44.0
Temporary employment	25.8	9.4	4.3
Rural casual labour	21.4	20.3	16.4
Self-employed	13.2	28.9	35.3
Total	100.0	100.0	100.0
Place of work (%)[1]			
Mombasa	49.1	37.5	35.3
Own location	35.2	44.5	48.3
Own district	7.5	10.2	11.2
Elsewhere	8.2	7.8	5.2
Total	100.0	100.0	100.0
Average earnings from off-farm employment (KSh/Worker)[2]	3,572	5,517	6,844

Source: Author's data

1. For notes concerning place of work see Table 1.
2. Income earned by part-time residents was estimated at 75 per cent of full earnings and that earned by non-residents as 25 per cent.

Education is No Guarantee of Economic Success

In general, parents in Kenya place a high premium on educating their children. In Coast Province, this tendency is less pronounced and average education levels are low. Table 7 shows that 56 per cent of all the workers had less than Standard 5 education, i.e. mid-way through primary school. In low-income households, this percentage is 63 per cent.

Table 7: Main Characteristics of Off-Farm Employment by Level of Education

	Level of education	
	< Standard 5	=> Standard 5
Total number	225	178
Type of work (%)		
Regular employment	30.2	55.6
Temporary employment	12.0	17.4
Rural casual labour	22.2	16.3
Self-employed	35.6	10.7
Total	100.0	100.0
Place of work (%)[1]		
Mombasa	38.2	45.5
Own location	49.3	32.6
Own district	8.0	11.2
Elsewhere	4.4	10.7
Total	100.0	100.0
Average earnings from off-farm employment (KSh/Worker)[2]	4,626	5,770

Source: Author's data

1. For notes concerning place of work see Table 1.
2. Income earned by part-time residents was estimated at 75 per cent of full earnings and that earned by non-residents as 25 per cent.

There is a clear relationship between education and type of work. The chance of finding regular employment increases with more education while the inclination for self-employment declines. As a result, more of the less well-educated can be found in their home place with more of the better-educated working at some distance from home. However, there is no clear relationship between level of education and off-farm earnings, which may be a contributing factor to Coast Province parents' disinclination to invest in their children's education.

Household Livelihood Strategies Unravelled

Schematically, the three household income categories can be related to livelihood strategies which involve trade-offs between ultimate goals and time availability

(Druijven 1990; Dietz, Druijven and Foeken 1992) (Figure 2). The *goal* may be, on the one hand, the preservation of a certain way of life, and, on the other hand, the improvement of the household's standard of living. The *time perspective* may either be long- or short-term. The latter usually implies immediate action, but long-term can range from a few months, e.g. preventing seasonal stress for instance, to a number of years representing an accumulation process. Each category in the typology reflects a broad type of livelihood strategy. The importance of the distinctions lies not in the typology itself, but in the possibility of relating various household characteristics to each type of strategy.

Figure 2: Typology of Household Livelihood Strategies

	Time Perspective	
Goal	Short-term	Long-term
Preservation	**A** Recovery strategies	**B** Conservation strategies
Improvement	**C** Opportunistic strategies	**D** Structural improvement strategies

Source: Dietz, Druijven and Foeken (1992)

It is tempting to place low-income households in category A, middle-income households in category B, and high-income households in category D. For the sake of contrast, the following is limited to characterising the strategies of categories A and D.

Low-income households were defined as those with an annual income below the food poverty line. Most of these households are 'trapped in the vicious cycle of poverty' (Gill 1991): low energy intake leads to under-nutrition and to under-utilisation of labour, which, in turn, adversely affect agricultural production. This may also be the reason that, compared with the other two income categories, so few women were engaged in off-farm employment.

Other significant factors are the higher number of children and the lower level of education. It has been seen that those who perform off-farm employment are relatively young. All this results in a very limited resource base. Despite being low, agricultural production is still the main source of livelihood. Income from the sale of cash crops and/or livestock is almost negligible. In many instances cash needs have to be fulfilled by whatever work is available and this is often casual labour on nearby farms.

High-income households are those with an annual income at least three times the food poverty line. The value of the household's own food production, although much higher than in the low-income households, comprises only a small portion of the household's resource base. Off-farm employment is the main source of income. On average, two persons per household are engaged in some type of employment, one with a regular job and the other is self-employed. Moreover, workers are on average older and better-educated. The result is that earnings from both types of employment are comparatively high. This implies that the resource base is much wider and much more secure than in low-income households. Successful self-employment activities indicate that 'structural improvement' has been realised in at least some of these households.

The possibilities for poor households, however, are much more restricted because of such factors as a lack of education and labour power. Livelihood strategies are consequently primarily aimed at 'recovery', or perhaps 'conservation', albeit at a very low level, while better-off households can exploit the socio-economic environment in such a way that structural improvement is realised.

Conclusion: Where Rural and Urban Boundaries Blur

The de-agrarianisation process at household level has been underway for decades in Coast Province. Very few households depend solely on agriculture for their livelihood. In fact, on average, off-farm income is more important than earnings derived from the sale of own farm produce. Migration to towns, mainly Mombasa, where most of the off-farm employment opportunities are found, is a common phenomenon.

Diversification of household resources means first of all an income from one or more off-farm activities. It is widely recognised that for a number of reasons 'betting on one horse', traditionally agriculture, is no longer a feasible livelihood strategy for most Kenyan rural households. More affluent households have a comparatively broad range of income sources, both agricultural and non-agricultural. This implies that alleviating poverty in rural areas can only succeed if sufficient non-agricultural income, off-farm opportunities are available.

The notion that a regular job in town offers the best possibility for a rural household to 'conserve' its status quo, or perhaps even to 'improve' it, has to be qualified based on the findings of the present study. On average, rural employment was actually more rewarding financially than urban employment. One reason for this was that workers in town spend a large proportion of their earnings on simply living there, while all earnings from workers living at the homestead potentially reach the household.

Urban employment prospects are contingent on personal characteristics such as sex, age and education. In turn, these factors condition the scope and success of the diversification of rural household resources. Men have a regular job more often than women, which is partly due to their higher education and partly to culturally-determined labour allocation patterns. The large majority of women depend on rural employment, either some modest kind of self-employment or casual labour on a nearby farm for their cash income. The men have a much wider geographical scope for realising their income-generating ambitions, migration to town being a very common option. For many men in Coast Province, rural-urban labour migration at a relatively young age can be seen as a kind of apprenticeship facilitating a more lucrative livelihood strategy aimed at structural improvement once they return to the rural homestead. But this is a male career path only. Women very seldom have such opportunities.

Notes

* I am very grateful to Willem Veerman for providing the quantitative data used in this chapter.

1. In each agro-ecological zone, two villages were selected, one in Kilifi and one in Kwale. The three zones are: the coconut-cassava zone (CL3, with about 1,100-1,200 mm of rainfall per year); the cashewnut-cassava zone (CL4, 900-1,100 mm); and the livestock-millet zone (CL5, 600-900 mm) (Jaetzold & Schmidt 1983).

2. Exchange rate of the Kenya shilling in 1985 was 16 shillings to one US dollar.

3. This category also includes casual labour in town and casual labour on estates and plantations, since these two types of casual labour appeared to be of a temporary nature, i.e. often for a period of several months. Moreover, the average incomes are also comparable with those from temporary employment. Where *casual labour* is mentioned in the text it refers only to *rural* casual labour, which consists almost exclusively of agricultural work on neighbouring farms during peak labour periods.

4. At first sight, it may appear rather surprising to find one-quarter of the rural casual labourers working in Mombasa. However Mombasa refers to Mombasa District, i.e. Mombasa town and the peri-urban area surrounding it. Commercial farming, i.e. the

production of vegetables, fruit, etc. for the city market is common in the latter area, offering employment opportunities during peak seasons.

5. In absolute amounts, however, the value of food production in middle-income households was 70 per cent and in high-income households 155 per cent higher than in the low-income households. The same applies to the third source of income, i.e. cash crops and livestock.

6. For instance, in May/June 1986, i.e. in the peak labour period during the long rainy season, three-quarters of the energy intake of low-income households came from purchased food (Niemeijer, Foeken & Klaver 1991).

7. The 46.2 per cent of the men working in Mombasa are not the same as the 46.2 per cent with a regular job (see Table 1). The same applies to the 14.8 per cent of the women.

8. If the figures had not been corrected for residency, the difference would have been even greater.

References

CENTRAL BUREAU of STATISTICS (CBS) 1983, *Third Rural Child Nutrition Survey 1982*, Nairobi, Ministry of Planning and National Development

____, 1986, *Statistical Abstract 1986*, Nairobi, Ministry of Planning and National Development

____, 1994, *Kenya Population Census 1989, Volume 1*, Nairobi, Office of the Vice-President and Ministry of Planning and National Development

CBS/UNICEF 1984, *Situation Analysis of Children and Women in Kenya, Volume 4: The Well-being of Children*, Nairobi, Central Bureau of Statistics/UNICEF

DIETZ, T., P. DRUIJVEN & D. FOEKEN 1992, 'Coping Mechanisms and Livelihood Strategies; A Summary of Concepts', in H.A. Reitsma, T. Dietz and L. de Haan (eds), *Coping with Semiaridity. How the Rural Poor Survive in Dry-Season Environments*, Utrecht/Amsterdam, Netherlands Geographical Studies 146, Royal Dutch Geographical Society, 37-43

DRUIJVEN, P. 1990, *Mandenvlechters en Mezcalstokers in Mexico. Het Belang van Rurale Nijverheid in de Bestaansstrategie van Huishoudens in de Tlacolula Vallei, Oaxaca*, Amsterdam, Department of Human Geography, University of Amsterdam

FOEKEN, D. 1994, 'Climatic Seasonality in Kenya, with Special Reference to Coast Province', *Eastern and Southern Africa Geographical Journal*, vol. 5, no. 1, 28-43

FOEKEN, D., P. LEEGWATER, R. NIEMEIJER, W. VEERMAN & J. HOORWEG 1989, *Seasonality in the Coastal Lowlands of Kenya, Part 3: Socio-economic Profile*, Nairobi/Leiden, Ministry of Planning and National Development/African Studies Centre Food and Nutrition Studies Programme, Report no. 32

FOEKEN, D. & N. TELLEGEN 1992, *Household Resources and Nutrition of Farm Labourers in Trans Nzoia District, Kenya*, Nairobi/Leiden, Ministry of Planning and National Development/African Studies Centre, Food and Nutrition Studies Programme, Report no. 44

GILL, G.J. 1991, *Seasonality and Agriculture in the Developing World. A Problem of the Poor and Powerless*, Cambridge, Cambridge University Press

GREER, J. & E. THORBECKE 1986, *Food Poverty and Consumption Patterns in Kenya*, Geneva, International Labour Office

HOORWEG, J., T. KLIEST & R. NIEMEIJER 1988, *Seasonality in the Coastal Lowlands of Kenya, Part 1: Research Objectives and Study Design*, Nairobi/Leiden, Ministry of Planning and National Development/African Studies Centre, Food and Nutrition Studies Programme, Report no. 27

HOORWEG, J., R. NIEMEIJER, D. FOEKEN, W. OKELLO & W. VEERMAN 1991, *Economic and Nutritional Conditions at Settlement Schemes in Coast Province*, Nairobi/Leiden, Ministry of Planning and National Development/African Studies Centre, Food and Nutrition Studies Programme, Report no. 36

HOORWEG, J., D. FOEKEN, & W. KLAVER 1995, *Seasons and Nutrition at the Kenya Coast,* African Studies Centre Research Series 7/1995, Aldershot, Avebury

JAETZOLD, R. & H. SCHMIDT 1983, *Farm Management Handbook of Kenya, Volume II: Natural Conditions and Farm Management Information, Part C: East Kenya*, Nairobi, Ministry of Agriculture

MINISTRY of ENVIRONMENT & NATURAL RESOURCES (MENR) 1984a, *Kilifi District Environmental Assessment Report*, Nairobi, National Environment and Human Settlements Secretariat

____, 1984b, *Kwale District Environmental Assessment Report,* Nairobi, National Environment and Human Settlements Secretariat

MINISTRY of FINANCE & PLANNING 1984a, *Kilifi District Development Plan 1984-1988*, Nairobi

____, 1984b, *Kwale District Development Plan 1984-1988*, Nairobi

NIEMEIJER, R., D. FOEKEN & W. KLAVER 1991, *Seasonality in the Coastal Lowlands of Kenya, Part 4-5: Food Consumption and Anthropometry*, Nairobi/Leiden, Ministry of Planning and National Development/African Studies Centre, Food and Nutrition Studies Programme, Report no. 38

TELLEGEN, N., L. VERSTRATE & D. FOEKEN 1992, *Income Generation of Farm Labourers in Trans Nzoia District, Kenya: Rural Employment and Social Networks*, Nairobi/Leiden, Ministry of Planning and National Development/African Studies Centre, Food and Nutrition Studies Programme, Report no. 45

8

The Rural Informal Sector in Tanzania

Mboya S.D. Bagachwa

Tanzania has made substantial progress over recent years in restructuring its economy away from state controls and towards markets. The adjustment programme - known as the Economic Recovery Programme (ERP) - introduced after the mid-1980s, has aimed to liberalise internal and external trade and establish a market-determined exchange rate. Restructuring of the parastatals, civil service and financial institutions, and the encouragement of the private sector have also been integral parts of the ERP. Real GDP rose on average by 4 per cent and some increase in per capita income has been registered.

These aggregate impacts, however, conceal a number of shortcomings at the sectoral, household and firm levels. Crop marketing problems persist; deterioration in infrastructure is yet to be checked; inflation is still high; and social service delivery remains desultory. An employment squeeze and retrenchments have exacerbated the problem of unemployment. Within industry, the ERP effects have been mixed. Some firms have been revitalised through the availability of imported raw materials and spare parts, while others have been forced to close down (Bagachwa 1993a).

In rural areas, declining real farm incomes, increasing pressure on land, and opportunities created by economic liberalisation have given rise to a dynamic rural informal sector (RIS). It has become an important source for jobs and income and presently employs about 21 per cent of the nation's labour force compared to only 7 per cent employed in the rural formal sector. The characteristics and dynamics of this sector are not yet fully understood and this chapter attempts to fill the gap. The first section presents an outline of the Tanzanian rural economy while the next two sections focus on the rural informal sector. The fourth section examines the impact of recent economic reforms on the RIS.

Tanzanian Rural Population

Approximately 85 per cent of the Tanzanian population reside in rural areas (URT 1993). There are about 3.5 million farm families working on smallholdings where the area cultivated averages 0.9 hectares with 93 per cent cultivating less than two hectares (URT 1990). The proportion of the active labour force engaged in agriculture has declined slightly from 91 per cent in 1965 to 84 per cent in 1991. The equivalent figures for industry show an increase from 3 to 5 per cent and for services from 6 to 10 per cent. Tanzania's economy is thus predominantly rural-based. Agriculture is not only the largest employer of the labour force but also the largest contributor to GDP (60 per cent in 1992).

The average annual rate of growth of the rural population was estimated at 2.7 per cent during the 1978-88 intercensal period. This was much lower than the 4.1 per cent for all urban districts combined. Corresponding rates for the previous decade suggest a slow-down in urban migration (2.3 and 9.3 per cent for rural and urban migration respectively during 1978-88).

Poverty and Rural Households

Most studies show the rural population to be significantly poorer than the urban population. Rural Tanzanians have bigger families than their urban counterparts (World Bank 1993a). Nearly three-fifths of rural inhabitants are in households below the poverty line. Poverty is most severe in regions with unreliable rainfall, poor infrastructural development and poor access to markets. Such regions include Dodoma, Lindi, Kigoma, Singida, Rukwa and Ruvuma.

Comprehensive time series data on changes in the extent of poverty in both rural and urban Tanzania are lacking. Even the little information that exists is contentious. Bevan et al. (1990) found an increase in rural per capita real incomes between 1969 and 1976-7, a very substantial drop between 1976-7 and 1979-80 and a further small drop between 1982 and 1983. Real incomes at the end of the 1980s were significantly below those of 1976. This assertion has been questioned by Sarris and van den Brink (1993) on the grounds that much of the economic activity of Tanzania went underground and was not captured in official statistics. What is quite indisputable however is that rural-urban disparity has declined, because of the catastrophic declines in urban wages, in the face of protected self-provisioned food production in the rural areas. This point was made as early as 1977 in ILO/JASPA's employment report (ILO/JASPA 1978) and pursued in their

1982 basic needs report (ILO/JASPA 1982). The background studies have been elaborated in various articles by Jamal (1982; 1986; 1989; Jamal and Weeks 1993).

Migration and Rural Differentiation

An analysis of inter-regional population movements between 1967 and 1988 reveals rapid growth[1] of Dar es Salaam, followed by Arusha, Rukwa, Mbeya and Ruvuma regions. Regions which experienced high levels of exodus were Mtwara, Coast, Tanga, Lindi and Mwanza. These movements can be explained from two perspectives. First, Dar es Salaam, with the highest per capita income in the country, has been receiving the largest number of internal migrants because of the normal forces of rural-urban migration. The net growth of Arusha, Rukwa, Mbeya and Ruvuma may be due to pressure on good land in the neighbouring regions of Kilimanjaro, Singida and Mtwara respectively. Other regions such as Lindi, Morogoro, Iringa, Shinyanga and Kigoma have low levels of infrastructural development, and very low incomes which contribute to the voluntary out-migration. According to Collier et al. (1986) the process of voluntary migration involves people leaving the village and coming back again. Some 27 per cent of the households surveyed had family members who had left the village. Out of those who had left, some 39 per cent returned. Thus population pressure, shortages of good agricultural land and low income opportunities have induced the rural population to migrate to new areas with good agricultural potential and increased income-earning opportunities.

De-agrarianisation and Changing Rural Markets

There is evidence that farming is the major occupation of the majority of people. Both the Collier et al. survey in 1980 and the 1991 Cornell/Economics Research Bureau (ERB) survey (Tinios et al. 1993) found that between 70 and 73 per cent of the respondents cited farming as their main occupation. According to Collier et al., however, up to the early 1980s the development of the Tanzanian rural labour market was limited. Labour involved on the family and communal *ujamaa* farms, and in other village activities resulted in little surplus labour. Very few households participated in the labour market (Collier et al. 1986, Bryceson 1990).

The situation appears to have changed since 1980 with wage labour assuming an increasingly important role in the rural economy. The 1991 Cornell/ERB survey reveals that 10-12 per cent of the rural population earned cash wages in either the agricultural or the non-agricultural labour market. Only 20 per cent of all wage income was earned in agricultural activities, the bulk (80 per cent) being from the rural informal sector. The ADIS[2] survey corroborates this evidence with the finding that the share of holdings hiring labour ranged from between 16 and 43 per cent in the years between 1988 and 1991.

Increased participation in the rural labour market suggests that the process of de-agrarianisation is accelerating. An analysis of rural cash incomes based on the 1969 and 1976-7 household budget surveys, the 1979-80 ILO survey, and the 1982-3 Collier et al. survey confirms the growing importance of the rural non-farm sector in the generation of rural incomes. The proportion of non-farm cash incomes in total cash income per household rose from 25 per cent in 1969 to 33 per cent in 1977, 38 per cent in 1980, and 47 per cent in 1983 (Sarris and van den Brink 1993). The authors conclude that 87 per cent of all rural households have some cash income from trade, enterprise or professions. The 1986-7 Agricultural Sample Survey of Tanzania Mainland showed that about 31 per cent of rural households depended wholly on non-farm sources of income (URT 1990), while the 1991 labour force survey indicated that almost one out of four rural households had at least one person self-employed in the informal sector during the year (URT 1993).

The seasonality of Tanzania's agriculture has always permitted farmers to engage in non-farm activities in conjunction with farming. However, it is apparent that the increased importance of the current rural non-farm sector has been induced by the deterioration in real official incomes. As the economic crisis deepened, prices of consumer goods in rural areas rose sharply due to shortages, official rationing and inflation. Concurrently, appreciation in the real exchange rate reduced the prices of cash crops. Besides, agriculture was stagnating in the face of weaknesses in the transport and marketing systems and the subsequent rising marketing margins of the official systems that resulted in large transfers from peasants to the state. As a consequence, average rural official income per household was estimated to have fallen by 48 per cent over the period 1977-83 (Bevan et al. 1990). Rural wage rates also declined substantially over the period. The average off-farm wage in 1980 was about TSh36 per day compared to TSh42 per day in 1983, a fall in real terms of 29 per cent (Collier et al. 1986). The high rate of inflation, averaging 30 per cent annually, and the implicit taxation on export crops through currency overvaluation destroyed the parity between export crops and food crops and induced farmers to switch from cash crops to food crops which could be traded in the parallel market. As real farm incomes declined, more and more farmers began to derive an increasing part of their cash incomes from non-farm sources including migrant remittances, giving rise to a thriving rural informal sector.

Between 1986 and 1993 the ERP appears to have arrested the decline in official rural incomes and rural standards probably improved. Farmers' incomes from traditional export crops increased in line with their production despite a decline in their share of export prices. As for non-traditional exports, prices improved considerably as did total production. Liberalisation increased both real incomes from maize and rice and improved their availability. Rural and urban consumers benefited from the greater availability of consumer goods (Bevan et al. 1989 and 1990, Booth et al. 1993, Bryceson 1993, Mans 1994).

Thus the ERP seems to have facilitated the de-agrarianisation process in two ways. First, the relatively low but rising rural incomes constitute an essential incentive for rising non-agricultural production (i.e. through increased demand and hence expanded markets). Second, the greater availability of raw materials and spares has facilitated this. There has been a boom in rural forward-linkage industries such as grain mills, oil presses, coffee and cashew nut processing, and saw mills (Bagachwa 1991, UNDP et al. 1988). As Booth et al. (1993) report:

> There is evidence...that liberalisation has stimulated village economies on the production side. However, changes in production and income generation appear in the main to have followed the pattern set down earlier...diversification of *miradi* [income-earning activities] at the household level...rather than that of structural adjustment [recovery/ innovation in export].

Importance of the Rural Informal Sector

The informal sector remains an elusive concept.[3] In this chapter the term is used interchangeably with the microenterprise sector to refer to very small-scale private units employing less than 10 persons and involved in the production and distribution of goods and services. They are informal in the sense that they are unregistered, omitted from official statistics and have little access to organised markets, credit institutions, formal education and most public services. Not being recognised or supported by government they are often compelled to operate illegally (ILO 1991).

The rural informal sector is taken to be synonymous with non-farm or non-agricultural small-scale activities, including manufacturing, construction, mining, fishing, transport, commerce and other services. Non-farm activities are included irrespective of whether they are carried out as main or secondary activities. Rural settlements are defined broadly to include villages and small towns which are not regional headquarters and whose economic functions directly relate to the agricultural hinterland.

The Tanzanian rural informal sector hosts diverse production and service activities. These activities play five important roles: first, providing employment and income opportunities at low capital investment per worker in the face of an expanding labour force and shrinking land base; second, providing seasonal and part-time employment during off-peak times; third, generating backward and forward linkages; fourth, providing low-priced goods and services; and finally, providing and upgrading entrepreneurial skills through on-the-job skill transmission.

Employment Creation

In Tanzania Mainland the 1991 National Informal Sector Survey (NISS) revealed that there were 1.8 million informal enterprises employing a total of 2.4 million people. Over one million of the establishments were located in rural areas, employing 1.4 million persons, i.e. about 60 per cent of the total informal sector employment. Nearly two-thirds of informal employees were males (Table 1) and 1.6 million households (34 per cent) had at least one member in the informal sector.

The 1990-91 Labour Force Survey (LFS) showed that there were 11.3 million people economically active in all sectors of the economy with around 83 per cent in rural areas, suggesting that about 21 per cent of the national labour force was employed in the informal sector. Twenty-eight per cent of the employed males and 15 per cent of the employed females were engaged in the informal sector at some time of the year. In rural areas 15 per cent of the total labour force was employed in the informal sector while in urban areas this proportion was 38 per cent.

Even in Zanzibar, informal sector activities were a significant source of employment for an estimated 124,088 persons who constituted 39 per cent of the labour force in 1990. The informal sector was even more prominent in rural areas where it employed 56 per cent of the total rural labour force. In urban areas the informal sector provided employment to 44 per cent of the available labour force.

Compared to the 21 per cent of the total labour force engaged in the informal sector, the formal wage employment sector employed only 6.7 per cent of the total labour force. Thus, the bulk of the informal sector employment potential is found in rural areas which account for 60 per cent of the total informal employment in Tanzania Mainland and 70 per cent in Zanzibar.

Table 1: Distribution of Informal Sector Employment in Tanzania

	Urban (1991)		*Rural (1992)*		*Total*		*Males*	*Females*
	Number	%	Number	%	Number	%	Number	Number
Tanzania Mainland								
Agric. & Fishing	126,325	13.3	110,052	7.8	236,377	10.0	188,063	48,314
Mining & Quarry	17,400	1.8	4,321	*	21,721	0.9	18,723	2,998
Manufacturing	121,748	12.8	404,501	28.5	526,249	22.2	395,247	131,002
Construction	51,112	5.4	112,326	7.9	163,438	6.9	162,216	1,222
Trade/Rest/Hotels	562,525	59.2	651,175	45.9	1,213,700	51.2	575,389	638,311
Transport	12,177	1.3	65,893	4.6	78,070	3.3	75,292	2,778
Community & Personal Services	58,816	6.2	71,009	3.3	129,825	5.5	116,164	13,661
Total	950,103	100.0	1,419,277	100.0	2,369,380	100.0	1,531,094	838,286
% of Total	40.1		59.9		100.0		64.6	35.4
Zanzibar (1990)								
Agric & Fishing	480	1.3	e	e	480	0.4	439	41
Mining & Quarry	92	*	2,948	3.4	3,040	2.4	2,625	415
Manufacturing	12,037	32.6	35,585	40.8	47,622	38.4	20,527	27,095
Construction	2,725	7.4	5,932	6.8	8,657	7.0	8,489	168
Trade/Rest/Hotels	17,871	48.4	36,490	41.8	54,361	43.8	33,522	20,839
Transport	1,181	3.3	4,330	5.0	5,511	4.4	5,443	68
Community & Personal Services	2,556	6.9	1,861	2.1	4,417	3.6	3,786	631
Total	36,942	100.0	87,146	100.0	124,088	100.0	74,831	49,257
% of Total	29.8		70.2		100.0		60.3	39.7

Sources: Tanzania urban 1991 from URT 1991; Tanzania rural 1992 from Bagachwa 1993a, Zanzibar 1990 from Zanzibar Revolutionary Government 1990

* insignificant
e excluded by survey design

Contribution to Output

One important role played by the informal sector is the provision of cheap and low quality goods and services compatible with the incomes of the majority of the population. According to the 1991 NISS the total value added (profits, wages and incomes in kind) by the informal sector came to TSh183.4 billion which was 32 per cent of the total official economy's value added (TSh580.7 billion). In activities like manufacturing, commerce and personal services, the value added generated in informal activities exceeded that generated in the formal sector. This suggests that the informal sector is not a marginalised sector but a major source of income and employment opportunities. About 57 per cent of the informal sector's value added originated from trade, restaurant and hotel activities. This subsector also accounted for 52 per cent of the total informal sector establishments in the country. Manufacturing is the second largest subsector accounting for 16 per cent of the total informal sector value added and 24 per cent of the total establishments.

Of the total informal sector value added, 40 per cent was contributed by the rural informal sector, equivalent to 13 per cent of the official economy's value added. Although urban areas account for 15 per cent of the total population, they generated 60 per cent of the informal sector's total value added and hosted 36 per cent of the total informal sector establishments. The relatively disproportionate concentration of informal sector activities in urban areas can be attributed to three factors. Firstly, not unlike larger firms, informal sector establishments appear to be responsive to the existing economies of scale of urban agglomeration as well as their array of infrastructural facilities with easy accessibility to industrial inputs, especially imports, and guaranteed markets. Secondly, higher urban per capita income and population density help to boost effective demand. Thirdly, support from government institutions and NGOs tends to be beamed at urban-based activities because they are easier to reach and monitor and therefore involve fewer administrative costs. Fourthly, it is believed that rural dwellers' prospects for alternative employment in agriculture are brighter than those of the urban population vis-à-vis urban-based industry.

Income Generation

Informal sector activities play an important role in absolute poverty alleviation by providing additional cash income to households. In rural Tanzania, average incomes generated by households engaged in rural non-farm activities exceed those generated by full-time farming households by 41 per cent (Chuta and Liedholm 1985). Collier et al. (1986) reported that non-farm work is paid three times the daily rate of farm work. Studies on the urban informal sector have also observed that informal sector earnings are substantial. Tripp (1988) found that the minimum income for an average household of six persons was over six times the average formal worker's monthly income. Much of this was contributed by the informal sector: one self-employed person in a household brought in around ten times more than the average formal sector worker. Even self-employed women, who generally earn less from their enterprises than men, made close to four times more than their employed husbands.

The Zanzibar informal sector survey also revealed that average monthly earnings per employee in the parastatal public sector were lower (TSh3,198) than those of a paid worker in the informal sector (TSh4,229). Likewise in Tanzania Mainland, average monthly earnings were reported to be 1.8, 2.6 and 1.2 times higher respectively than the monthly urban minimum wage in Tanzania Mainland. Even the average monthly informal sector wage (cash payments) was higher than the minimum urban wage of TSh3,500 in all subsectors except in trade/restaurants/hotels (URT 1991).

The relatively high value added in the informal sector is a clear indication that several people are employed in the sector, wages are relatively high and capital resources gainfully employed. It also suggests that there is a sufficient surplus being generated for the owner's capital and that it is wrong to always equate poverty with the informal sector as has been the tradition. Indeed there are a number of informal sector operators whose incomes are comparable to or higher than those of workers engaged in similar activities in the formal sector. Moreover, to the extent that a significant portion of informal sector incomes accrues to disadvantaged groups such as women, the landless and youths, it tends to have an income-equalising effect.

Skill Formation and Human Resource Development

The main source of skills for operating and managing informal enterprises comes from the informal sector itself. Such skills are self-taught or acquired on the job through experience and learning from relatives or other craftsmen. Various informal sector surveys (summarised in Bagachwa 1993a) indicate that between 80 and 95 per cent of the artisanal entrepreneurs received such training prior to establishing their enterprises.

Anatomy of the Rural Informal Sector

Table 2 shows the importance of RIS in terms of shares, number of enterprises and employment. The two largest activities are trade/restaurants/hotels and manufacturing. The former predominate in terms of both the number of establishments and employment, accounting for 40-45 per cent of the total. Manufacturing is the second largest subsector constituting between 31 and 41 per cent of the total estimated establishments and between 29 and 40 per cent of total employment. Other important activities include construction, community and personal services, and transportation.

Table 2: Distribution of Rural Informal Sector Activities and Employment, Tanzania and Selected African Countries

	Tanzania mainland				*Other countries*			
	% of total employment		*% of total establishments*		*% of total establishments*			
	Urban 1991	Rural 1992	Urban 1991	Rural 1992	Botswana 1992	Malawi 1992	Lesotho 1991	Kenya 1988
Agric. & Fishing	13.3	7.8	7	0.4	e	e	e	e
Mining & Quarry	1.8	*	*	0.8	e	e	e	e
Manufacturing	12.8	28.5	31	40.5	31.3	34.8	61.9	21.9
Construction	5.4	7.9	8	2.3	0.0	0.4	5.3	e
Trade/Rest/Hotel	59.2	45.9	45	40.1	66.1	61.0	26.8	65.8
Transport	1.3	4.6	3	2.0	0.3	0.4	0.4	e
Community & Personal Services	6.2	5.3	6	13.9	2.3	3.4	5.6	12.3
Total	100.0	100.0	100	100.0	100.0	100.0	100.0	100.0

Sources: Tanzania urban from URT 1991; Tanzania rural 1992 from Bagachwa 1993a; Other countries from Liedholm and Mead 1993

* insignificant
e excluded by survey design

The relative insignificance of agricultural activities is by survey design since those located in rural areas were excluded from the survey. The predominance of trade-oriented and light manufacturing activities in Tanzania's rural informal sector is consistent with the stylised pattern of microenterprises in Eastern and Southern Africa (as shown in Table 2), and elsewhere in Sub-Saharan Africa (Bagachwa and Stewart 1992, Liedholm and Mead 1993).

Size, Ownership, and Labour Force

Informal sector enterprises are mostly small. According to the 1992 Rural Informal Sector Survey (RISS) the 998 sample rural informal firms employed a total of 1,633 persons implying an average of 1.6 persons per establishment (Bagachwa 1993a). Over 85 per cent were single-person enterprises. The 1991 Mainland NISS enumerated a total of 1.15 million rural enterprises with 1.42 million people, an average of 1.3 persons per establishment. This average is identical to the figure emerging from the Zanzibar informal sector survey (1990). Urban informal sector units show similar traits, registering 1.3 and 1.5 persons per establishment in Zanzibar and mainland Tanzania respectively (URT 1991). Individual or sole proprietorships dominate.[4] In rural areas various estimates put this proportion at 98 or 99 per cent (URT 1991 and 1993). Group ownership and partnerships outside the household are not common.

Employment in the informal sector comprises working proprietors or operators, paid employees, apprentices, and paid and unpaid relatives. Since most are one-person enterprises, operators dominate the labour force. In rural areas on the mainland, working proprietors account for three-quarters of the total employment and in urban areas almost two-thirds. In Zanzibar this figure approaches 75 per cent in both rural and urban areas.

The second largest category in the labour force is unpaid, mostly family, employees, constituting 11 per cent and 18 per cent of total employment in rural and urban mainland areas respectively. Overall, unpaid workers and apprentices account for over 50 per cent of all employees in the informal sector.

The proportion of hired labour in total employment (including operators) averages 8 per cent in rural Tanzania Mainland. There is a clear tendency for this share to increase as one moves from rural to urban areas and as the size of the market grows and specialisation increases. In urban Tanzania consequently, the proportion of paid workers in total employment averages 15 per cent of total informal urban employment or 42 per cent of total employees.

Location, Infrastructure and Capital Structure

The results of the 1992 RISS revealed that 42 per cent of the rural informal enterprises operated from fixed premises (mainly within the house or dwelling of the operator), 16 per cent from temporary structures and 31 per cent were mobile (Bagachwa 1993a). The 1991 NISS also showed that 39 per cent of the rural informal establishments operated from fixed premises, 18 per cent from temporary premises, and 37 per cent were mobile. Operating from fixed premises is advantageous because the sites are easy to locate and hence easy to target for public support.

Generally speaking, rural informal establishments lack access to essential utilities such as water and electricity. Only 20 per cent of the firms had water and 14 per cent electricity and all of these were located in small towns (URT 1991). Electricity was mainly used for lighting and not for running operations, except in a few processes such as grain milling and metal fabrication, and in garages and repair workshops. The general lack of availability of power in rural areas is a major constraint on the development of the rural informal sector since it hinders the adoption of modern small-scale power-operated machinery. Where power was available there was relatively more capacity utilisation since operations could be extended into night shifts (e.g. in grain milling). Inadequate physical infrastructure at sites, make-shift buildings, and lack of office space and basic utilities such as water made it difficult for informal sector operators to qualify for business registration and licences since they did not meet the required standards.

The initial capital requirement in the informal sector varies with the type of activity but is generally low. In rural areas between 55 to 60 per cent of the enterprises start business with a total fixed and working capital of less than TSh1,000 (US$2), while only 19 per cent start with a total capital of TSh20,000 (US$4) or more. Initial capital requirements are relatively higher in urban areas than in rural areas. Only 26 per cent of urban enterprises indicated starting business with more than TSh20,000. Even then, given that most firms were less than five years old at the time of the survey, initial capital requirements are much lower compared to a typical formal sector firm.

Evidence from various surveys (Bagachwa 1993a) shows that savings are the major source for financing informal sector enterprise, with between 40 to 80 per cent of urban enterprises and 74 to 80 per cent of rural firms reporting self-financing of their operations from savings. This can limit the scope, expansion and diversification and the type and quality of capital equipment procured since private savings are usually minimal.

Market Demand

There are three main sources of demand for informal sector products: individual households, other informal sector enterprises, and other sectors of the formal economy such as large-scale industry and government institutions. A minor and potential source of demand is from exports.

Markets are highly localised. In rural areas, both the 1991 NISS and the 1992 RISS revealed that almost all sales were made in local areas and exports were practically non-existent (URT 1991; Bagachwa 1993a). The pattern was similar in urban areas and in both areas the overwhelming bulk of the goods and services were sold directly to individual consumers. A second, but less important source of demand for informal sector products came from small enterprises. Such sales were reported by 4 per cent of the firms in rural areas and 6 per cent in urban areas. Only 1 per cent of all enterprises reported having made sales to government and parastatal institutions.

Constraints

Survey findings regarding entrepreneurs' perceptions about the constraints they face must be interpreted cautiously (Liedholm and Mead 1993). Entrepreneurs may exaggerate their problems in the hope of securing both moral and material support. Alternatively, they could be defensive in order to hide their inadequacies. With this in mind, the survey evidence reveals a shortage of finance or credit, especially for working capital, as the most severe problem at start-up and during business operations. This problem was also implied by the predominance of self-finance at the time of initial investment and when expanding the business.

A second set of problems mentioned related to shortage of inputs, i.e. raw materials, equipment and spare parts. On average 20 per cent of all enterprises considered this to be the most severe problem as it relates to the high cost of inputs as well as their unavailability. Inputs are expensive because of the overall inflationary situation, the impact of currency devaluation and the fact that most operators in the informal sector do not have direct access to supplies at factory prices.

A third set of problems involved demand bottlenecks. These were usually expressed as 'no customers' and poor marketing systems, including a lack of publicity, excessive competition from other informal sector and protected formal sector firms, and also sheer ignorance about existing markets.

A fourth set of problems cited was a lack of appropriate sites and public utilities. The former includes problems such as poorly constructed structures, with limited space or inaccessibility to markets. The situation is even worse for those not operating in areas approved by local or municipal authorities who face continual harassment from city authorities. Since the suitability of the building is a prerequisite to the issuing of licences, insecure sheds cause not only operational inconvenience but are also a constraint to legality. Surprisingly, government regulations (i.e. taxation, licensing registration, municipal fees, etc.) were not perceived as a major constraint by most entrepreneurs.

Informal Sector under Adjustment

Table 3 presents survey results on the impact of ERP on production and employment as perceived by rural entrepreneurs. The impacts have been mixed. Rural informal firms which reported increased output predominated in trade/restaurants/hotels (69 per cent), community and personal services (65 per cent), and manufacturing (57 per cent). Stagnation (no change) was reported to be highest in the mining and quarrying sector (68 per cent of firms) and construction (59 per cent). Generally ERP had a limited impact on employment. The highest proportion of firms in which employment increased was construction (30 per cent), manufacturing (22 per cent) and transport (22 per cent). This reinforces the point that internal expansion of informal sector enterprises in terms of employment is generally limited. Expansion occurs in the form of new establishments.

Table 3: Impact of ERP on Employment and Output in the Informal Sector 1988-91 (Percentage of Enterprises)

	Change in Output			*Change in Employment*		
	Increase	No Change	Decrease	Increase	No Change	Decrease
Agriculture & Fishing	37	52	11	14	83	3
Mining & Quarrying	24	68	8	10	79	11
Manufacturing	57	13	30	22	61	18
Construction	33	59	8	30	42	28
Trade/Rest/Hotels	69	15	16	19	55	26
Transport	41	35	24	22	65	13
Community & Personal Services	65	21	14	17	68	15

Source: Bagachwa 1993a

The biggest impact of ERP has been in terms of availability of inputs. Over half of the firms reported that it was easier to obtain imported and domestic inputs after ERP. This enabled informal sector firms to raise capacity utilisation levels and improve quality. For example, access to new imported steel enabled numerous enterprises which had previously been dependent on limited scrap materials to make more and a wider range of higher quality products (Bagachwa 1993b). The new liberal environment also enabled capital formation to take place through new investment. Over half of the firms in manufacturing, transport, and community and personal services purchased new equipment and/or expanded their operations.

Table 4: Impact of ERP on Rural Informal Sector Accessibility to Resources and Degree of Competition, 1986-1991

	Easier to obtain					
	Imported inputs	Domestic inputs	Harder to get Credit	Greater competition	Purchase of new equipmt	Change in product mix
Agriculture & Fishing	37	52	11	14	83	3
Mining & Quarrying	24	68	8	10	79	11
Manufacturing	57	13	30	22	61	18
Construction	33	59	8	30	42	28
Trade/Rest/ Hotels	69	15	16	19	55	26
Transport	41	35	24	22	65	13
Community & Personal Services	65	21	14	17	68	15

Source: Bagachwa 1993a

Table 4 also shows that competition increased substantially during the ERP period. This is mainly due to the increased availability of both domestic and imported inputs as reported earlier. Increased competition and increases in the prices of inputs arising from devaluation forced some firms to lose their markets.

In summary, the medium- and long-term effects of the ERP reforms on small-scale enterprises are not yet clear. The emerging evidence, however, indicates that the reforms have served as a double-edged sword, threatening some firms' markets through greater imports and domestic competition and revitalising others by providing freely available raw materials and spares. The most adversely affected firms have been those which have been unable to innovate or rely on imported inputs, including a number of small engineering firms. Also affected have been firms lacking strong sectoral linkages. For such firms the principal sources of decline in demand have been: first, increased prices of imported raw materials and inputs due to the inflationary effects of devaluation; second, falling real incomes and depressed purchasing power among urban and rural households; and third, increased imports and domestic competition resulting in a lower volume of sales. The beneficiaries of the reforms have been mostly microenterprises using mainly domestic resources and those able to diversify into new product lines.

Conclusion

Two developments are assuming increasing importance within the Tanzanian rural economy. These are the increase in the number of household members participating in the labour market and the rural informal sector. The pronounced seasonality of agriculture has always resulted in slack periods which have permitted farming communities to engage temporarily in non-farm activities. The new developments are, however, partly a response to the economic crisis of the early 1980s, partly a response to the opportunities created by the new liberal policy environment under the economic recovery programme adopted since 1986, and partly a response to increasing pressure on good land. These alternative rural strategies are not merely survival strategies or passing phenomena. Rather they represent rational dynamic choices under changing structural, institutional and policy circumstances in rural areas.

Notes

1. Net population movement is calculated by comparing population growth by region with the average growth for the country (World Bank 1993b).
2. Agricultural Diversification and Intensification Study (ADIS 1992).
3. Paettie (1987) and Livingstone (1991) present a good survey of the concept while the ILO (1993) discusses the practical problems involved in measuring the informal sector.
4. Single person microenterprises were found to account for 80 per cent of all microenterprises in Lesotho, 70 per cent in Zimbabwe, 69 per cent in Swaziland, and 65 per cent in Botswana (Liedholm and Mead 1993).

References

ADIS (Agricultural Diversification and Intensification Study) 1992, *Final Report*, Oxford, Food Studies Group and Morogoro, Sokoine University

BAGACHWA, M.S.D. 1991, *Choice of Technology Industry: The Economics of Grain Milling in Tanzania*, Ottawa, International Development Research Centre (IDRC)

____, 1993a, *The Rural Informal Sector in Tanzania*, Economic Research Bureau, Dar es Salaam mimeo

____, 1993b 'Impact of Structural Adjustment on the Small Enterprise Sector in Tanzania' in A.H.J. Helmsing & Th. Kolstee (eds), *Small Enterprises and Changing Policies*, London, Intermediate Technology Publications, 91-113

BAGACHWA, M.S.D. & F. STEWART 1992, 'Rural Industries and Rural Linkages in Sub-Saharan Africa', in F. Stewart, S. Lall & S.M. Wangwe (eds), *Alternative Development Strategies in Sub-Saharan Africa*, London, Macmillan, 145-84

BEVAN, D.L., P. COLLIER & J.W. GUNNING, with A. BIGSTEN & P. HORSNELL 1989, *Peasants and Government, An Economic Analysis*, Oxford, Clarendon Press

____, 1990, *Controlled Open Economies: A Neoclassical Approach to Structuralism*, Oxford, Clarendon Press

BOOTH, D., F. LUGANGIRA, P. MASANJA, A. MVUNGI, R. MWAIPOPO, J. MWAMI, & A. REDMAYNE 1993, *Social Economic and Cultural Change in Contemporary Tanzania: A People-Oriented Focus*, Stockholm, SIDA

BRYCESON, D.F. 1990, *Food Insecurity and the Social Division of Labour in Tanzania, 1919-1985*, London, Macmillan

____, 1993, *Liberalizing Tanzania's Food Trade: Public and Private Faces of Urban Marketing Policy, 1939-1988*, London, James Currey

CHUTA, E. & C. LIEDHOLM 1985, *Employment Growth in Small-Scale Industry: Empirical Evidence and Policy Assessment from Sierra Leone*, New York, St. Martin's Press

COLLIER, P., S. RADWAN & S. WANGWE with A. WAGNER 1986, *Labour and Poverty in Rural Tanzania*, Oxford, Clarendon Press

INTERNATIONAL LABOUR ORGANIZATION (ILO) 1991, *The Dilemma of the Informal Sector*, Report to the Director General (Part I), International Labour Conference, 78th Session, Geneva, ILO

____, 1993, *Statistics of Employment in the Informal Sector*, Report to the Fifteenth International Labour Conference of Labour Statisticians, Geneva, ILO

ILO/JASPA 1978, *Towards Self-Reliance: Development, Employment and Equity Issues in Tanzania*, Addis Ababa, ILO/JASPA

____, 1982, *Basic Needs in Danger: A Basic Needs Oriented Development Strategy for Tanzania*, Addis Ababa, ILO/JASPA

JAMAL, V. 1982, *Rural-Urban Gap and Income Distribution: The Case of Tanzania*, Addis Ababa, ILO/JASPA

____. 1986, 'The Economics of Devaluation: The Case of Tanzania', *Labour and Society*, vol 11, no. 3

____. 1989, 'The Demise of the Labor Aristocracy in Africa: Structural Adjustment in Tanzania', in J. Weeks (ed.) *Debt Disaster? Governments, Banks and Multilaterals Face the Crisis*, Cambridge, Mass., Ballinger

JAMAL, V. & J. WEEKS 1993, *Africa Misunderstood or Whatever Happened to the Rural-Urban Gap?*, London, Macmillan

LIEDHOLM, C. & D. MEAD 1993, *The Structure and Growth of Microenterprises in Southern and Eastern Africa: Evidence from Recent Surveys*, GEMINI Working Paper no. 36

LIVINGSTONE, I. 1991, 'A Reassessment of Kenya's Rural and Urban Informal Sector', *World Development*, vol. 19, no. 6, 651-670

MANS, D. 1994, 'Tanzania Resolute Action', in Hussain, I. and R. Faruqee (eds), *Adjustment in Africa*, Washington, World Bank, 353-426

PAETTIE, L. 1987, 'An Idea in Good Currency and How it Grows: The Informal Sector', *World Development*, vol. 15, no. 7, 851-860

SARRIS, A.H. & R. van den BRINK 1993, *Economic Policy and Household Welfare during Crisis and Adjustment in Tanzania*, New York, New York University Press

TINIOS, P., A.H. SARRIS, H.K.R. AMANI & W. MARO 1993, 'Household Consumption and Poverty in Tanzania: Results from the 1991 National Cornell-ERB Survey', Paper prepared under the auspices of the Cornell Food and Nutrition Policy Program Africa Economic Policies Project supported by USAID

TRIPP, A.M. 1988, 'Defending the Right to Subsist: The State vs. the Urban Informal Economy in Tanzania', Paper presented at the African Studies Association Annual Meeting, Chicago

UNDP/UNIDO/ILO/GOVERNMENT of the NETHERLANDS 1988, *The Thematic Evaluation of Technical Cooperation in Support of Rural Small Enterprises in Tanzania*, Vienna, UNDP

UNITED REPUBLIC of TANZANIA (URT) 1988, *1988 Population Census*, Dar es Salaam, Bureau of Statistics

____, 1990, *Agricultural Sample Survey of Tanzania Mainland 1987-88*, Dar es Salaam, Bureau of Statistics

____, 1991, *Tanzania: The Informal Sector 1991*, Dar es Salaam, Planning Commission and Ministry of Labour and Youth Development , Government Printer

____, 1993, *Tanzania (Mainland): The Labour Force Survey*, Dar es Salaam

WORLD BANK 1993a, *Tanzania - A Poverty Profile*, Population and Human Resources Division, East Africa Department draft, Washington, World Bank

____, 1993b, *Tanzania, Agriculture Sector Memorandum*, Agriculture and Environment Operations Division, East Africa Department Report no. 12294 TA, Washington, World Bank

ZANZIBAR REVOLUTIONARY GOVERNMENT (ZRG) 1990, *Zanzibar The Informal Sector 1990*, Zanzibar

V

SOUTHERN AFRICA

9

Non-Farm Activities and Gender in Zimbabwe

Rudo B. Gaidzanwa

The aim of this chapter is to raise some conceptual issues relating to de-agrarianisation. Empirical evidence from Zimbabwe is examined in order to clarify and specify the contexts, processes and consequences of de-agrarianisation. If de-agrarianisation is taken to be the 'shedding of the agricultural population to the towns and to the rural non-farm sector', it is necessary to examine its extent and the process through which it happens. In the context of the labour migrant economies of Southern Africa, de-agrarianisation may take specific forms which do not necessarily entail one-off and enduring movements of populations out of the rural farm sector. Instead, out-migration may occur during economically stressful periods only to be reversed or to slow down during periods of relative economic growth and prosperity.

In Zimbabwe, a cheap labour procurement policy dating from the colonial period has involved the cyclical migration of men between 16 and 60, with young persons out-migrating and older men returning from wage labour who are reincorporated into village life. The returnees tend to have cash reserves which can be invested in small trade and commercial enterprises to sustain them on retirement.

De-agrarianisation may not be linked to rural non-farm expansion in the positive sense of growth, rather it may reflect impoverishment, landlessness and the displacement of those people marginalised within the rural farm sector. Furthermore, de-agrarianisation may be more strongly evident in the expansion of the urban wage and non-wage sectors rather than rural sector expansion. A proliferation of studies on Africa indicates increasing diversification of rural economic activities. Zimbabwe is no exception. Since 1991, micro- and small-scale enterprises in rural areas have been increasing at twice the rate of urban areas (GEMINI 1994). Thus, an increase in the involvement of people in rural non-farm activities is likely. Whether this can be taken to indicate that de-agrarianisation is taking place is an issue that needs to be examined in the light of studies of specific areas and survey data.

De-agrarianisation is directly related to the state of people's relationship to land, markets, and to credit and other services which are necessary for making a living within the agricultural sector. When these factors combine to render survival unsustainable in the agricultural sector, people are likely to adjust by seeking alternatives both within and outside, depending on the situation of the individuals and households. Climate, location, and agricultural policies and practices influence people's decisions about whether to continue to operate in the agricultural sector full-time, part-time, or to move out of agriculture altogether. Individuals may diversify their enterprises within rural areas in order to include other activities in the non-farm sector. In conceptualising de-agrarianisation, it is important to understand the motivations, class and social positions of the different entrants to the non-farm sectors in rural areas.

Zimbabwean Economy, Polity and Society

The population of Zimbabwe was estimated at 10 million in 1992, growing at an annual rate of 3.2 per cent, which is projected to more than double the population to 23 million by the year 2005. In 1992, the percentage of the population under 15 was 42 per cent, that of people over 65 only 3 per cent, and those between 16 and 64 was 56 per cent.

The urban population is estimated at 26 per cent of the total and its annual growth rate over 7 per cent. The rural population is dominated by elderly and young people because of the colonially-induced labour migration system which siphoned off the economically active males, and later also females into the urban areas.

In 1989, average GDP per capita was around Z$1,000 with the average in communal areas at Z$200 and Z$400, a third of this originating from wage labour and crop sales and the rest from subsistence agriculture. Landholdings are highly skewed, with large-scale commercial farmers, mostly white, holding nearly 50 per cent of all agricultural land while comprising less than 0.5 per cent of the total population. The remaining agricultural land, most of low quality, is apportioned among three million peasant farmers under communal tenure. There is growing recognition that some rural areas in Zimbabwe cannot be food self-sufficient and that alternative ways of sustaining the population have to be devised. Debates surrounding the land reform programme reinforce this view. Thus, the issue of de-agrarianisation is firmly on the agenda with respect to those areas that are not suitable for more intensive cropping.

Men have primary user rights to land while women have secondary user rights to communal land through marriage although they are primarily responsible for most of the work in the agricultural sector. A majority of the economically active female population work in agriculture with only 19 per cent in industry and services in the formal sector. There is a higher proportion of the male population in industry (15 per cent) and in services (21 per cent). Data on unemployment and underemployment are scarce. A guesstimate of unemployment is at 35 per cent, reinforced by a 15 per cent decline in waged agricultural employment between 1980 and 1987 and 14 per cent in mining. Trade liberalisation and price decontrol have contributed to a rise in consumer prices. The decontrol of labour regulations, redundancies and retrenchments have accelerated in the wage sector. The formal economy creates 7,000 jobs while the education system generates 100,000 school-leavers per year, most of whom are not able to find wage jobs in the formal sector of the economy (Zimbabwe 1993).

This then is the context of the debate on micro- and small-scale enterprises in Zimbabwe. While the GEMINI survey has attempted to enumerate the scope of these small businesses, its exclusion of agriculture renders it less than useful in determining the linkages between the urban and rural agricultural sectors. Thus arriving at some conclusions about de-agrarianisation requires examining existing surveys and qualitative studies of the rural non-farm and urban sectors.

Non-Farm Activities in Rural Households

Several surveys and studies have been conducted in order to specify the extent of rural non-farm activities in various Zimbabwean localities. Not all were conducted specifically on non-farm rural activities. Jackson, Collier and Conti (1988) investigated insecurity and income amongst 600 rural households in Zimbabwe's communal lands. They found that diversification and versatility of household labour raised the incomes of rural households. Most households which diversified into non-subsistence activities were able to escape poverty. Wage remittances insulated rural households from food deficits and poverty demonstrating the strong link between wage income, non-farm income and food security. Some households assured their security and increased their incomes through migration into wage labour in rural and urban areas, while others went into rural wage labour when their subsistence crops failed to ensure basic survival. Those households where remittances were relatively high, that is over Z$1,000 per year, were able to invest in off-farm activities as a way of diversifying their resource base. It was not the mere occurrence of remittances but their size that increased the possibility for households to set up non-farm enterprises in rural areas.

The study did not specify the types of enterprises that were set up in rural areas nor did it reveal the specialisations that rural households pursued in the rural non-farm sector. However, the data did show a clear divide between farmers with high incomes (derived from remittances, off-farm wage employment, cropping, livestock and self-employment) who were able to embark on non-farm enterprises, while poorer households were more likely to seek wage labour in rural areas to supplement their subsistence-based cropping and livestock activities.

Another survey by Sunga et al. (1989) looked at resource structures and socio-economic features of communal agriculture, based on 759 households in eight provinces across Zimbabwe's six environmental zones. One-fifth cited wages and salaries as an important source of income, although the authors expressed scepticism about this given the assumed lack of wage employment opportunities in rural areas. The survey overlooked many of the off-farm activities that rural people engaged in and failed to attach significance to the levels of income they contributed. The survey findings indicate that many households engage in commercial pottery, basket making, beer brewing, sculpture and craft work. A third engaged in a residual unspecified category termed 'other' income earning, although it cannot be inferred from the survey who they are and what they earn since a number of anomalous activities were grouped together in this category including brick moulding, contract ploughing and bridewealth. The study did not consider all rural off-farm income-generating activities. By comparison 48 per cent of the households indicated crop sales as a source of income, while 31 per cent received remittances.

GEMINI (1994), the most recent survey, recorded a higher growth of micro- and small-scale enterprises in rural areas (7.1 per cent) than in urban areas (3.6 per cent). This growth was associated with the inception of the structural adjustment programme. Rural micro- and small-scale enterprises employed an increasing percentage of people in vending, retail, bars, pubs and unlicensed *shebeens*, the last three representing high-profit sectors. However, there has been a decline in the manufacturing and construction sectors in rural areas with the greatest decrease registered in flour mills, tailoring, bakeries and other repairs, all of which were adversely affected by competition from established urban millers, and second-hand clothes traders specialising in imported clothes and textiles. In areas where growth was registered, it tended to be in metal and leather work which are relatively high-growth and high-profit activities and in pottery and crocheting which are low-growth, low-profit activities.

Given that the results of the survey were not disaggregated by gender and area, it appears that most of the new rural enterprises were influenced by the ready supply of labour. Many rural people trying to secure their survival went into easy-entry non-farm activities requiring low investment as a result of their increasing impoverishment in the face of the economic stringency of structural adjustment. Survey findings on firm closures show that the highest numbers occurred in vending, crocheting, basket making, knitting, and beer brewing, activities of low profit that are commonly undertaken by rural women. However, in 1992, a year of low economic growth, there was a high business mortality rate in welding, brick making and garment retail, all of which are high-profit activities that are accessed primarily by men in rural Zimbabwe.

In terms of employment creation, the GEMINI survey noted that the development patterns of individual firms showed little promise. Firms making low profits often disappeared. Very few of the firms expanded to create significant employment. The firms that were most likely to expand were those in brick making, construction, services and auto repairs. In 1992, most of the rural micro- and small-scale enterprises were adversely affected by drought and structural adjustment. This was seen in problems in input procurement for beer brewing, grass and cane work, food vending, and livestock retailing, all of which are closely related to agriculture. This reinforces the observation that the fate of many non-farm rural enterprises is closely tied to that of the agricultural sector in Zimbabwe.

Legal and Regulatory Measures

There is a plethora of legal and regulatory measures that have affected the development of non-farm enterprises in Zimbabwe. The effect of these measures differs between rural and urban areas due to the differing degrees of enforcement. Accessing space for trading and manufacturing activities is but the first step along the long legal road to an acceptable business operation. Zonal restrictions are more stringent in urban than in rural areas. The major consequences of rural zoning regulations are that those operating in the zoned areas prefer to be near bus stops and other public amenities where customers normally congregate but where they must pay rent and are precluded from acquiring title deeds to their premises. This restricts their access to credit and other resources whose availability is premised on having a traceable business address.

Regulations on shop hours are easier to flaunt in rural areas than in towns since the enforcement agencies are more lax and distant from central government influence. However, the licensing procedures needed for trading activities in fixed rural locales require literacy and numeracy and often patronage of local bosses in traditional or government positions of power. Thus the legal operation of off-farm ventures is now a profoundly politicised activity needing patronage and sophistication in the manipulation of the various actors who operate as gatekeepers in legal licensing and registration (Zhou 1993). Such registration also acts as a filter since most financial institutions restrict credit to licensed entrepreneurs. Credit and financial markets are also bound up with their own rules regarding the viability of proposed activities, projected cash flow, etc. All these preconditions play an important role in influencing rural business operators' ability to enter into commercial and manufacturing activities.

The activities that showed the highest possibilities for growth were brick making, construction, and services. Their growth is linked to rising incomes amongst some rural strata who are investing in brick houses. There is also significant construction activity as a result of government-initiated projects to build schools, clinics, toilets, roads and other public infrastructure with the use of labour-intensive technologies. Employment-creating food-for-work schemes comprise a significant proportion of the off-farm activities in rural Zimbabwe, especially in those areas that regularly experience low rainfall and are supported by government food supplements and drought relief. These programmes absorb considerable labour although a systematic enumeration has yet to be undertaken. Their sustainability is likely to be influenced by the continued ability of the government to support infrastructural development, especially in the more underdeveloped rural areas.

Gendered Nature of Non-Farm Activities

There is a paucity of qualitative studies and data that disaggregate off-farm activities in rural areas by gender, with the notable exception of Zhou's 1993 study of Mataga growth point in Mberengwa, a small market centre serving two large rural irrigation schemes. Rural dwellers are attracted to Mataga both to sell their produce and to buy consumer goods. Zhou found that the majority of trade activities are undertaken by women but less than 27 per cent of the settlement's trading space is allocated to them. Agro-processing and trade activities, which are a 'natural' extension of women's activities in agriculture, are not accommodated at the centre.

Both men and women are involved in agricultural production in Mataga's hinterland, women more intensively than men. There are barriers against the extension and integration of women's agricultural commodity processing and trade due to the gendered nature of the allocation of stands. The district council, which is the allocative body, works closely with the politically elected ward councillors through development committees. Thus, when applications for space are considered, traditional leaders and councillors attempt to represent their constituents' interests and in the absence of transparent criteria for vetting applications, councillors use their discretion in allocating stands. Personal prejudices and politics obviously play a role, often overshadowing purely economic criteria for determining project viability. Based on past outcomes, projects owned by politically connected men, who are in fact engaged in wage employment elsewhere, win approval. As non-residents, they prefer businesses that can be delegated to relatively unskilled and lowly educated relatives. Most of the people so delegated are women who, as 'dependants' of the owners, are presumed to be obedient and trustworthy and not have business ambitions of their own.

Women attempting to operate on their own account face numerous social impediments. For example, when a woman tries to obtain guarantors as proof of access to funds, conflict can erupt with her spouse. She may face accusations of infidelity when asking for help from a man to set up her business. Single women are denied trading space on the grounds that they are 'unstable' because of their marital status. Some elderly widows who were plot holders in the irrigation schemes and thus had collateral were not permitted to rent space in Mataga. Only 17 per cent of the commercial and industrial stands have been allocated to women. All twelve women who were able to obtain stands had affiliations with council employees and councillors and some were actually proxies for their spouses to dissimulate the flagrant self-allocation of choice commercial and industrial stands. Despite these obstacles, at least ten women are operating significant businesses on their own account, including one wholesale general dealership.

Gender ideologies of both men and women are at the centre of the gatekeeping institutions that determine the course of enterprise development. Women usually form the majority of the economically active adult rural population because of the continuing tradition of male out-migration. By restricting women's entrepreneurial activities, these gender ideologies undermine growth, employment creation and the vertical and horizontal integration of entire local rural economies.

Gender bias is at the root of female entrepreneurs' inability to expand their enterprises or move them to better locations. Married women fear having their successful enterprises taken over by their husbands or male kin. Thus many women attempt to falsify and minimise the incomes that they derive from their enterprises as a way of circumventing the gender politics surrounding the control over incomes in patrilineal households. This strategy of stunting enterprise growth or diversifying into many small enterprises where returns can be concealed has negative consequences for the growth of non-farm enterprises run by women.

The question of gender bias must be addressed in any policy intervention to determine the scope and trajectory of de-agrarianisation, with a view to supporting those enterprises that have growth potential (Gaidzanwa 1993). With official awareness of the problem being limited, the risk of misguided interventions is ever-present. Currently, women with business acumen have difficulty accessing inputs and services necessary for their off-farm enterprises.

Mataga thus provides a good example of the inadequacies of the current definitions and conceptualisation of employment, unemployment and economic activities. According to census figures, 48 per cent of the women resident in Mataga were unemployed, whereas Zhou found that virtually all Mataga women were involved in trading or other commercial activities and only wives of civil servants were economically inactive. Even in those activities that had a low-growth potential, women tended to reinvest locally more than men. Businesswomen at Mataga supported three times as many dependants in their businesses as men.

Zhou suggests that with better management support and skills training, Mataga's predominantly female entrepreneurs could be playing their rightful role in generating local growth and creating off-farm employment. Their current lack of knowledge of basic technologies for processing, production and manufacturing explained the absence of industrial expansion. Most also had no systematic formal or informal advice on enterprise options. Their ideas for business opportunities came from observing neighbours and relatives, resulting in a continual duplication of economic activities.

Conclusion

The form and content of de-agrarianisation is governed by historical, social and economic circumstances of specific areas. Rural non-farm expansion in Zimbabwe has been affected by the colonial land grab in the late nineteenth century, the subsequent linking of rural and urban subsistence to a migrant wage labour system and the problems of agricultural sustainability in communal areas. Initially, the Zimbabwean de-agrarianisation process was primarily conditioned by the policy of cheap labour procurement, but the loss of agrarian labour was not necessarily permanent. More often it was cyclical, with males tending to move out of rural areas during their most productive years and rejoining their rural households on retirement or when they had accumulated enough resources to set up small trade or commercial rural enterprises.

At present, the sustained movement of young men and women out of rural areas continues, but the character of de-agrarianisation is changing in form and substance. Fewer emigrants return to set up homes in rural areas in their old age while the attempt by people who have accumulated surpluses from agriculture to invest in small enterprises in the rural areas is a relatively recent development which points to a significant change in the cycle of investment. Those rural households that invest in rural non-farm enterprises have diverse income sources which enhance their security. Simultaneously, poorer households also try to gain income by trading some of their agricultural produce within the rural areas outside official and/or established commodity marketing. As entrepreneurs, they have different aspirations in terms of the scale of their businesses. Their micro-activities focus on survival, while those of the traders, manufacturers and commercial operators have the potential for growth.

However, political and gender biases in local institutions limit the growth and employment creation of some of these categories of entrepreneurs. Industrial extension is also lacking and its availability together with better credit and other support services would go some way towards sensitising high-potential entrepreneurs to opportunities for expanding their enterprises. While the structural adjustment programme has eroded the purchasing power of some rural consumers, it has also facilitated the entry of some entrepreneurs into the rural non-farm sector.

The situation is highly fluid and elusive. Statistical documentation, official policies and general awareness of the rural non-farm sector are based on unwarranted assumptions about employment, unemployment and economic activity. These assumptions are contradicted by the realities revealed by small, localised, qualitative studies. It is clear that further in-depth qualitative research is needed as a guide to policy-making for the rural non-farm sector in Zimbabwe.

References

GAIDZANWA, R.B. 1993, 'Women Entrepreneurs, Donor Promotion and Domestic Policies', in A.H.J. Helmsing and T. Kolstee (eds), *Small Enterprises and Changing Policies*, London, IT Publications

GEMINI 1994, *Changes in the Small-Scale Enterprise Sector from 1991 to 1993: Results of a Second Nationwide Survey in Zimbabwe*, Bethesda, Maryland

JACKSON, J., P. COLLIER & A. CONTI 1988, *Rural Development Policies and Food Security in Zimbabwe: Part 2*, Geneva, International Labour Office

SUNGA, E. et al. 1989, *Farm Extension Baseline Survey Results*, Zimbabwe Institute of Development Studies, Department of Agricultural and Rural Development

ZHOU, A.O. 1993, *Enabling Economic Initiatives of Women Entrepreneurs at Growth Points in Zimbabwe: A Case Study of Mataga*, University of Zimbabwe, Department of Rural and Urban Planning, Unpublished M.Sc. Thesis

ZIMBABWE, GOVERNMENT of 1993, *Zimbabwe Annual Review of Manpower*, Harare

10

Rural Diversification in Zimbabwe

Poul Ove Pedersen

Rural households in Sub-Saharan Africa have increasingly engaged in non-agricultural activities in order to supplement their agricultural incomes. Such activities represent a grey zone and a potential linkage between agriculture and urban areas. Their development depends on the structure both of agriculture and of the urban system. As an analytical category, 'rural non-agricultural activities' (RNAs), is, like its close kin the urban informal sector, heterogeneous, consisting of activities with potentially differing impacts on the development of rural areas. One reason for this is that RNAs are defined by what they are not, rather than what they are. Helmsing (1991) distinguished two types of RNAs:

> *Type 1:* Microenterprises operated from the farmstead or home and therefore dispersed all over rural areas, often operated on a part-time or seasonal basis and secondary to agriculture. The labour force comprises owners and unpaid family members. They serve a local market, often consisting primarily of the extended family and neighbours. Many of the activities are based on traditional rural raw materials and knowledge and require limited capital.
>
> *Type 2:* Small to medium-sized enterprises operated on a full- or part-time basis, but even on a part-time basis usually more important than agriculture or other activities. They may employ both family and wage labour. They serve larger markets and are typically located in small rural centres or towns. Most are privately owned but they may also be cooperatives or branches of larger public or private organisations. They are often linked to the higher levels of the urban hierarchy.

In areas where agriculture is seasonal, peasant farmers will engage in Type 1 RNAs when the economy becomes more commercialised. In fact, many of these are activities which peasant farmers pursue in the low season, except that they were traditionally carried out in work parties together with family, friends and neighbours, while now they are performed for the market, albeit local (Bessant and Muringai 1993). Many of the Type 1 activities rely on traditional cultural values and technologies.

Type 2 RNAs are a response to a general surplus of labour in rural areas resulting from a growing population, a lack of new farm land, and the introduction of labour-saving farm technologies, rather than from the seasonality of agriculture *per se*. However, the seasonal effects of agriculture are also mirrored in the non-farm economy by virtue of the population's fluctuating purchasing power and labour supply. Small-town entrepreneurs and workers often return home for agricultural work. The seasonality of RNAs, especially Type 1, results in inefficient capital utilisation and therefore low capitalisation. On the other hand, when agricultural and non-agricultural seasons do not complement each other, agricultural seasonality results in larger seasonal unemployment.

The two types of RNAs may develop in symbiosis with each other, agriculture or higher level urban activities, in mutually supportive ways. But they may also compete destructively. Which type dominates will vary according to place, sector, and time. Demand and supply for the goods and services produced play a determining role as well as the structure of labour surplus in agriculture.

This chapter investigates the development of RNAs in rural areas and small towns based on empirical data from Zimbabwe. The first section reviews some of the theoretical literature and is followed by a presentation of data on the development of RNAs in the post-independence period and a detailed investigation of fluctuations under the impact of structural adjustment and drought. The final section places the findings in a theoretical framework.

Changing Theoretical Perceptions of Rural Non-Agricultural Activities

The way development theories have perceived the role of RNAs in the interaction between agriculture and the urban system has changed dramatically over the past three decades. In the modernisation theories of the 1960s, household-based Type 1 RNAs were seen to be transitory. The linkages between agriculture and the urban system were, through the eyes of Christaller's central place theory, seen to be channelled through the small rural towns and Type 2 RNAs, and they were generally thought to be harmonious and symbiotic.

Clearly, this view did not reflect the reality of newly independent African countries, where the urban system was largely monopolised by colonial interests and non-African traders. Hence, by the end of the 1960s, this harmonious view of rural-urban relations gave way to dependency theories. Small rural towns were seen not as rural service centres, but as centres of exploitation through which resources and surpluses were sucked out of rural areas by a rural petit bourgeoisie linked to the colonial power (Southall 1979; 1988). Exploitative rural towns had to be bypassed and services provided by the government directly to rural households in order to bring about genuine rural development. The farm household with Type 1 household-based activities became the focus of attention. The objective was increased decentralisation and the empowerment of farmers. However, the result was often quite the opposite as decision-making became concentrated in the hands of central government and donors, all located in the capital city.

Bypassing small towns did not reduce the exploitation of rural areas because the exploitative forces were not rooted in the small-town activities themselves, but rather in the central powers which they served as agents. The new independent states required no fewer resources than the colonial states. The major part of these resources had to come from the agricultural sector. Monopolistic government-controlled parastatals which bought agricultural products at prices often far below world market prices were the instrument for this. The result was a massive transfer of resources to the urban areas, development of a centralised agricultural processing and marketing industry, and support to Type 1 non-agricultural activities catering to basic needs, but seldom reaching beyond a semi-subsistence level. Type 2 small and medium-sized enterprises, which could have been the basis for rural industrialisation, were suppressed. The pattern was upheld by donors and NGOs, with donors espousing large-scale processing and production controlled by parastatals and cooperatives and NGOs supporting Type 1 small projects operated by local cooperatives and women's groups. Type 2 small and medium-sized enterprises were generally neglected.

Around 1980 views on rural development and non-agricultural activities changed as a reaction to the notion of 'urban bias' (Lipton 1977; Harris and Moore 1984; Varshney 1993; Jamal and Weeks 1993). This attack on urban bias was incorporated in the World Bank's structural adjustment policies, with its crusade for trade liberalisation, parastatal privatisation and market-based prices.

However, the adjustment packages have been a mixed blessing for rural areas. Trade liberalisation and devaluation led to price increases for many consumer goods. Although large farmers with an agricultural surplus benefited, small farmers mostly lost out. Secondly, the privatisation of parastatals also did not lead to the hoped-for decentralisation of the economy because government monopolies were often taken over by large private enterprises. Thirdly, internal trade liberalisation and small-enterprise support schemes which should foster economic decentralisation were slower to develop than price and foreign trade liberalisation. They also mostly failed to reach smaller towns.

Thus although the policies of the 1980s became anti-statist and decentralist, the geographic dimensions of decentralisation were not sufficiently stressed. The emphasis remained on reform of macroeconomic policies. Only since the end of the 1980s has there been an increased focus on local government reforms, small-enterprise development schemes, and small-town development.

Despite the earlier and more or less continuing bias, non-agricultural activities both in rural areas and small towns developed more rapidly during the 1980s than the 1970s (Pedersen 1991). The 1980s saw a changed and more positive view of small towns and their potential role in rural development (Rondinelli 1985; 1988; 1990). As in the 1960s, this viewpoint was again built partly on Christaller's central place theory, but much more focus was put on rural-urban linkages and the role of small towns in increasing rural productivity, and much less on linkages with the higher levels of the urban hierarchy (Pedersen 1992).

To understand and explain de-agrarianisation and the development of RNAs in rural areas and small towns, a theory is needed which sees non-agricultural activities neither as completely independent nor as marginalised, powerless pawns of the large-scale sector; a theory which recognises both the active role small enterprises can play in rural development and their partial dependency on the large-scale sector. The final section outlines such a framework based on new theories of flexible specialisation and enterprise networks. But first, attention is focused on data on Zimbabwean rural development, particularly the development of non-agricultural activities since independence in 1980.

RNAs in Zimbabwe since Independence

Rural Context

Most agricultural land in Zimbabwe is divided between large-scale commercial farms and communal areas. Although some resettlement has happened since independence it has not affected the major outline of land distribution, where about 4,500 very large farms occupy about two-fifths of Zimbabwe's most fertile lands and with relatively stable rainfall, and 800,000 smallholders own 42 per cent of the land in communal areas with low and irregular rainfall. During the colonial period practically all investment in transport and agricultural infrastructure and all urban development took place in the large farm areas. Not surprisingly, almost the entire marketed agricultural surplus was produced there. The large farms were closely linked to the highly centralised manufacturing industry and urban areas. They were owned by white farmers, although some have since been taken over by African politicians and businessmen.

Until independence, communal areas were mostly bereft of transport and agricultural infrastructure but since then concerted efforts have been made to increase cash-crop production in communal areas and road access, agricultural services and marketing facilities have been improved accordingly. Agricultural research and development policies have shifted from a focus on large-scale commercial farms to catering also to the needs of communal and small-scale commercial farmers. This has led to considerable increases in both yields and marketed output, especially in years with good rainfall; by the end of the 1980s, communal areas produced more than half of the maize and cotton marketed in Zimbabwe, indicating a considerable increase in rural cash incomes. However, just 18 out of 170 communal areas accounted for most of the marketed surplus (Amin 1989) and 10 per cent of communal farmers controlled half of the marketed surplus while 40 per cent had a deficit, even in an average year (Jackson and Collier 1991). Thus, although agricultural cash incomes have increased, they are still very limited for most rural households.

Income from cash-crop production is also very unevenly distributed seasonally because of erratic rainfall and most rural households depend on wages, non-agricultural activities, and remittances from urban-based family members for cash incomes. In 1982 about half of the income in communal areas was derived from remittances (World Bank 1982; Bonnevie 1987). Since then the percentage has undoubtedly declined because both agricultural and local non-agricultural incomes have increased. Jackson and Collier (1991) found that 19 per cent of total rural household income was due to remittances, with 37 per cent of all households being recipients. Thus, remittances are still important and probably increasing in absolute terms.

Growth and Structure of RNAs

Rural non-agricultural activities were less prevalent in Zimbabwe before independence than in many other African countries. The World Bank (1982) estimated that at the start of the 1980s only 3-4 per cent of rural households were engaged in non-agricultural activities. This can be explained by Zimbabwe's well-developed, but also very centralised, pre-independence manufacturing sector which, combined with large work migration to towns, ensured that many of the commodities consumed in rural areas were purchased in towns.

Since independence, RNAs have been growing rapidly. Helmsing (1991) found in a 1983-4 survey that 15 per cent of rural households ran such activities, while the 1991 GEMINI study reported that around 40 per cent of all rural households undertook at least one non-agricultural activity (McPherson 1991). This corresponds to a growth in the average number of enterprises per household of 3-3.5 per cent annually. The GEMINI II (1994) study found that the number of RNAs had grown annually by 7 per cent between 1991 and 1993. With a population growth of 3 per cent, this corresponds to a growth in the average number of enterprises per household of 4 per cent, or about the same as during the period before 1991.

By comparing the two GEMINI studies with Helmsing's study, Table 1 attempts to give a picture of the development trends of different subsectors, although differences in sampling procedures preclude a strict comparison. Helmsing's data only covered the rural areas proper and were based on simple averages, while the GEMINI study included the small towns and was based on population-weighted averages. Account also has to be taken of the fact that the total number of small enterprises increased dramatically between 1986 and 1991, both because the average numbers of RNAs per household doubled and because the rural population increased. Thus between these years, the absolute number of enterprises increased by 50 to 100 per cent depending on the sector, and from 1991 to 1993 by an average of 12 per cent overall. Given this, only subsectors where the percentage figure for 1991 is under 50 per cent of the 1986 figure are likely to have experienced an absolute decline.

As the table indicates, manufacturing is the most important sector, constituting more than 80 per cent of RNAs in 1986 but falling to about 66 per cent in 1993. Manufacturing activities are highly concentrated in a few subsectors: beer brewing (8 per cent in 1991), dressmaking and tailoring (6 per cent), knitting (9 per cent), crocheting (8 per cent), grass and cane products (20 per cent), and wood carving (5 per cent). In total these six subsectors comprise 56 per cent of all the enterprises.

Table 1: Sectoral Distribution of Rural Non-Agricultural Activities

Sector	1986[1]	1991[2]	1993[2]	*Changes* 1986-91	1991-93
Flour milling	0.7	1.0	0.4	+	-
Beer brewing	6.3	8.2	2.9	+	-
Tailoring + dressmaking	13.9	5.8	3.2	-	-
Knitting	10.4	9.2	7.3	-	-
Crocheting	6.9	7.5	12.4	+	+
Shoe works/repairs	2.4	1.0	1.1	-	-
Grass + cane	11.1	20.0	16.4	+	-
Wood carving	5.8	5.1	4.6	-	-
Carpentry	2.1	2.4	2.6	+	+
Pottery	6.7	2.5	3.6	-	+
Brick making	1.7	2.6	1.9	+	-
Tin smithing	1.7	1.3	1.2	-	-
Welding + other metal work	5.9	0.6	2.4	-	+
Other manufacturing	4.9	6.7	7.4	+	+
Total manufacturing	82.0	73.9	67.4	-	-
Construction	7.6	5.5	3.8	-	-
Trade	8.3	18.1	25.5	+	+
Services	2.1	2.8	3.3	+	+
Total	100	100	100		
Total sample size	288	1815	1830		

Sources: Helmsing (1991), GEMINI (1994)

1. Helmsing 1991 excludes small towns.
2. GEMINI 1994 includes small towns. Exclusion of small towns from the 1991 and 1993 data would in general narrow the gap between the 1986 and 1991 data slightly but without changing the structure of the data. The size of the 1993 rural sample is not given, but the total sample including urban areas was 16 per cent lower than in 1991.

Trading activities are second in importance and grew rapidly from only 8 per cent in 1986 to 25 per cent in 1993. The construction sector constituted less than 8 per cent in 1986 and was reduced to half as much in 1993, probably because building-material production had been taken over by enterprises outside the construction sector. Services play a minor although increasing role. A comparison of the main sectors shows that the direction of change is the same in the two periods 1986-91 and 1991-3, with a relative contraction of manufacturing and construction and expansion of trade and services, but the speed of change was faster during the second period.

On dissecting the manufacturing sector, substantial variations emerge. Tailoring and dressmaking, knitting, wood carving, and tin smithing declined relatively during the two periods, tailoring probably also in absolute terms. Knitting and wood carving declined more slowly and quite likely increased in absolute terms during the first period. These subsectors face less competition from the industrial sector than tailoring because of the quality of the products they produce. They also have access to tourist and informal export markets.

Crocheting, carpentry and other manufacturing grew in relative terms in both periods. Crocheting is the most important of these sectors. Its growth can probably be attributed to expanding informal import trade with South Africa and Botswana (Brand et al. 1994). Other manufacturing grew rapidly in both periods, indicating an increased diversification of the manufacturing sector.

The subsectors of food processing, grass and cane products, and brick making increased their share during the upturn and contracted during the downturn. This could be an indication of a pro-cyclical market orientation. However, for food processing the contraction was most likely caused by a lack of local grain rather than markets since the drought relief provided for rural areas came in the form of mealy meal which had already been milled in urban mills. The contraction of grass and cane products in the second period may also be due to a lack of inputs during the drought. However, as the production in this subsector tends to be concentrated in specific areas, the large expansion during the first period may be at least partly caused by the different sampling areas used in the Helmsing and GEMINI studies. Finally pottery, welding, and shoe works and repair contracted during the upturn and expanded during the downturn, indicating that they might follow what could be called a labour-supply or unemployment hypothesis. However, this is problematic because neither pottery nor welding are typical easy-entry sectors.

The data thus indicate that both the general expansion of the rural small-enterprise sector and trends at the subsector level were primarily caused by long-term structural changes and only to a smaller extent by short-term cyclical changes. This conclusion contrasts with many current studies of small enterprises which on the basis of cross section or short period studies see small-enterprise development as a short-term crisis phenomenon, e.g. Brand et al. (1994) and GEMINI (1994).

Dynamics of District Service Centre Growth

At the time of independence, the few urban centres in communal areas were very small but since then the Zimbabwe government has pursued various policies to develop district service centres or 'growth points' in communal areas (Wekwete 1991; Gasper 1988). These policies have especially focused on investments in:

- agricultural services and marketing depots,
- infrastructure, linking most of the district service centres to national hard-surface road and electricity networks and investments in local water and sewage systems, market places, and bus terminals,
- public services, especially in primary and secondary education and health services, and
- housing schemes, especially for the increasing number of public and parastatal employees who have moved to district centres, but also to some extent for lower income households.

These policies have in tandem with increased rural incomes from agriculture and remittances led to considerable growth in many district service centres, with the largest expanding to towns of 10,000 inhabitants or more. Both public services and trade have increased rapidly while growth in manufacturing has been much slower (Pedersen 1991).

Based on detailed studies of two of the larger district service centres (Gutu-Mupandawana and Gokwe), three waves of growth can be identified (Pedersen 1997a and b). Timewise they were initiated in consecutive periods between the droughts in 1984, 1988 and 1992. The first of these waves consisted of the establishment of agricultural and public services, parastatal depots and branch offices, and public administration. Benefiting from this development, traditional rural traders invested primarily in general-dealer shops, and in bottle stores and butcheries which require special licences. This public-sector driven growth continued into the second wave, but the more important players became the large national and regional retail chains, which established branch stores in many district service centres so as to take advantage of the growing rural markets, especially in clothing and hardware (Zinyama 1990). Most of these retail chains operated with uniform national prices and thereby forced prices down.[1] The increased competition led some of the larger traders to diversify into specialised shops, especially in clothing, furniture and hardware. Wholesalers serving rural dealers were also established. Despite increased competition from the branch stores, the number of local retailers continued to grow, because the small towns captured part of the trade that had previously gone to Harare.

The third wave which started towards the end of the 1980s was carried partly by a growing number of often very small, specialised retail and service enterprises, e.g. photography, records, women's dresses, hairdressers, dry-cleaning outlets, newspapers, magazines and books, repair services, accountancy, training courses, etc. and partly by a still small but growing number of medium-sized manufacturing industries with 10-40 employees. How far this development will proceed depends on the effects of the structural adjustment policies introduced in 1991 and the droughts which hit Zimbabwe during the early 1990s.

Impact of Structural Adjustment and Drought

The combined effect of structural adjustment policies and the severe 1992 drought dramatically reduced levels of income and economic activity at the same time as prices skyrocketed. Enterprises in two centres, Gutu-Mapandawana and Gokwe, were interviewed during November and December 1993 to ascertain the impact. There was confirmation of a decline in economic activity during 1992 but not uniformly.

Clothing

The clothing sector was hard hit. Sales dropped by between 20-50 per cent, but almost all the shops survived. The more expensive shops were especially vulnerable to falling demand during the drought.[2] Some started dealing in low quality clothes or even second-hand clothes to lower their prices. However, in general, second-hand clothes have so far not played as important a role in the district service centres as they may have done in rural areas.[3]

Half of the small, male repair tailors operating in the centres closed down. Also many of the small, female knitters or dressmakers operating independently in the centres moved their business to their homes in order to reduce costs. The private dressmaking and knitting training centres in Gutu survived, although they had very few trainees during 1992. In 1993 the two clothing factories in Gutu were still in operation. In general, sales seemed to be recovering although it was estimated that it would take at least another year for them to reach pre-drought levels.

Food Processing and Retailing

The different subsectors in food retailing and agro-processing and marketing responded differently to the crisis, and their fortunes changed several times during the drought period, partly due to changing food subsidies and partly to the deregulation of the sector.

General dealers were hit by falling demand, as were other traders, but made up for it by increased sales of mealy meal, often at increased prices, to maize-deficit farmers. This also had a tremendous impact on the milling sector. Most small service mills operating in rural areas and small towns had to close down or curtail their operations. On the other hand, the large urban commercial roller mills benefited from the drought. They were administering the food subsidy introduced to alleviate the effects of the drought, and were operating at full capacity, processing imported maize. After the drought, the situation was completely reversed with the stabilisation of the smaller service mills. Small-town commercial mills were kept out of the market because of the large milling companies' practice of bonded sales. Intermediate-sized hammer mills established since 1990, which can operate both as service and commercial mills, basically survived as service mills.

A number of small commercial oil presses were established after 1990. Some of these had to close down during the drought due to a lack of oilseeds, but in 1993 most were still operating although confronted by monopolistic competition from larger oil mills. This, however, is not likely to be as big a problem as for maize milling because capacity still matches demand.

Other food products experienced lower demand. Escalating bread prices due to the removal of grain subsidies caused a decline in bakery sales. Similarly, rapid increases in meat prices led to decreases in butchers' sales as consumers switched to fish from Lake Kariba. Most of the surviving butchers operated their businesses in conjunction with cattle farming. Under liberalisation, the capacity utilisation of the Cold Storage Commission's abattoirs was reduced by half because commercial farmers increasingly sold to private abattoirs, whereas communal farmers had few cattle to sell after the drought.

Building Materials

The building sector experienced surprisingly little adverse impact. A visual inspection indicated that many buildings in the centres had been repaired and new ones built during and after the drought. One reason was that prices of some building materials actually decreased due to structural adjustment. Another may be that many businessmen with permanent employees who could not be used in their ordinary jobs during the drought engaged them in building improvements.

Farm Inputs

The trade in farm inputs appears, especially in Gutu, to have been increasing rapidly since the 1993 harvest. Sales of seeds and fertilisers were obviously very low during the drought season of 1991-2. However during the 1992-3 season, the government distributed large amounts of free fertilisers and during the 1993-4 season, sales increased rapidly. The main reason was that maize prices increased much more than fertiliser prices and therefore encouraged the use of fertilisers. But quite evidently only the larger farmers with a marketed maize surplus benefited. This helps to explain the seeming paradox of depressed sales in food and clothes and booming sales in the building and farm implements sectors. Sales of ox-carts, used by farmers for transporting crops between home and fields and to the market, increased rapidly in the post-drought period as well. Small welders prospered and increased their numbers, especially after the relatively good harvest of 1993.

Specialised Retail Trade and Services

Many of the specialised retail and service businesses did not survive the drought, but others have opened since. Both in Gutu and Gokwe, new private training institutions were established in fields other than dressmaking and knitting, e.g. O-level courses, secretarial and business studies, and welding. Kiosks selling radios and other goods imported from Botswana or South Africa also sprang up, yet another indication of the skewed impact of structural adjustment and drought. Legal and debt-collection services were launched in both Gutu and Gokwe. In Gutu a local newly established security firm out-competed the non-local security firms and quickly developed into Gutu's largest enterprise, employing 140 young men and women as uniformed security guards.

Small-Scale Industries

The picture here is quite mixed, varying from sector to sector and also from Gutu to Gokwe. In Gutu, all the enterprises survived the drought year, although with losses, and seemed quite optimistic about the future, with the exception of the roller mill and bakery. Plans were afoot to set up new enterprises. In Gokwe, the industrial sector is smaller than in Gutu and seemed worse hit. Three enterprises - a building-material producer, a mill, and one of the three bakeries - were out of business at the end of 1993. Also plans for establishing a large cotton ginnery and textile factory in Gokwe had temporarily been shelved. This, however, was due to a lack of water and electricity infrastructure in the area rather than because of the drought and structural adjustment. On the other hand, a new local oil mill had been established during the drought. The business optimism which existed in Gokwe before the drought has evaporated.

Overall Trend

Type 1 and 2 small-scale non-agricultural activities compete in the rural market at present in Zimbabwe, both with each other and with the large urban-based commercial and industrial enterprises. The expectation was that the expansion of the large-scale retail sector in rural areas since independence would have impeded the development of small rural enterprises, but this has not transpired. Small rural enterprises appear to have grown rapidly during most of the post-independence period and this growth has not just been a crisis phenomenon. The large-scale retail sector has appropriated an increasing share of the rural commercial market, but the growth of the overall market has left room for small enterprises to develop.

Two reasons can be cited for this market growth. First, rural incomes have increased due to expansion in commercial agriculture, remittances and rural wages. Second, the spread of branch stores which mostly operate with uniform national prices has forced prices down and in so doing has increased rural purchasing power and, most importantly, the circulation of incomes within rural areas. Thus contrary to expectations, the increasing level of commercialisation emanating from the expansion of the large-scale retail sector seems to have been a stimulus to the development of Type 1 and 2 RNAs. However, it has also led to a gradual restructuring of RNAs. When the drought occurred, the restructuring, already underway, was influenced by the crisis.

The effect of drought and structural adjustment in the district service centres seems to have been much smaller and the recovery much quicker than could have been expected, given the severity of the drought and the negative impact of structural adjustment on incomes and prices. Although the majority of enterprises suffered, only a few actually closed, most due to illness, old age or death, and therefore would have done so in any case. Many survived the crisis by switching to new and cheaper commodities or new activities. After the drought, enterprises with growing demand were established in new areas. Thus the number of enterprises in the two centres has continued to grow, with only a short interruption during the height of the drought. At the same time, considerable structural change has taken place.

The trend towards more specialised retail trade and services visible during the last years before the drought has clearly continued. It is, however, still too early to say if the small-scale industrial sector will finally take off in small towns. The rapid restructuring which has already occurred in agro-processing and the increasing focus on small-enterprise development and indigenisation of the economy certainly support the process. The effect of structural adjustment policies on the industrialisation of small towns so far has been sector-specific, depending on the speed and sequence of trade liberalisation, the development of the home market, and the extent to which larger industries focus on the export market.

Conclusion

In general, the Zimbabwean rural economy has three main characteristics. Firstly, large and small enterprises using many different production and distribution technologies coexist. Secondly, market segmentation is based not so much on product specialisation as on differences in delivery services, i.e. credit, transport and location. Thirdly, the development process is not just proceeding from small to large enterprises but equally the other way.

This pattern does not conform to theories derived from development and dependency paradigms, which see large-scale production as efficient and small-scale production as anomalous set to wither away with development. Such paradigms led to development policies based on what could be called an industrial monoculture and worked against economic diversification. In contrast, new theories of industrial development based on flexible specialisation and networks of enterprises see the coexistence of different production technologies and organisations as the norm, rather than an aberration, and a precondition for development in an unstable economic environment (Rasmussen, Schmitz and van Dijk 1992; Pedersen, Sverrisson and van Dijk 1994; Pedersen 1996).

Large mass-producing enterprises require stable markets and production environments to be viable. Such conditions are rare in Africa, where there are low and unreliable incomes, poorly-developed infrastructure, arbitrary political and legal systems, and strong seasonal, climatic and cyclical swings in the economy. Large mass-producing enterprises trying to expand into such environments become less efficient, even if they operate within a government-supported monopoly. Large enterprises will mostly try to avoid serving the smallest markets, leaving the peripheral rural areas poorly served by the large-scale sector, whether private or parastatal.

Smaller enterprises may successfully enter such markets, but they need to follow strategies which make them less sensitive to the unstable environment, notably:

- *Investment in multi-purpose machinery and employment of skilled labour* which makes it possible to shift production between different markets and thus creates an overall stable market for the enterprise even though individual markets may be unstable. The term flexible specialisation is used to describe this strategy. Such enterprises make up the core of integrated enterprise networks in industrialised countries but they are infrequent in Africa.

- *Reduction of fixed investments to a minimum and employment of family labour or unskilled labour* which can be hired and fired at short notice. Thus, fixed costs can be reduced and firms survive by expanding and contracting their production capacity concurrently with the swings in the market. Enterprises following this strategy include so-called sweatshops. They often operate as simple subcontractors.

- *Investment in small, household-based enterprises* where the enterprise owner and family members may spread risks by drawing on other income sources from agriculture or from formal or informal wage labour while working in the enterprise. Small Type 1 activities typically follow this course.

These different strategies make up a hierarchy with large-scale production at the top, requiring more capital and better skills. Entry is difficult and profits correspondingly higher.

Where peripheral development has succeeded in newly-industrialising countries, it has often been based on small and medium-sized enterprises growing on sweatshop or flexible specialisation strategies, or a combination of the two. In most African countries however, post-independence industrial policy attempted to create industrialisation based on large-scale enterprises with government-assured monopoly powers and most have been operating inefficiently. In response to this, a sector of often very small enterprises surviving on semi-subsistence strategies has developed at the rim of the large-scale sector, but small and medium-sized enterprises based on sweatshop or flexible specialisation strategies have yet to develop. Donors and NGOs tended to reinforce this pattern by focusing their development efforts either on large parastatal enterprises or on enterprises in strictly rural areas.

Structural adjustment programmes in theory favour the development of small and medium-sized enterprises given their stress on creating an enabling business environment. However, in practice, Zimbabwe's adjustment programmes have often had precisely the opposite effect. Privatisation has tended to focus on large state enterprises and foreign investments rather than on investment in small enterprises based on local resources. Macroeconomic policies have attempted to make the export industry more competitive on the world market, rather than to increase productivity in production for the home market. At the same time, increasing food prices and retrenchments in both the state and large-scale private sectors have caused a rapid contraction of the home market, to the particular detriment of small enterprises.

Structural adjustment policies have especially focused on short-term contractionary macroeconomic measures. Such measures have been based on very unrealistic assumptions about long-term stable development with insufficient consideration of the climatic and economic shocks of short-term adjustment. This is illustrated by the setbacks experienced when structural adjustment policies coincided with the 1992 drought. Changes in public policies at the local level to encourage small enterprises are practically absent and in any case take much longer to bear effect.

In conclusion, agro-industrial relations and industrial structures are the result of long-term interactions between enterprises, labour markets, social structures and the public sector. These interactions are governed by more or less hierarchical networks as well as by market relations. To change this structure will take time. The public sector can play an important role in this by instituting sectoral and local policies which support local private investments, employment generation, and organisation of local labour markets. Deregulation of administrative practices which is stressed in structural adjustment programmes is a necessary but minor part of this. It is of greatest importance that the public sector change from being only a central decision maker to being a participant in grass-roots development. This does not mean that macroeconomic policies are unimportant. They have, undoubtedly, been necessary to change production conditions but they do not in themselves lead to the transformation of economic and industrial structures which can enhance rural standards of living.

Notes

1. In a 1982 study, Göttlischer (1986) found that retail prices of basic commodities in the district service centres were 10-20 per cent higher depending on the distance from Harare, and prices in small rural business centres were 10-15 per cent higher than in district service centres.
2. One shop specialising in expensive women's dresses in Gutu was converted into a grocery store during the drought and now specialises in farm-input supplies for which there is a growing market.
3. District councils were all reluctant to grant licences to the second-hand clothing trade in service centres.

References

AMIN, N. 1989, *Market Reform in Zimbabwe: Peasantry, Maize Marketing and Food Security*, Geneva, UNRISD Seminar on Food Pricing and Marketing Reforms

BESSANT, L. & E. MURINGAI 1993, 'Peasant, Businessmen and Moral Economy in the Chiweshe Reserve, Colonial Zimbabwe 1930-68', *Journal of Southern African Studies*, vol. 19, no. 4, 551-92

BONNEVIE, H. 1987, *Migration and Malformation - Case Studies from Zimbabwe*, Copenhagen, Centre for Development, Research Project Paper A.87.1

BRAND, V., R. MUPEDZISWA & P. GUMBO 1994, *Structural Adjustment, Women and Informal Trade in Harare, Zimbabwe*, Uppsala, Scandinavian Institute of African Studies, Research Report

GASPER, D. 1988, 'Rural Growth Points and Rural Industries in Zimbabwe: Ideologies and Policies', *Development and Change*, vol. 19, no. 3, 425-66

GEMINI 1994, *Changes in the Small-Scale Enterprise Sector from 1991 to 1993: Results of a Second Nationwide Survey in Zimbabwe*, Bethesda, Maryland

GÖTTLICHER, M. 1986, *Zentrale orte im koncept der ändlichen regionalentwicklung -dargestellt an beispielen aus das communal land gebieten Zimbabwes*, Bonn, Rheinischen Friedrich-Wilhelms-Universität Dissertation

HARRIS, J. & M. MOORE (eds) 1984, 'Development and the Rural Urban Divide', *Journal of Development Studies*, vol. 20, no. 3

HELMSING, A.H.J. 1991, 'Rural Industries and Growth Points: Issues in an Ongoing Debate', in N.D. Mutizwa-Mangiza and A.H.J. Helmsing (eds), *Rural Development and Planning in Zimbabwe*, Aldershot, UK, Avebury

____, 1991, 'Non-Agricultural Enterprises in the Communal Lands of Zimbabwe', in N.D. Mutizwa-Mangiza and A.H.J. Helmsing (eds), *Rural Development and Planning in Zimbabwe*, Aldershot, UK, Avebury

JACKSON, J.C. & P. COLLIER 1991, 'Incomes, Poverty and Food Security in the Communal Lands of Zimbabwe, in N.D. Mutizwa-Mangiza and A.H.J. Helmsing (eds), *Rural Development and Planning in Zimbabwe*, Aldershot, UK, Avebury

JAMAL, V. & J. WEEKS 1993, *Africa Misunderstood or Whatever Happened to the Rural-Urban Gap?*, London, Macmillan

LIPTON, M. 1977, *Why Poor People Stay Poor: Urban Bias in World Development*, Cambridge, Massachusetts, Harvard University Press

MCPHERSON, M.A. 1991, *Micro and Small-Scale Enterprises in Zimbabwe: The Results of a Country-Wide Survey*, Bethesda, Maryland, GEMINI Technical Report 25

PEDERSEN, P.O. 1997b, *Small African Towns - Between Rural Networks and Urban Hierarchies*, Aldershot, UK, Avebury

____, 1997a, 'The Structure of the Economy of Small Towns in Zimbabwe', in Wilbert Gooneratne and R.A. Obudho (eds), *Contemporary Issues in Regional Development Policy. Perspectives from Eastern and Southern Africa*, Aldershot, UK, Avebury

____, 1996, 'Flexibility and Networking in a European and an African Context', in D. McCormick and P.O. Pedersen (eds), *Small Enterprises, Flexibility and Networking in an African Context*, Nairobi, Longhorn Publishers

____, 1992, 'The Structure of Small Service Centres under Conditions of Uncertain Supplies', *International Regional Science Review*, vol. 14, no. 3, 307-16

____, 1991, 'The Restructuring of Wholesale and Retail Trade in Zimbabwe's New District Service Centres', *African Urban Quarterly*, vol. 6, no. 3-4, 292-303

PEDERSEN, P.O., A. SVERRISSON & M.P. van DIJK (eds) 1994, *Flexible Specialization and Other Approaches to the Dynamics of Small-Scale Industries in the South*, Rugby, UK, Intermediate Technology Publication

RASMUSSEN, J., H. SCHMITZ & M.P. van DIJK 1992, 'Introduction: Exploring a New Approach to Small-Scale Industry', *IDS Bulletin*, vol. 23, no. 3, 2-7

RONDINELLI, A.D. 1990, 'Locational Planning and Regional Economic Development: Appropriate Methods in Developing Countries', *International Regional Science Review*, vol. 13, 241-8

____, 1988, 'Market Towns and Agriculture in Africa: The Role of Small Urban Centres in Economic Development', *African Urban Quarterly*, vol. 3, no. 1-2

____, 1985, *Applied Methods of Regional Analysis: The Spatial Dimension of Development Theory*, Boulder, Westview Press

SOUTHALL, A. (ed.) 1988, 'Small Towns in Africa Revisited', *African Studies Review*, vol. 31, no. 3

____, (ed.) 1979, 'Small Towns in African Development', *Africa*, vol. 49, no. 3

VARSHNEY, A. 1993, 'Beyond Urban Bias', *The Journal of Development Studies*, vol. 29, no. 4

WEKWETE, K. 1991, 'Growth Centre Policy in Zimbabwe: with Special Reference to District Service Centres', in N.D. Mutizwa-Mangiza and A.H.J. Helmsing (eds), *Rural Development and Planning in Zimbabwe*, Aldershot, UK, Avebury

WORLD BANK 1982, *Zimbabwe Agricultural Sector Study*, Harare, mimeo

11

Of Livestock and Deadstock: Entrepreneurship and Tradition on the South African Highveld

*Leslie Bank**

Entrepreneurs often come from immigrant groups in many rural areas of Africa (Barth 1967; Oberschall 1973; Kennedy 1988). In South Africa, the policy of Separate Development aimed to *prevent* outsiders from gaining access to commercial opportunities inside the bantustans. In order to encourage ethnic entrepreneurs in these areas, the Apartheid state created the Bantu Investment Corporation (BIC) in 1959. One of the main objectives of the BIC was to expropriate European trading concerns in the reserves and to hand them over to Africans. The BIC was also charged with the responsibility of training and financing new commercial ventures undertaken by Africans. To encourage African entrepreneurship in the homelands, the state also tightened restrictions on African commercial and industrial undertakings in white urban areas (Southall 1980). The aim of this policy was to direct urban-based African businessmen towards the homelands areas.

On the basis of these measures and state initiatives, it soon became conventional wisdom that the expansion of rural entrepreneurship in the bantustans emerged as a result of continuous and generous state support on the one hand, and the rapid shift of urban skills, capital and resources towards rural areas on the other. This argument, which has been amazingly influential in studies of rural class formation in South Africa, is actually based on rather flimsy evidence. Indeed, Nolutshungu (1982) made the point that the amount of state support given to African entrepreneurs relative to white industrialists who wished to relocate to the homelands was very small. In the Qwaqwa bantustan, which is the focus of this chapter, the state-run Development Corporation spent 26 million rands on the interests of (white) industrialists between 1977 and 1985, while over the same period less than 1 million rands were allocated to African entrepreneurs - hardly sufficient funds to support arguments about state-driven entrepreneurial class formation.

Furthermore, Sarakinsky (1989) has suggested that few urban African entrepreneurs were evicted from urban areas. Urban African entrepreneurs of the 1960s were able to entrench themselves in the cities. There was no major movement of urban entrepreneurs to rural areas despite state policies of the 1960s and 1970s with that objective. This leaves some interesting questions, the foremost of which is: if the state did not create and mould the new entrepreneurs of the bantustans and they were not from urban areas, where did they come from, what motivated them, and how did they get into business?

Many scholars have tried to explain rural entrepreneurship in the bantustans in terms of *extrinsic* factors while largely ignoring *endogenous* forces and ideologies which have been generated within rural areas themselves. It is only by looking at processes of rural transformation and, specifically de-agrarianisation, that it is possible to begin to understand the nature and character of entrepreneurship in the former Qwaqwa bantustan, the ethnic national unit of the South Sotho group. A large number of the entrepreneurs who set up retail businesses in Qwaqwa in the 1970s and 1980s were either former labour tenants or sharecroppers from farms in the Orange Free State or were the sons of such individuals: the dependants of a semi-autonomous peasantry recently displaced by mechanisation and relocation.

The entrepreneurial responses of these individuals were largely built around rural resources, experiences and aspirations. Many individuals broke into retailing by shifting their material assets from livestock to 'deadstock', i.e. commerce. The decisions of ex-labour tenants to enter the retail business were based more on their desire to retain some measure of cultural and economic autonomy from the apartheid economy, than on any abstract desire for modernity and self-improvement. By conflating the processes of entrepreneurship with those of modernity in former bantustan areas, there is the risk of misunderstanding these complex phenomena. Rural stores in Qwaqwa have culturally-defined agrarian associations.

This chapter's analysis of rural entrepreneurship begins in the 1940s when the first trading licences were granted to Africans in the Witsieshoek Native Reserve (later the Qwaqwa homeland) in the north-eastern Orange Free State region. Thereafter, attention is directed to conditions on white-owned farms in the surrounding Orange Free State countryside, the main source of relocation into Qwaqwa in the 1970s and 1980s. In considering the shift from farm to bantustan, the focus is on the entrepreneurial strategies of rural households and the shift from livestock to deadstock. In the final section, the complex relationship between entrepreneurship, culture and the identity politics of Qwaqwa in the 1980s is explored.

Between Cattle and Commerce

In the 1930s, Witsieshoek was one of the most impoverished rural reserves in South Africa. Located on the rocky, infertile slopes of the Maluti mountains surrounding Lesotho, the Native Economic Commission described the levels of agricultural production in the reserve as 'pathetically low' in 1932. By the 1940s the situation had changed little, despite concerted efforts by the state to raise productivity (Badenhorst 1950). The consequence of this was that Witsieshoek residents depended heavily on labour migration for survival.

Reflecting on the economic orientation of households during the late 1940s, the chief state agricultural officer for Witsieshoek, R. M. Roberts, reported that, although the vast majority of men spent most of the time in urban areas:

> The Natives, by custom, are what is best described as 'peasants'. It is more accurate to say that they would like to be peasants, practising mixed farming. Actually by far the greater proportion find it impossible to exist as such... They hold land, building sites and cattle in the Reserve but earn their living in industry outside the Reserve, to which they periodically return, and to which they *eventually retire* (Roberts 1950).

Behind this image of Witsieshoek as a peasant society locked into a well-established pattern of labour migration lay a reality of marked economic differentiation. The growing inequalities in the reserve economy caused concern among state authorities who wished to see Witsieshoek retain its *subsistence functions* in the broader political economy of labour migration. To address the situation, agricultural 'betterment schemes' were introduced. Land was reallocated to ensure that all households had access to three morgen lots (2.5 hectares) and attempts were made to impose cattle-culling on the local population (Maroney 1977; Kotze 1982). Official culling met with flat refusal throughout the 1940s by stock owners. Tension escalated, culminating in a state of anarchy. In 1950 a heavily armed squad of police was sent to disperse an anti-culling protest meeting, but the villagers refused to submit to their authority. The police opened fire and killed at least 16 men and women, a blood bath that left a lasting imprint on the reserve (Maroney 1977; Lodge 1983; Kotze 1982).

Following an official Commission of Enquiry into the rebellion, the liberalisation of trading practices in the reserve provoked considerable local interest. In the Orange Free State, access to trading rights for Africans had long been a thorny issue. The 1923 Native Urban Areas Act, clearly stated that urban authorities 'may let sites within the location or native village for trading purposes... provided that no site shall be let to a person who is not a Native' (Hart 1971), but the racist Orange Free State Municipal Congress resolutely refused to implement the 1923 legislation. Despite complaints from chiefs and even the Acting Native Commissioner, the issuing of African trading rights in Witsieshoek did not begin until after the 1950 rebellion made it imperative.

By the end of the 1950s, 40 local applications had been submitted for trading premises. Most were made by middle-aged men with little or no formal education who were heads of large rural households with considerable cash or livestock assets. They were usually individual stock farmers who were in a *structurally* different position from the vast majority of impoverished households in the reserve. Many claimed that they would rely on their sons working in urban areas to help them run their new businesses. Entry into commerce in their case could be achieved simply by shifting resources from one economic sphere to another.

In effect, they were engaged in economic diversification and were seldom prepared to sell off all their livestock to finance their retail businesses in case their new stores did not succeed. Many put their wives and sons in charge of the shop and continued to concentrate on stock farming. The Bantu Investment Corporation (BIC), in charge of promoting African commerce, interpreted this caution as evidence of 'a lack of entrepreneurial potential in the area' and continuously used this as an excuse to retain white trading businesses in the reserve.

The shift from livestock to deadstock was not easy in a situation where personal status and importance were derived largely from an individual's ability to control agricultural resources, especially livestock. Indeed, in 1949, the resident agricultural officer claimed that peasants in Witsieshoek still 'worshipped' their cattle and 'regard it as insult for anyone to lay a hand on them'. The officer went on to report that there were strong cultural barriers preventing the exchange of cattle for cash in the reserve. Referring specifically to credit arrangements between migrants and local traders, he observed that:

> It has become recognised practise for a Native to hand over a beast in security against purchases or debts. With very few exceptions these animals are eventually redeemed, but the lapse of time is often considerable. Until they are redeemed these animals are

> considered to be the property of the trader, but with a difference. The trader is *morally bound not to sell the beast* to recover his money (quoted in Roberts 1950).

These observations were endorsed by local commentator Mopeli-Paulus, who also wrote at the time that people had a 'natural aversion' to selling cattle in Witsieshoek (undated: 112). The most graphic illustration of local commitment to cattle was seen during the Witsieshoek Rebellion of 1950, when police opened fire on hundreds of migrants and peasants gathered at Nohoa village to protect their cattle from culling. One dying victim exclaimed to Mopeli-Paulus at the site of the massacre: 'We die for our cattle!'

That cattle remained a primary symbol of power, status and social cohesion in Witsieshoek in the 1950s seems clear. Migrants went to extraordinary lengths to defend their herds, which served them both as icons and assets. However, while the notion of selling cattle for cash went against the grain for many Basotho entrepreneurs in Witsieshoek, by the 1950s it had become a stark reality for anyone who wished to establish a life of security and relative autonomy outside the Apartheid economy.

Mass Relocation and Market Anarchy of the Bantustan Era

Throughout the 1960s, the BIC in Witsieshoek blocked African entrepreneurship. Of the 16 new applications received by the BIC between 1960 and 1968 it turned down 14 on the grounds that the reserve was 'over-traded'. Conditions in Witsieshoek changed dramatically in the 1970s. Qwaqwa was designated as an official homeland in 1969 making it home to over 3 million people classified as South Sotho. As a result, the population of Qwaqwa quadrupled from 24,000 to over 100,000 between 1970 and 1975. By 1980, it stood in excess of 200,000. The major geographical source of this influx was the white farmlands of the north-eastern and north-western Orange Free State. Financial incentives offered to white farmers by the state-funded Land Bank in this area during the 1960s had encouraged many former absentee landowners to take up occupancy of their land and embark on large-scale mechanisation. This was followed by legislation in 1964 which empowered farmers to forcibly remove tenants from their land (Hathorn and Hutchinson 1990). On some farms mechanisation occurred very rapidly. A former labour tenant explained:

> One year the tractors just appeared on the land we used for our cattle. The farmer said that this was good land and that we must now use the land the tractors couldn't reach. But he kept a lot of good grazing for himself, and I could see he wanted to drive my cattle into the hills as if they were goats (quoted in Sharp undated).

The independence and the ability of African labour tenants to command substantial resources of their own was steadily undermined. The large tracts of land that African tenant families had formerly devoted to their own crops were now trimmed to tiny household gardens, while many farm workers lost access to land altogether. Even more damaging was the assault on livestock. The African herd of the north-eastern Orange Free State declined from 287,000 in 1958 to a mere 120,000 (Sharp undated). Few farm households were allowed to keep more than five head of cattle. The entrenchment of this pattern of dispossession resulted in a growing interest among farm workers in the changes that were taking place inside the Witsieshoek reserve (Mapena 1970). Mass lay-offs and grinding poverty led African farm workers to relocate themselves to the bantustan.

This unexpected influx of farm refugees, as well as a smaller proportion of forcibly resettled people from white urban areas, threw the homeland administration into complete confusion. The tribal authorities were overwhelmed and the BIC came under scathing attack for its inability to prepare the homeland for tens of thousands of new consumers.

Market anarchy replaced state control as the growing homeland consumer market was left in the hands of anyone who had the resources and the inclination to exploit it. In the 1970s, with the moribund local administration devoid of any clear economic policy, a mushrooming second economy began to appear as scores of people set themselves up as hawkers, backyard grocers, taxi-drivers, wood and coal dealers, brick makers, etc. To assert some control over the situation, legislation was passed in 1976 by the new Qwaqwa Legislative Assembly (QLA) to liberalise access to trading licences. The result was a tenfold increase in African-owned businesses in Qwaqwa over the next decade. Table 1 correlates the number of business licences issued with population growth between 1960 and 1986. The ratio of storekeepers to consumers is also provided.

Table 1: Trading Licensing and Population Increase in Qwaqwa, 1960-1986

Year	No. of stores	Estimated population	Population per store
1960	33	15,000	455
1970	35	24,000	700
1976	76	120,000	1,579
1978	168	200,000	1,190
1980	295	300,000	1,017
1982	389	350,000	900
1984	532	400,000	715
1986	675	425,000	630

Sources: Qwaqwa Department for the Interior records and the Qwaqwa Development Corporation records. Figures for the pre-1976 period were drawn from the BENSO *Qwaqwa Economic Review* of 1978. Population figures are drawn from Sharp 1982 and estimates provided by the district magistrate's office in Qwaqwa.

This table highlights a number of key features about commercial development in Qwaqwa. The first point to note is the rapidity with which new licences were issued after 1976. The figures show that, on average, more than 60 new licences were granted annually between 1976 and 1986. The second point to note is the high store-consumer ratio throughout the 1970s. Local reports suggest that the queues outside village retail stores in the 1970s often extended hundreds of yards down the streets. As a result, this was a period in which storekeepers' profits soared. The picture for the 1980s shows a steady decline in store-consumer ratio as new licences were issued.

From Labour Tenants in the White Countryside to Bantustan Entrepreneurs

Turning to the question of the social origins and economic backgrounds of these new traders, it is useful to draw on the findings of 80 detailed life histories of traders in the rural retail sector collected in the mid-1980s. The vast majority of these interviews were with the storekeepers who had set up their businesses in

Qwaqwa in the 1970s. What is significant about these findings is that they correlate so closely with the evidence presented for the 1950s. Over 70 per cent of the owners interviewed were former livestock owners on white-owned farms in the Orange Free State. In fact, many were the sons of successful sharecroppers of the 1910s and 1920s and had recent experience as labour tenants on white land. Like their counterparts in Witsieshoek, they had little formal education and had even less experience of the migrant labour market. Some of these individuals were still running large herds of cattle in the 1960s and had retained their status as quasi-independent rural producers until their arrival in Qwaqwa. The second category, comprising approximately 30 per cent of the sample, was made up of a mixture of ex-labour migrants, school teachers, clerks, and bureaucrats who entered commerce through urban wage labour. In the following discussion the focus is on the former category of operators who form the majority of storekeepers.

Research among the new arrivals indicates that they were mainly wealthy labour-tenant households from white-owned farms. They included individuals, such as George Mokwena, who left the farm on which he had worked for four decades in 1965 with 30 head of cattle and 20 sheep. He was among many labour tenants who now looked to Witsieshoek as a last resort to re-establish themselves as independent rural producers on tribal land. Those, like George, who were lucky enough to gain entry into the fledgling homeland and were given arable land temporarily, achieved their objective. But as relocation from white farms into Witsieshoek accelerated in the 1970s, their hopes were dashed by rampant stock theft and over-population. In reformulating their strategies, these former labour tenants began to follow the path opened up by livestock farmers two decades earlier.

To illustrate how this process typically occurred, it is useful to consider the case of George Mokwena in detail. He arrived in Witsieshoek in 1965 with his wife and their three sons and was settled in the village of Makwane, established on newly incorporated white farmland. In the first two years after resettlement, George worked hard to transform the three-morgen plot (2.5 hectares) allocated to him by the Bakwena tribal authority, into a viable family farm. In the meantime, George's sons went out to work on the Witwatersrand, remitting home part of their monthly earnings to help their father. The land allocated to George was fertile and initially showed potential but, by the end of 1969, when Makwane village was transformed into a 'closer settlement' village George began to question his future as a farmer.

The theft of his harvest and four cattle in 1970 did little to allay his fears. As George's dream of returning to agriculture began to disappear, he took greater notice of his sons' suggestion that he should consider selling off his cattle and reinvesting in a rural store. They proposed that he open a wood and coal business in Makwane. At first George found the suggestion almost unbelievable. According to one of his sons, his initial response was: 'I cannot understand why anyone would be stupid enough to sell cattle to buy wood. I will not do it'. But, by 1972, he had changed his mind and decided to submit an application to the tribal authority for a wood and coal licence. When interviewed in 1985, George had acquired two additional stores in the village, both run by his sons who had withdrawn from the labour market.

The success of these ex-labour tenants in making the transition to commerce in the 1970s depended critically on their willingness to give up their livestock quickly and to reinvest their savings in new ways. In the above case, mass relocation to Makwane village made this decision easy. But in other villages where the effects of relocation were less immediate, the pressures on small farmers to sell stock were not as great. In these cases, stock owners were inclined to hold onto their stock for longer, and in the process often lost the opportunity to make a smooth transition to commerce. The failure of older men to take advice from their working sons was a frequent cause of their delayed response. Last-minute attempts to sell off stock and prolonged domestic squabbles between male householders over the appropriate allocation of household resources was often a recipe for disaster. In one case recorded in Tseseng village, the stubborn refusal of an ex-labour tenant, Thabo Moloi, to sell his cattle eventually led to the breakdown of his extended family. As his three sons went off in their own directions, Thabo lost his ability to move out of farming. When interviewed in the 1980s, he was an old and sickly man and claimed that he would rather die than relinquish his cattle. But there was a bitterness in his words which revealed a sense of deep regret.

George Mokwena and Thabo Moloi had chosen different paths. There was clearly nothing inevitable about the shift from livestock to storekeeping. Both informants had the opportunity. For those labour tenants who remained on white-owned farms during the 1960s and only relocated to Qwaqwa in the 1970s, the luxury of shifting their assets from one sphere to another was, however, no longer a possibility. Most of these households were poverty-stricken on arrival in Qwaqwa having lost most, if not all, of their rural resources prior to their arrival. The sale of the few cattle these families had left by the 1970s barely covered the costs of relocation. Despite their painful experiences of dispossession on white farms, few of these households had lost their *desire* for autonomy and independence, although they no longer had the material resources to operationalise it. This was clearly demonstrated by the persistent attempts of ex-farm workers to 'exit' the migrant labour economy after arrival in Qwaqwa. In the early 1980s, one TEBA official reported that Qwaqwa had the poorest rate of contract completion in South Africa and said that it was for this reason that the TEBA had decided to cut its labour quota for Qwaqwa.

In the vast majority of cases, worker strategies to *exit* the migrant labour system proved disastrous and within months they were back in labour queues. But some did succeed in breaking out and taking advantage of the commercial opportunities of Qwaqwa during the 1970s. The secret to success lay in a variety of factors: access to a stable, well-paid migrant job which was not abandoned prematurely; the existence of a low household dependency ratio, and the ability of the male household head to exert tight control over family labour. The latter factor was critically important since without careful coordination and control of household resources, the quest for autonomy was bound to fail. The three-generational structure of ex-labour tenant households and the ability of the household head to exert tight control over family labour placed this category of households at an advantage over more fragmented and impoverished households. In the case studies recorded, it was most often the ability of ex-labour tenants to divert the labour of women away from the domestic sphere into more productive avenues which proved to be the foundation for entrepreneurial success. In the closer settlements, numerous cases were recorded where women were forced to market consumer goods purchased with male wages (Bank 1994a).

The deployment of female labour in pursuit of male objectives was, however, not confined to retailing. In the local brick manufacturing sector, rural men were also able to translate domestic power into profits. The division of labour was strictly along lines of age and gender, with women and children doing the manual work of digging, carting the clay and moulding bricks, while men looked for migrant jobs or secured contracts for the supply of raw materials to keep their wives productive.

The prominence of ex-labour tenant families among the so-called 'new commercial elite' in Qwaqwa during the 1970s was the product of three related factors. Firstly, the access of these households to residual resources such as livestock at the time of relocation gave these households distinct advantages in the pursuit of commercial opportunities. Secondly, entrepreneurs were able to achieve their objectives precisely because of their ability to hold together their often large domestic groups under difficult conditions. The ability of rural men to resuscitate older notions of the patriarchal family rooted in a bygone era of independence in the white countryside was an important resource. Thirdly, and perhaps most importantly, these operators were able to make the transition from cattle to commerce because they were driven by a *desire to retain or recapture their autonomy as self-reliant producers* able to operate outside the framework of the Apartheid economy.

Commerce and Consciousness: Entrepreneurship and Social Identity

Fredrik Barth (1963) defined entrepreneurship in terms of three criteria: (1) the single-minded maximisation of *one type of value* (this need not be economic profit), (2) the use of a *deductive prognosis* of results which does not conform to expectations based on institutionalised experience, and (3) the willingness to take *risks*. In terms of this definition, it seems clear that the majority of individuals cited in this chapter must be defined as entrepreneurs. There can, for instance, be little doubt that they were involved in the maximisation of value, although the primary value they sought to maximise was not economic profit but *autonomy*. Moreover, in setting out to achieve their aim, former livestock owners employed deductive reasoning which involved weighing up the pros and cons of holding onto their livestock. By selling livestock to open retail stores, they broke away from established customary expectations and exposed themselves to great social and economic risk. These risks involved the constant threat of social ostracism and the possibility of economic failure.

But the value of Barth's work lies in the emphasis he places on the social context of entrepreneurial activity. When considering the social context of entrepreneurship in Witsieshoek in the 1950s and in Qwaqwa in the 1970s and 1980s, one is struck by significant differences. In the 1950s one of the main dilemmas for entrepreneurial households was the fear of repudiating community values. Cattle were then still widely perceived as community resources used to cement social and economic relations between households. It was also believed that those who owned many cattle should be prepared to loan them to others in times of need. Such beliefs were manifested through the ubiquitous sharecropping and *mafisa* cattle-lending agreements that existed in Witsieshoek.[1] Mapena (1970) was still able to observe some of this cooperation in the 1960s:

> There are hardly any people who still use the hoe for ploughing their lands. Some men have oxen and ploughs, and use them for ploughing their lands. When a man has oxen, but no plough, he puts his oxen at the disposal of his neighbour or relative who has a plough, and in that way gets his field ploughed. The same cooperative farming is seen when a man has a plough and few oxen.

By selling their cattle to enter commerce, wealthier households implicitly threatened to disrupt good neighbourly and community relations. As a result, entrepreneurs feared that if they did not acknowledge community values, they might easily be accused of witchcraft or face consumer action. It was for this reason, among others, that many of the new entrepreneurs of the 1950s retained some of their livestock. The art of successful entrepreneurship was therefore a matter of being able to walk a social tight-rope between acceptance and rejection in one's community.

In the 1970s, the situation was very different. During the phase of mass relocation, rural villages were totally overrun by new arrivals, existing social relations broke down and the moral fabric of village life changed dramatically. One of the most important changes was that the pre-existing ideology of shared poverty quickly fell away and was replaced by a much more individualised approach to the predicament of poverty. Spiegel and Sharp (1985) argue that the loss of residual rural resources such as land and cattle, and the absence of reliable sources of cash income in most households radically eroded the material basis for generalised reciprocity - even to the extent that kin relations were difficult to maintain. In reflecting on this evidence, one might suspect that Qwaqwa provided an ideal environment for the emergence of a self-serving capitalist class. Ironically, the entrepreneurs of the 1970s did not see themselves in this way, and consistently presented themselves as the 'guardians of community values' and *Sesotho* traditions. The point is well demonstrated with reference to changing patterns of store naming in the area.

In the 1950s rural stores were always named after the owners or after the village in which they were situated. Throughout this period owners made little use of their stores as a means of confirming or asserting a local identity. Traders had enough difficulty distancing themselves from demands on their resources without providing a further invitation to rural villagers to exploit the pervasive ideology of shared poverty. By the 1970s, the naming of stores had become a much more elaborate process. Storekeepers now went to great lengths and expense to create an identity that suited their purpose. For example, they started painting imposing murals on the walls of their stores depicting clan totems or idyllic rural scenes.

These images stood in contrast to the *anomie* of closer settlement life and appealed to images of an era when villages still constituted communities.

The use of clan totems was particularly significant. Clan totems were loaded political symbols in Qwaqwa since many of the immigrants who arrived in the bantustan during this period were not members of either the Bakwena or the Batlokwa, the two dominant tribal groupings. People from the white farms in north-eastern Orange Free State defined themselves as 'Makholokoe', a sub-division of the larger Batlokwa, and in the period immediately preceding mass farm relocation, members of this 'tribe' had petitioned the South African state for access to independent tribal land. Their struggle for land failed and many families were still bitter about this issue on arrival in Qwaqwa in the 1970s. The decision by storekeepers to highlight clan totems as symbols of identity thus lodged them firmly within a local discourse of difference (Bank 1995).

The iconography of rural stores reflected a complex mixture of social identities in Qwaqwa's rural villages in the 1970s. For instance, it was common for storekeepers to draw attention to their own specific clan totems, while at the same time naming their stores in ways that appealed to a broader ethnic identity and an ideology of sharing. Names such as *Thusanang Basotho* (Help each other Basotho), *Ratanang Basotho* (Love each other Basotho) or even Thaka *Bafutsana* (Among the poor) were in vogue in the 1970s. The irony is that the traders of the 1970s were using precisely the kinds of symbols that their counterparts in the 1950s were so eager to avoid. It can, of course, be proposed that they were simply using these images and symbols to attract customers. But, as Table 1 shows, there was no need for aggressive marketing in the 1970s. Indeed, during this period some storekeepers actually complained to the Qwaqwa Government that they could not cope with the large number of consumers queuing outside their shops.

By emphasising their *Sesotho* identity, as opposed to simply their clan origins, entrepreneurs offered support for the process of ethnicity building in Qwaqwa in the 1970s. They strongly endorsed the campaign of the ruling party to stress the Sesetho ethos of *re a thusana* (help each other) as the social basis for 'Sotho Sotho' homeland development (Bank 1995). They also supported attempts by the local elite to manipulate the contrast between *sesotho* (sotho ways) and *sekgowa* (white ways) as a way of building ethnic consciousness in the area. Rural entrepreneurs in Qwaqwa realised that white traders and businesses continued to pose a threat to their enterprises. As a result, they frequently emphasised that they were not like the 'exploitative white traders' who never cared for the Basotho people. Rural traders insisted that they offered 'proper credit' to their clients and based their business practice on 'true Basotho values'. Furthermore traders viewed the parastatal Qwaqwa Development Corporation (QDC), which was still dominated by white bureaucrats in the 1970s as the embodiment of *sekgowa* in Qwaqwa. As with the BIC before it, they said that it had been brought to the homeland to deceive and exploit genuine Basotho entrepreneurs. For them it was 'a wolf in a sheepskin' (Bank 1994b).

Some entrepreneurs embellished these narratives, stating that they had opened businesses to avoid being subjected to the unpredictability and cruelty of whites. They said that they did not want to work for whites nor did they wish to expose themselves to the unnecessary hardship of labour migrancy. 'What you see here,' one owner stated, 'might not seem like much, but it belongs to me and it gives me the freedom to make my own decisions; there is no white *baas* (boss) telling me what to do.' In reconstructing their social identities in Qwaqwa, these owners were involved in a deeply political process which often involved associating themselves closely with the values of *Sesotho* while at the same time rejecting state definitions of modernity and development.

Beyond the Bovine Mystique: Entrepreneurship and Cultural Process

Thus the expansion of entrepreneurship in Qwaqwa was driven forward neither on the basis of state funds and support nor through the relocation of urban entrepreneurs to rural areas. Instead, the entrepreneurial responses were consistently built around rural resources, objectives and initiatives. A family labour system, which underwrote earlier sharecropping and labour tenancy relationships in the white countryside, was reimposed in Qwaqwa's closer settlement villages to facilitate entry into the rural retail sector. Indeed, the ability of rural entrepreneurs to stay in business often depended on their ability to exploit family labour by manipulating older notions of patriarchal control. As a result, the rural retail sector in Qwaqwa was characterised by a virtual absence of wage labour in the 1980s. Throughout the 1970s and into the 1980s, many rural storekeepers were strongly opposed to the employment of wage labour in their businesses and sometimes went to extraordinary lengths to avoid the employment of non-kin in their stores. To achieve this, traders even resorted to fostering street children as a means of acquiring kin.

Besides the importance of family labour within the business, very few store owners were prepared to enter into business partnerships. In the late 1970s, this became a highly sensitive issue when selected white retail businesses were given permission to open outlets in Qwaqwa. In the wake of this announcement, QDC officials and members of the Qwaqwa government urged rural traders to pool their resources in order to establish village supermarkets. These never materialised. The only exceptions recorded involved partnerships between close kin, such as spouses or brothers. The tendency was to keep business within the family at all costs, even if this jeopardised the profitability of an enterprise. There was a widespread perception that profits in business were essentially made through savings rather than reinvestments. In other word, these rural entrepreneurs viewed saving, parsimony and thrift as the main source of profit. This orientation towards saving rather than investment supported the existing tendency towards 'one man, one shop'. In most of the stores visited there was no organised system of bookkeeping and thus no conceptual separation between 'domestic' and 'business' expenditure. Money was transferred to and fro between the domestic and business spheres.

How does one interpret these patterns? Drawing on the work of Ferguson (1992), who observed that property is not a relationship between people and things, but rather a relationship *between people concerning things*, it can be argued that rural entrepreneurs not only built up their stores by transforming livestock into deadstock, but actually conceptualised them as imaginary herds, as *truly social commodities*, which were at once social and economic. Ashton (1952) notes that livestock in rural Lesotho were always divided into 'women's animals' (pigs and fowl) and 'men's animals' (cattle, sheep, and goats). These were different categories of property. The former were conventionally viewed as individual property, which belonged to *particular women* and were to be used by women to meet their personal needs, whereas the latter were seen less as individual property, but as a social or collective resource. Cattle did belong to particular men, but they were also considered to be a household resource open to the claims of all household members. As a collective resource, it was completely within the rights of the household head to call on other household members to care for this resource.

Ex-labour tenants and former stock owners conceptualised their stores precisely within this framework. They viewed them as their personal property in the first instance and as household property in the second. It was on this basis that they were able to convince their wives, children and relatives to work in their stores without remuneration. By constructing their stores as imaginary herds, many rural entrepreneurs in Qwaqwa were able to exploit family labour. However, by using this idiom they were also forced to keep the business within the family. In terms of Basotho custom, it is not possible for cattle to be *jointly owned by unrelated men.* It seems that the same rule was applied to stores. Moreover, as already seen above, many rural entrepreneurs used their stores to express their collective identity and clan allegiance. In this sense, a store much like a migrant's herd operated as a visible marker of social identity. It was a public statement of belonging and status. Culturally, it was a smooth transition from livestock to deadstock.

Conclusion

The case study presented in this chapter challenges the conventional 'modernist' interpretations of entrepreneurship in rural South Africa. It is misleading to view the development of commerce in Witsieshoek/Qwaqwa as a rejection of *Sesotho* tradition and an embrace with modernity. To impose such ideologically loaded categories on this process of economic restructuring is not only to deny continuities in rural market responses over time, but also to run the risk of seriously misinterpreting processes of consciousness and identity formation.

The general failure of researchers in South Africa to take consciousness and social identity in rural areas seriously has resulted in persistent attempts to squeeze rural entrepreneurs into inappropriate social and political categories. It has, for instance, frequently been postulated that rural entrepreneurs, by virtue of their 'privileged' economic position, must be the 'natural' political allies of other rural elites, such as teachers and bureaucrats. After all, they are said to share the same 'class positions'. But this perspective clouds rather than illuminates our understanding of the rise of entrepreneurship in rural South Africa.

In the 1980s, for instance, when the ruling elite in Qwaqwa eventually toned down its campaign to build a broad 'South Sotho' ethnic identity in the homeland and opted for the shorter route of consolidating power around a narrower Bakwena tribal base, it immediately lost the support of the traders, who remained committed to ethnic national projects in Qwaqwa throughout the 1980s (Bank 1994). Rural traders seemed impervious to local criticism of their position and even when the African National Congress (ANC) finally set up offices in Qwaqwa in the early 1990s, many rural traders refused to join the ANC. Many of those interviewed in the early 1990s said that they did not care much for the ANC's inclusive ideology of non-racialism. They said that among the national political parties they preferred the Africanist orientation of the Pan-African Congress (PAC), which 'at least, had respect for tradition'.

Finally, the example of African entrepreneurship in Witsieshoek/Qwaqwa illustrates that de-agrarianisation can never be read as a straight-line journey between two polar opposites, be it rural and urban, or tradition and modernity. It is a far more nuanced and paradoxical process. Strong agrarian identities can be retained and even elaborated upon long after occupational pursuits have switched to non-agrarian activities.

Notes

* The author would like to thank Dr Colin Murray for his useful comments on an earlier version of this paper and Dr Deborah Bryceson for her editorial skill in drastically slimming a much longer original version of this paper.

1. According to Sheddick (1954) *mafisa* is 'the practice whereby a stock owner entrusts a portion of his stock to the care of another who, while he is in no way a hired employee, acts as the caretaker of that stock in return for certain rights of usufruct over the stock' (in Murray 1981: 92).

References

ASHTON, H. 1967 *The Basotho: A Social Study of Traditional and Modern Lesotho*, second edition, New York, Oxford University Press

BADENHORST, C. 1950, *Witsieshoek: n' Project vir Staat en Kerk*, University of Stellenbosch, unpublished MA dissertation

BANK, L. 1994a, 'Angry Men and Working Women: Violence and Economic Change in Qwaqwa in the 1980s', *African Studies*, vol. 53, no. 1, 89-114

____, 1994b, 'Between Traders and Tribalists: Imposition and the Politics of Disjuncture in a South African Bantustan', *African Affairs*, vol. 93, 75-98

____, 1995, 'The Failure of Ethnic Nationalism: Land, Power and the Politics of Clanship on the South African Highveld, 1860-1990', *Africa*, vol. 65, no. 4, 565-91

BARTH, F. (ed.) 1963, *The Role of the Entrepreneur in Social Change in Northern Norway*, Bergen, Norwegian University Press

____, 1967, 'Economic Spheres in Darfur' in R. Firth (ed.), *Themes in Economic Anthropology*, London, Tavistock

BENSO 1978, *Qwaqwa Economic Review*, Pretoria, Bureau for Economic Research and National Development, Government Printers

FERGUSON, J. 1992, 'The Cultural Topography of Wealth: Commodity Paths and the Structure of Property in Rural Lesotho', *American Anthropologist*, vol. 94, 55-73

HART, G. 1971, *Some Socio-Economic Aspects of African Entrepreneurship*, Rhodes University, Institute of Social and Economic Research

HATHORN, M. & D. HUTCHINSON 1990, 'Labour Tenants and the Law' in C. Murray and C. O'Regan (eds.), *No Place to Rest: Forced Relocations and the Law in South Africa*, Cape Town, Oxford University Press

KENNEDY, P. 1988, *African Capitalism; The Struggle of Ascendency*, Cambridge, Cambridge University Press

KOTZE, D.A. 1982, 'The Witsieshoek Revolt, 1940-1960', *African Studies*, vol. 41, 127-41

LODGE, T. 1983, *Black Politics in South Africa since 1945*, Johannesburg, Ravan Press

MAPENA, P.O.I. 1970, *The Native Administration of Witsieshoek*, University of South Africa, unpublished MA thesis

MARONEY, S. 1977, 'The 1950 Witsieshoek Rebellion', *Africa Perspective*, vol. 2, no. 3

MOPELI-PAULUS, A. undated, *The World and the Cattle*, University of the Witwatersrand, African Studies Library, unpublished manuscript

MOPELI-PAULUS, A. & P. LANHAM 1953, *Blanket Boys Moon*, Cape Town, David Philip

MURRAY, C. 1981, *Families Divided*, Cambridge, Cambridge University Press

NOLUNTSHUNGU, S. 1982, *Changing South Africa*, Cape Town, Blackshaws

OBERSCHALL, A. 1973, 'African Traders and Businessmen in Lusaka', *African Social Research*, vol. 16

QWAQWA LEGISLATIVE ASSEMBLY (QLA) 1970-88, Verbatim Reports, Government Publishers, Pretoria

ROBERTS, R.M. 1950, *Letters. Witsieshoek Collection*, Bloemfontien Archives, South Africa

SARAKINSKY, M. 1989, *The Changing Urban Class Structure in South Africa: 1970-1985*, University of the Witwatersrand, unpublished MA dissertation

SHARP, J. undated, *Agricultural Transformation, the State and the Politics of Identity: The Influx from Orange Free State Farms to Qwaqwa in the 1970s*, unpublished manuscript

____, 1982, 'Relocation and the Problem of Survival in Qwaqwa', *Social Dynamics*, vol. 8, 11-29

SHARP, J. & A. SPIEGEL 1985, 'Vulnerability to Impoverishment in South African Rural Areas: the Erosion of Kinship and Neighbourhood as Social Resources', *Africa*, vol. 55, 133-52

SOUTHALL, R. 1980, 'African Capitalism in Contemporary South Africa', *Journal of South African Studies*, vol. 7

VI

CONTINENTAL POLICY ISSUES

12

Rural Industries in Africa: Hope and Hype

Ian Livingstone

There is no question regarding the desirability of developing non-agricultural rural employment in Africa. Such economic activity offers a number of favourable attributes, including labour-intensity, urban-migration reduction and an enhancement of rural household viability by providing, in conjunction with services, multiple sources of income. Non-agricultural activities are also an increasing necessity in the face of declining land availability. How much real economic development can be expected from the non-agricultural sector, and in particular from rural small-scale industry, however, is quite uncertain.

It is possible that a parallel debate between pessimists and optimists may develop as happened in the case of the urban informal sector. As may be recalled, the pessimistic view saw the informal sector as a 'sink' for those unable to secure formal sector jobs: a low-income alternative to unemployment, made up of shoe shiners, car washers and the like. The expansion of the sector was involutionary rather than evolutionary. There was an absorption of increasing numbers but with diminishing marginal productivity, as more and more producers competed within a limited market. The optimists' position was partly emotional or even ideological. Known as 'informal sectorists' (Davies 1978), they saw the sector as a dynamic sector of 'entrepreneurs' and small-scale capitalists, significantly underestimated by official statistics, with a vast potential for employment generation.

Lines are already being drawn with respect to rural small-scale enterprises, although up to now mostly the optimistic view is being heard. A whole literature talks of the 'rural non-farm economy' (Kilby 1986) and of 'rural microenterprises' (Liedholm, Mead and others in the Michigan State University/GEMINI research group), certainly much more attractive labels than 'informal sector'. It has been suggested that as much as 80 to 90 per cent of industrial employment in African countries may be rural. The pessimists have been rather slow to respond to this expanding literature, although Hunt (1983) presents a strongly contrary view of rural possibilities based on the situation of Kenya: 'despite recent suggestions to the contrary this scope [for absorbing the growing labour force of one low-income economy, Kenya, into non-farm employment] is limited if the intention is to ensure incomes above the poverty line'.

Against this background, this chapter takes a closer look at some of the statistical evidence on rural industries. A much more cautious view of the current contribution and future prospects of rural industries in Africa emerges.

Re-examining Rural Industries

Much of the confusion surrounding rural small-scale enterprises stems from the considerable problems of data collection and interpretation. Microenterprises are defined as firms which employ less than ten persons, but usually less than four. It is rare for such small firms to keep records. Surveys which centre on market centres fail to capture much of the activity which is carried on outside these centres, notably construction and transport. Different data-gathering procedures associated with household versus enterprise surveys, and censuses versus local surveys yield very different results, related, as Kilby (1986) notes, to the invisibility of non-farm activities. Furthermore, most rural industries are carried out on a part-time basis. The dispersed as well as invisible nature of rural industries increases the costs of data collection. This results in varying coverage which affects comparability as well as accuracy.

The central finding of studies by 'optimists' is that rural small-scale industries in Africa are extremely important. Kilby (1986) refers to the 'surprising dominance of rural industry in total manufacturing employment'. Liedholm (1990) states similarly that 'a surprising, yet important finding is that in most countries the vast majority (of small industries) are located in rural areas'. Table 1 shows the percentage of employment in manufacturing industries accounted for by rural areas in selected African and other countries.

Such statements are grossly misleading, albeit compensatory of neglect in the opposite direction. A false impression is sometimes created by quoting the distribution of numbers of establishments rather than numbers employed in small-scale industries. The vast number of one-person establishments greatly increases the number of establishments in proportion to numbers employed. This is illustrated in Table 2 from Liedholm (1993) and Table 3 based on Bagachwa and Stewart

(1990). Liedholm (1994) goes even further, stating in relation to Lesotho that almost 90 per cent of medium and small enterprises are located in rural areas.

The impression of rural dominance changes when numbers employed are given. For example, the recent Ugandan Census of Business Establishments shows firms with 5-9 employees account for only 9 per cent of the total employed. Small firms of between 10-49 employees account for a further 29 per cent, medium establishments with 50-99 employees constitute another 9 per cent. Large firms in excess of 100 employees account for 53 per cent. The census excludes microenterprises employing 1-4 persons (Government of Uganda 1993).

The distinction between rural manufacturing enterprise as opposed to rural non-farm enterprise as a whole, including trade and services of all kinds, is often not made clear. Kilby (1986), for example, attempts to demonstrate 'the dominance of rural industry in total manufacturing employment' by citing the share of non-farm income from all sources in total household income as evidence to conclude that 'the non-farm sector ranges from one half to three-quarters the size of the agricultural sector'. While each is a separate statement, the impression is given, intentional or not, that rural *industry* constitutes an important share of total household income.

The distortion may be illustrated with reference to Kenya. According to the Household Budget Survey of 1981-2, non-farm income provided 17 per cent of the total income of rural households, compared with 48 per cent for farm income. This, however, is not all manufacturing. In the urban areas, the Small-scale Enterprise Survey showed that manufacturing accounted for only 17 per cent of total employment. If it is assumed that the same proportion were applied in the rural areas and that average incomes from manufacturing and non-manufacturing were equal then manufacturing's contribution to total rural household income would be just below 3 per cent (Livingstone 1991). This figure would be increased if part of a separate figure for 'paid employment' came from the informal sector. However if this part is taken as 30 per cent, as suggested by the World Bank (1987), the share of manufacturing increases to only about 4 per cent.

In a table derived from Haggblade (1987) and reproduced by Bagachwa and Stewart (1990) showing the composition of rural employment in 11 African countries (Table 4), manufacturing appears as a respectable 29 per cent of rural non-agricultural employment. However, non-agriculture's share was only 13.4 per cent of total rural employment so that in the final column manufacturing's share averages 3.8 per cent of total rural employment. The fact that Bagachwa and Stewart's paper, dealing with small-scale manufacturing, is introduced with this table but excludes the final column, gives the wrong impression of the quantitative importance of rural small-scale industries in Africa.

Table 1: Large and Small-scale Manufacturing Employment in Rural Areas in Selected African and Other Countries[1]

Country	Year	Percentage
Sierra Leone	1976	86
Indonesia	1976	80
Sri Lanka	1971	75
Jamaica	1980	74
Ghana	1973	72
Bangladesh	1974	68
Zambia	1985	64
Philippines	1976	61
India	1967	57
Pakistan	1975	52
Taiwan	1976	49
Malaysia	1970	46
Korea	1975	30

Source: Liedholm and Mead (1986)

1. 'Rural' is defined as all localities of less than 20,000 inhabitants.

Table 2: Location of Medium and Small Enterprises (percentage of total)

Location	Botswana[1]	Lesotho[2]	Malawi[3]	Swaziland[4]	Zimbabwe[5]
Major cities	10.2	12.0	9.0	15.5	32.0
Secondary towns	21.2	8.4	1.5	8.9	10.2
Rural areas	68.6	79.6	89.5	76.6	57.8

Source: Liedholm and Mead (1993)

1. The major city category is restricted to Gabarone, which was stratified into residential, commercial and industrial areas. There were two strata for secondary towns: medium and small. Rural areas consisted of large villages, small villages, and rural areas.
2. The survey distinguished between small towns (6.8 per cent of all employment) and rural towns (1.6 per cent), both considered here as secondary towns; and between 4 categories of rural areas: lowlands (29.7 per cent), foothills (28.4 per cent), mountains (9.7 per cent) and the Senqu River Valley (11.8 per cent).
3. Within urban and secondary towns, all markets, commercial areas, and industrial areas were enumerated completely to avoid a bias in population estimates.
4. The sampling in the two major towns distinguished between high-income (4.0 per cent), medium-income (3.7 per cent) and low-income (7.8 per cent) areas. The secondary towns included smaller towns (3.6 per cent) and company towns (5.3 per cent).
5. In Zimbabwe there were four urban strata for the major cities: high- and low-density areas (21.9 per cent and 6.1 per cent respectively), commercial districts (2.8 per cent) and industrial areas (1.5 per cent). Secondary towns included smaller towns (7.8 per cent) and growth points (3.5 per cent). Rural areas were subdivided between district councils (45.2 per cent) and rural councils (11.2 per cent).

Table 3: Locational Distribution of Rural Manufacturing Firms by Employment (percentage)

	Number of workers		
	Small	Medium	Large
Country	1-9	10-49	50 and above
Ghana (1970)	84[1]	1	15
Kenya (1969)	49[1]	10	41
Nigeria (1972)	59[1]	26	15
Sierra Leone (1974)	90	5	5
Tanzania (1978)	55[1]	8	37
Zambia (1985)	83	1	16

Sources: Bagachwa and Stewart (1990) based on Chuta and Liedholm (1979); Milimo and Fisseha (1986); United Republic of Tanzania, Survey of Industries (1979)

1. The residual, i.e. difference between employment recorded in labour force or population censuses and establishment surveys.

Table 4: Magnitude and Composition of Rural Employment[1]

	% total employment		*% of rural non-agricultural employment*				Rural mfg as % total
Countries (Survey date)	Agri-cultural	Non-agricult'l	Mining	Mfg	Constru ction	Ser-vices[2]	employ-ment
Cameroon (1976)	89.6	10.4	0.2	23.8	8.6	67.4	2.5
Malawi (1977)	89.0	11.0	0.8	24.9	14.9	59.3	2.7
Mali (1976)	91.7	8.3	0.8	39.8	0.8	58.6	3.3
Mauritania (1977)	79.2	20.8	1.9	17.3	5.8	75.0	3.6
Mozambique(1980)	91.0	9.0	0.0	50.9	5.6	43.5	4.6
Rwanda (1978)	95.1	4.9	9.5	23.4	13.2	53.9	1.1
Senegal (1970-1)	82.3	17.7	2.4	34.3	4.3	59.0	6.1
Sierra Leone (1974)	86.2	13.8	5.4	20.3	7.9	66.3	2,8
Tanzania (1978)	93.9	6.1	0.0	19.6	0.0	79.4	1.2
Togo (1970)	74.5	25.5	0.1	18.6	4.2	77.0	4.7
Zimbabwe (1982)	80.0	20.0	0.0	46.6	0.0	53.4	9.3
Mean	86.6	13.4	1.9	29.0	5.9	63.0	3.8

Source: Haggblade et al. (1987, Table 16, p.32), reproduced in Bagachwa and Stewart (1990), final column added.

1. Employment is defined as economically active population primarily engaged in each activity. This table includes data from 1970 onwards.
2. Includes transport, commerce and other services + 'other'.

As a final example, data showing that manufacturing accounts for 57 per cent of medium and small enterprises leads Liedholm (1994) to state that 'the dominance of manufacturing activity . . . is a striking feature of findings from Lesotho'. This statement owes much more to the non-development of the trading sector than positive development in small-scale manufacturing, which remains limited.

Nature of Rural Manufacturing

There is no disputing the expansion in the number of microenterprise establishments over time in Africa as in most least developed countries. The question that has to be addressed is whether this process is evolutionary or involutionary, that is, whether it represents actual or effective labour absorption. For this reason, it is important to examine the *content* of rural manufacturing.

Liedholm (1994) observes in rural Lesotho that: 'three activities dominate: food and beverages (beer brewing primarily), textiles and apparel, and wood and grass products. These "big three" sectors together are consistently the most important categories among micro and small enterprises around the world'.

It would be wrong to dismiss rural beer brewing as an unimportant productive activity. It bears all the characteristics of the informal sector, fulfilling the same function as the bottled formal sector equivalent, at a lower level of quality but at a price affordable by the mass of rural consumers. The equivalent volume of production in the formal sector would require a huge investment. However, most beer brewing is carried out by rural women as a part-time activity. The full-time equivalent employment involved is very much less than that suggested, perhaps a fifth.

Milimo and Fisseha's (1986) Zambian data (Table 5) shows 50 per cent of self-employed 'rural employees' in 1980 were engaged in beer brewing. Charcoal, an important commodity in Sub-Saharan Africa as the most common urban household energy source, appears to be an activity in which the marginal product of labour is extremely low. A recent study of charcoal makers supplying Kampala in Uganda (Opio-Okori 1994) found earnings per hour to be as low as 6 US cents per bag, due to the large number of hours required, including wood gathering. This is illustrative of the low value added in rural manufacturing. The part-time nature of the above kinds of production and the low value added in many activities will affect the relative rural and urban shares respectively in manufacturing employment and value added.

Table 5: Employment in Rural and Urban Manufacturing in Zambia

	Large-scale (1980)	*Small-scale (1985)*		
		Urban	*Rural*	
Industry	No. ('000)	No. ('000)	No. ('000)	%[1]
Textiles and clothing	10.2	19.8	11.7	4.5
Wood products	6.3	11.9	82.7	31.5
Metal products	6.3	7.6	10.3	3.9
Food	16.6	17.5	14.3	5.4
Beverages	3.8	8.4	132.4	50.4
Leather products	1.0	2.1	1.4	0.5
Non-metallic products	3.5	1.2	6.5	2.9
Chemicals	7.3	2.0	-	-
Machinery	1.0	(4.1)[2]	(1.4)[2]	(0.5)[2]
Electrical products	1.7	3.1	(0.9)[2]	(0.3)[2]
Transport equipment	1.3	8.0	-	-
Miscellaneous	0.2	2.5	0.8	0.3
Total	58.9	88.2	262.8	100.0
Persons engaged/ establishment	103	1.9	1.6	
Share in total mfg employment	15%	21%	64%	

Source: Milimo and Fisseha (1986)

1. This column is interpolated by Kilby (1986). Data for large-scale industry are not available since 1980, but employment and output are thought to have continued the decline that began in 1975.
2. The figures in parenthesis are primarily repair activities.

It could be disputed whether African rural enterprises can be defined as 'industry'. Indeed, industry was restrictively defined by the editor in the introduction of this book to 'occupationally specialised labour in factory organisations producing on the basis of science and technological advances spurred by the competitive forces of the world market'. Certainly, further research is needed to establish more precisely the present and potential contribution of rural small-scale industry in terms of productivity and growth. Thus, the question remains, do African enterprises represent evolution or involution?

Limited Rural Purchasing Power

The most important determinant of the scope for rural small-scale enterprises is the level of agricultural incomes, which determines the extent of local purchasing power from which forward 'demand linkages' are generated. This relationship is illustrated by results from a survey of rural enterprises in four districts of Kenya (Table 6) which shows wide variations in value added per person engaged. Value added per capita was more than four times as great in the best-placed district compared with the worst-placed. In microenterprises, value added per person is a good indicator of monthly earnings. It is significant to note that only 16 per cent of the establishments were engaged in manufacturing.

Table 6: Value Added in Rural Informal Sector Establishments in Kenya, 1986

District	Mean no. of persons engaged	Gross output per establishment (KShs/month)	Mean value added per establishment (KShs/month)	Value added per person engaged (KShs/month)[1]
Nyeri	1.50	14,401.5	3,092.3	2,062
Meru	2.06	12,936.0	2,491.3	1,209
Siaya	1.86	10,453.7	892.4	480
Uasin Gishu	1.82	9,152.0	1,026.7	563

Source: Ng'ethe et al. (1989)

1. The minimum wage outside Nairobi/Mombasa in June 1987 was KShs589.

Kilby (1986) quotes expenditure elasticities for local non-food items in Sierra Leone, Nigeria and Malaysia as 1.40, 1.34 and 2.05 respectively. While these promise well for the expansion of rural non-farm employment, the highest elasticities were associated with services, not manufacturing. In the case of Sierra Leone the elasticity for manufactured products originating from small-scale producers was only 0.85.

Demand limitations were evident in another survey in Sierra Leone which revealed substantial excess capacity among small-scale industries (Table 7). Significantly, the highest excess capacity existed in the rural areas and diminished as the population size of the locality increased. In localities below 2,000 inhabitants there was up to 45 per cent excess capacity. Data from Ghana and Tanzania also reflect general excess capacity.

Table 7: Estimates of Excess Capacity in African Rural Non-farm Enterprises (percentage)

	Tailoring	Carpentry	Metal work	Baking and milling
Ghana	34	58	41	52
Tanzania (Arusha Region)	55	41	61	59
Sierra Leone				
Localities < 2,000	45	45	43	-
Localities 2,000-20,000	34	33	47	41

Sources: Bagachwa and Stewart (1990) based on Liedholm and Chuta (1976) for Sierra Leone; Steel (1977) for Ghana; and Bagachwa (1981) for Tanzania

Apart from low incomes, Africa's dispersed settlement patterns with widely scattered homesteads and with poor road systems dilute whatever market exists and reduce the ratio of non-farm to farm income compared with Asia. The contrast with much of Asia is demonstrated by the following description of Pakistan:

> ... the size and dynamism of the rural small-scale industrial sub-sector are attributable to four basic characteristics of the economy. There is a strong and dynamic agricultural base, particularly in the Punjab; there is a strong tradition of rural industry; there are local concentrations of population in the most prosperous agricultural areas providing a corresponding concentration of accessible markets for non-farm goods and services; and there is a relatively well-developed transport and trade network (ILO 1990).

Influence of the Resource Base

Rural non-agricultural activities have direct forward linkages with agriculture in the form of agricultural processing and other manufacturing based on agricultural raw materials, whilst backward linkages are provided through the manufacture of agricultural equipment, tools and inputs. The type of agriculture and degree of agricultural intensification are critical factors affecting the extent of backward linkages. Given the dominance of hoe agriculture in so many parts of Africa, there are striking differences between the technological bases of Africa and Asia (Table 8).

Table 8: Characteristics of Agriculture in Sub-Saharan Africa and Other Developing Regions, 1982-84

Region	Arable land per agricultural worker (ha)	Arable land irrigated (percentage)	Fertiliser consumption per cultivated hectare (kg)	Cereal yield 1975-82 (kg/ha)	Tractors per 1,000 hectares 1978-80
SSA[1]	1.6	2	9	800	1.4
Asia	0.8	27	46	1,900	2.0
Near East					
North Africa	2.8	20	72	1,400	6.6
Latin America	4.9	7	53	2,000	5.4

Source: Jamal (1988)

1. Sub-Saharan Africa excludes South Africa.

In Africa, the percentage of arable land irrigated is only 2 per cent, compared with 27 per cent in Asia, while fertiliser consumption per cultivated hectare is 9 kg, compared with 46, both indicative of the much greater intensity of agriculture in Asia. In Asia, the widespread use of irrigation pumps, for example, and a more developed transport sector, in the form of trucks and buses, generates: 'an elaborate network of metal and welding workshops throughout the rural areas... in Bangladesh, even in small villages, they employ a remarkable number of lathe machines, drilling bores and electrical equipment, representing an enormous potential for further development of small enterprises' (Haan 1989). To demonstrate the contrast, in Kenya, one of the more agriculturally developed African countries, the Rural Household Budget Survey of 1981-2 showed that only 12 per cent of rural households owned even a plough.

The importance of forward linkages through agricultural processing is illustrated in the Ugandan Census of Business Establishments (Government of Uganda 1993). These census statistics exclude firms of 1-4 persons which comprise most of the microenterprise sector. The census reveals that in 1984 agro-processing, consisting of coffee processing, grain milling, tea processing, sugar and jaggery, and cotton ginning, accounted for 37 per cent of both value added and persons engaged in Ugandan firms of 5 or more persons.[1]

Three further natural resource-based activities, sawmilling, wood and straw products, and mineral products (brick making etc), provided a further 4 per cent of value added and 9 per cent of persons engaged. If these are combined with agricultural processing activities, a full 42 per cent of value added and 46 per cent of employment are resource-based. If the capital city, Kampala, and Jinja and Mukono are excluded, leaving a number of major urban areas of 40,000-60,000 persons, the share of resource-based industries rises to 82 per cent of value added and 66 per cent in terms of persons engaged (Government of Uganda 1993).

Livingstone (1991) identified differences between Kenya's urban and rural informal sectors, with the latter much more resource-based than the former. The following five categories of activities were more prevalent in the rural informal sector than in the urban informal sector:

- resource extraction activities such as fishing and wood cutting, which are strictly part of primary production rather than part of the informal sector, but tend equally to be neglected in analysing sources of income and employment,
- supply of building materials, including cement blocks and bricks, building poles and timber,
- household industry, particularly beer and cheap consumer goods based on local materials, such as mats, baskets, gourds, calabashes and goatskins,
- supply of fuel and water, i.e. charcoal making and water carrying, though these activities extend also into urban areas, and
- market vending.

A wider review (Livingstone 1992) compares similar evidence for other countries, such as Thailand, confirming that the extent and variety of rural industries varies directly with the richness of local natural resources.

The agricultural and natural resource base is thus critical. One cannot expect to develop significant rural industries in, for example, semi-arid areas, where there is only limited arable agriculture and little or no forest resources and where purchasing power barely exists. Ironically, the *need* to supplement low agricultural or livestock incomes in semi-arid areas is so great that governments and international agencies usually attempt to establish programmes for small-scale enterprises and small-scale industrial enterprise there, even though these areas offer the least favourable conditions.

Tendency for Urban Concentration

If rural industries are defined as those geographically located outside urban areas of 20,000 or more persons, then a further constraint arises in relation to the *location* of small-scale industrial enterprises. It is true that some resource-based industries must necessarily be dispersed within rural areas to be cost-effective because they are weight-losing. Saw mills are a good example. However, any locational advantage a rural area may have is often outweighed by the scale advantage of urban areas. Thus, even weight-losing agricultural processing establishments are frequently in major towns. The Ugandan Census of Business Establishments cited above shows that 80 per cent of value added and 60 per cent of employment are concentrated in the three major towns, Kampala, Jinja and Mukono. Furthermore, the value added per person in these towns was nearly triple that of other areas.

In their investigation of manufacturing microenterprises in Northern Nigeria, Liedholm and Parker (1989) surveyed the same microenterprises in 1974 and 1980. They found that none of the village establishments had expanded in terms of employment, while 13 per cent of firms in rural towns and 31 per cent in urban centres had. This indicates *some* growth of firms, but primarily in urban areas.

While the tendency for large-scale industrial concerns to polarise into urban centres is self-evident, it has recently been observed that microenterprises similarly tend to form agglomerations or clusters in urban areas, sometimes voluminously (IFAD 1990). This spontaneous clustering, very often divided according to particular trades and specialisations, is no doubt indicative of externalities perceived by small producers, as in the case of their large-scale counterparts. The same report identifies the clusters as possible vehicles for the dissemination of new technologies and other promotional measures. This suggests that the most effective approach to the promotion of microenterprises and small-scale industry need not primarily have a rural area focus, though it could have a rural town dimension. Thus, it may be more effective to develop a symbiotic relationship between rural towns and their agricultural hinterlands with, for example, the production of agricultural equipment, processing equipment, and inputs, all of which can be produced through either large-scale formal or small-scale informal sector enterprise.

Non-Farm Income and Household Welfare

The fact that even 'rural' industries tend to be located in rural towns and rural trading centres, but away from the rural household raises the question of how many households are *effectively* touched by access to rural industry or non-farm activities in general. What is the relative contribution to rural household welfare of non-farm activities within the rural household as opposed to those concentrated in rural or urban towns? Livingstone (1991) notes the large proportion of 'divided households' in which the husband, or other family members, are employed in town while the smallholding is maintained by the female 'head', who also receives remittances. To what extent can remittances be considered a significant and reliable source? Types of non-farming earnings and remittance patterns vary within a country as well as between countries. Much more research is needed to distinguish the patterns as it is obviously important in determining the role of small-scale industries and non-farm activities in rural poverty alleviation, with or without increasing population pressure.

Where there are no local opportunities for non-farm income nor remittances from urban-based employment, households may simply become poor as holding size diminishes. Recent village surveys in Uganda covering 238 households in one sub-parish of Hoima District and 300 in Mukono District largely confirm this (Table 9). The first is a relatively poor area with low farm incomes in which it would be hoped that households would find non-farm activities to supplement their income. In fact 170 enterprises were being carried out by 238 households, but the list is unimpressive - beer brewing and the production of other drinks, pancakes (*chapatis*), mat making and brick making. Few of these activities were likely to generate high levels of additional income.

More significant non-farm activities were expected to prevail in Mukono, one of the most fertile parts of Uganda, and therefore an area likely to generate demand and other linkages with rural industry. Mukono was experiencing strong population pressure and inhabitants had very small farm plots, necessitating supplementary non-farm income. In the 300 interviewed households, 167 enterprises were found but the activities were similar to those in Hoima. These findings are illustrative of the constraints on the development of rural non-agricultural activities that have been outlined in this chapter.

Table 9: Proportion of Households Involved in Various Non-farm Activities in Uganda, 1992-93

Activity	*No. of times mentioned*		*% of total households*		*% of total FHHs*[1]	
	Hoima	Mukono	Hoima	Mukono	Hoima	Mukono
Size of Sample	238	300	238	300	57	82
Retail trading	83	66	-	-	-	-
Food	52	26	20.1	8.7	24.6	12.2
Non-food	14	14	5.4	4.7	1.8	4.9
Fish	7	6	2.7	2.0	1.8	1.2
Banana juice	0	7	0.0	2.3	0.0	3.7
Charcoal & Firewood	10	13	3.9	4.3	1.8	-
Production and Trading	32	29	-	-	-	-
Banana juice	6	6	2.3	2.0	3.5	3.7
Alcoholic drinks	11	4	4.3	1.3	8.8	4.9
Pancake selling	9	6	3.5	2.0	8.8	3.7
Native medicines	6	3	2.3	1.0	-	-
Charcoal	-	10	-	3.3	-	-
Mfg and Crafts	50	53	-	-	10.5	-
Beer brewing	23	4	8.9	1.3	-	3.7
Brick making	9	9	3.5	3.0	8.8	1.2
Mat making	5	25	1.9	8.3	-	19.5
Basket making	1	1	0.4	0.3	-	1.2
Tailoring	3	0	1.2	0.0	-	0.0
Carpentry	3	2	1.2	0.7	-	-
Blacksmithing	1	2	0.4	0.7	-	-
Maize milling	1	0	0.4	0.0	-	0.0
Bicycle repair	4	0	1.6	0.0	-	0.0
Repairs	0	7	0.0	2.3	0.0	1.2
Leather manufacture	0	1	0.0	0.3	0.0	-
Shoe making	0	2	0.0	0.7	0.0	-
Services	-	12	-	4.0	-	2.4
Other	5	7	-	-	-	-
Pitsawing	2	0	0.8	0.0	-	0.0
Saw milling	0	1	0.0	0.3	0.0	-
Sand collection	0	1	0.0	0.3	0.0	-
Building & Construction	2	5	0.8	1.7	-	-
Tractor hire	1	0	0.4	0.0	-	0.0

Sources: Bategeka (1993) and Ogar (1994)

1. 'FHH' refers to female headed household.

Conclusion

This brief critical review of the literature may seem unduly pessimistic about the scope for rural industry, but there is, in fact, considerable opportunity for a wide range of initiatives in small-scale and rural industry development. Rural non-farm activities must remain an important vehicle for labour-intensive growth and for meeting the basic needs of low-income rural and urban populations. Rural industries and non-farm activities are extremely heterogeneous in character and potential, while the scope for their development varies widely according to their agricultural and natural resource base and geographical location. Recent literature has done much to correct previous neglect and quantitative underestimation of the rural non-farm sector, but the quantities, productivities and locations of rural industries need to be kept in perspective if programmes for poverty alleviation are to be realistic.

Notes

1. Despite this deficiency, as a national census it is a valuable source of data as opposed to survey data which are so often defective by virtue of sampling biases and the non-comparability of categories between surveys.

References

BAGACHWA, M.D. & F. STEWART 1990, *Rural Industries and Rural Linkages in Sub-Saharan Africa: A Survey*, Oxford, Queen Elizabeth House Development Studies Working Paper no. 23

BATEGEKA, L. 1993, *Sources of Income as Related to Poverty in Karongo Village, Hoima District*, M.A. Dissertation, Makerere University, Economics Department

CHUTA, E. & C. LIEDHOLM 1985, *Employment Growth in Small-Scale Industry Empirical Evidence and Policy Assessment from Sierra Leone*, New York, St. Martin's Press

DAVIES, R. 1978, *The Informal Sector: A Solution to Unemployment?*, London, Catholic Institute for International Relations

HAAN, C. 1989, *Small Scale/Micro Enterprises and Rural Non-Farm Employment in Africa: Options for IFAD Involvement*, Rome, IFAD

HUNT, D. 1983, 'The Limited Scope for Poverty Reduction through Non-Farm Employment', *Employment, Peripheral Activities and Development*, Manchester Papers on Development, Issue no. 7

IFAD 1990, *Kenya: Special Programming/General Identification Mission on Small Scale Enterprises,* Rome, Report no. 0204-KE, 2 vols

ILO 1990, *Rural Small Scale Industries and Non-Farm Employment*, Geneva, ILO, Technology and Employment Branch

JAMAL, V. 1988, 'Getting the crisis right: missing perspectives on Africa', *International Labour Review*, vol. 127, no. 6

KILBY, P. 1986, *The Non-farm Rural Economy*, Washington DC, World Bank EDI Course Note

LIEDHOLM, C. 1990, *Small Scale Industry in Africa: Dynamic Issues and the Role of Policy*, Oxford, Queen Elizabeth House Development Studies Working Papers

____, 1994, *Micro and Small Enterprises in Lesotho: The Informal Sector,* Maseru, Workshop on Development of Support and Advisory Institutions to the Small and Medium Enterprise Sector of Lesotho

LIEDHOLM C. & D. MEAD 1986, *Small Scale Enterprises in Developing Countries: A Review of the State of the Art,* Michigan State University, MSU International Development Paper no. 30

____, 1993, The *Structure and Growth of Microenterprises in Southern and Eastern Africa,* Washington, GEMINI Working Paper no. 36

LIEDHOLM C. & J. PARKER 1993, *Small Scale Manufacturing Growth in Africa: Initial Evidence,* Michigan State University, MSU International Development Working Paper no. 33

LIVINGSTONE, I. 1991, 'A Reassessment of Kenya's Rural and Urban Informal Sector', *World Development*, vol. 19, no. 6

____, 1992, *Rural Industries and Poverty Alleviation*, Working Group on Industrial Contribution to Rural Development, ACC Task Force on Rural Development, UNIDO/FAO/IFAD/ILO/UNCHS

MILIMO, J & Y. FISSEHA 1986, *Rural Small Scale Enterprises in Zambia: Results of a 1985 Country-wide Survey,* Michigan State University, MSU International Development Paper no. 28

NG'ETHE, N., J.G. WAHAMA & G. NDUA 1989, *The Rural Informal Sector in Kenya: A Study of Microenterprises in Nyeri, Meru, Uasin Gishu and Siaya Districts,* Nairobi, IDS Occasional Paper no. 54

OGAR, S. 1994, *Sources of Farm and Non-farm Income in Mukono District and the Analysis of Rural Poverty,* M.A. Dissertation, Makerere University, Economics Department

OPIO-OKORI, H. 1994, *Satisfying Household Energy Consumption in Uganda and Greater Kampala: Demand, Supply and Future Prospects*, M.A. Dissertation, Makerere University Economics Department

UGANDA, GOVERNMENT of 1993, *Census of Business Establishments, Uganda, 1989. Manufacturing Sector Report,* Entebbe, Statistics Department, Ministry of Finance and Economic Planning

WORLD BANK 1987, *Kenya: Industrial Sector Policies for Investment and Export Growth,* Washington, Report no. 6711-KE

13

Labour Diversification in Rural Africa: Implications for Public Works Programmes

Tesfaye Teklu

Recent experiences of labour-intensive public works programmes in Sub-Saharan Africa (von Braun, Teklu and Webb 1992) have prompted this chapter. Their interface with the topic of de-agrarianisation is provided by the fact that public works programmes constitute one form of income and labour diversification in Africa and hence of de-agrarianisation. Labour market conditions which permit this diversification are thus relevant to understanding the process of de-agrarianisation. The key assumption in the design of public works programmes is that employment in rural areas is strictly demand driven, i.e. labour is readily available in rural areas as long as there are additional employment opportunities. This assumption is also implicit in the hopes being put on rural non-farm activities as a remedy for some of Africa's economic problems. The assumption however conflicts with current evidence from Africa. Various labour force studies indicate a tight aggregate labour supply, as measured by rates of unemployment and underemployment (Botswana Central Statistical Office 1986, Ethiopia Central Statistical Office 1985, Kenya Central Bureau of Statistics 1990). Other sample-based rural studies also confirm a low margin of surplus labour in rural areas (Collier et al. 1986).

This chapter presents a brief survey of this evidence. It begins with a synopsis of household labour portfolios and their variations. Sources of labour supply and responsiveness to changing labour demand are examined. The final part highlights the need to improve our understanding of the functioning of rural labour markets with reference to rural labour policy, in particular public works programmes.

Diversification Practices: Micro Level Evidence

Labour constitutes the main source of income in rural Africa and the share of labour income is greater for the poor. Thus, income diversification practices are strongly reflected in labour patterns. While farm work constitutes a large proportion of total work time, rural labour is typically diversified. The data presented in Table 1 confirm the tendency for rural households to diversify their income sources. The Tanzania case may be considered as typical. Farm income constitutes the major source of income while wage income accounts for a much smaller share.[1] Wage income, however, tends to be higher in drought-prone countries such as Botswana or densely populated countries such as Rwanda. Landlessness and unequal land distribution are also factors, as illustrated by the Kenya data; the juxtapositioning of landlessness and large farms pushes people into employment on neighbourhood farms.

Table 1: Rural Household Income by Source (percentage)

Country/Zone	Year	*Self-employment* Farm	Non-farm	Wage Employment	Transfers
Botswana	1974-5	38.7	25.8	21.5	14.0[1]
	1985-6	23.4	13.4	34.5[2]	28.7[1]
North-west Rwanda	1985-6	41.5	-	43.5[3]	15.0[1]
Tanzania	1979-80	72.6	23.1	n.a.	4.3
	1982-3	62.7	26.3	6.4	4.8
South-western Kenya	1985-7	53.5	27.0	15.8	3.7
Niger: Sudanian-Sahelian	1989-90	48.0	46.0	2.0	4.0
Niger: Sudano-Guinean	1989-90	57.0	35.0	6.0	2.0
Western Sudan	1985-8	45.6	25.9	10.1	18.4[1]

Sources: von Braun and Pandya-Lorch 1991; Colclough and Fallon 1983; Botswana CSO 1988; Reardon et al. 1993; Collier, et al. 1986; Bevan et al. 1988

1. Includes transfers and remittances.
2. Wage income from labour-intensive relief work is included.
3. Off-farm includes wage earnings and non-farm self-employment.

The extent of income diversification measured in terms of the percentage of non-farm income to total income varies. As with wage income, the shares tend to be high in arid and semi-arid zones where cropping income is risky, as for example in Botswana and in the Sahelo-Sudanian zone of Niger and Western Sudan, or, alternatively, where land-to-labour ratios are low due to population pressure. Within the same country, the shift to non-farm income tends to be intensified in drought years. By way of illustration, a large decline in farm income in rural Botswana during the drought years of 1982-7 precipitated a greater increase in the share of non-farm income.

When income diversification is related to income, it shows a positive relation in an environment where income is growth-driven. As income levels increase, especially in growth-mediated environments where consumption and production linkages are in effect, the level of diversification increases. Typically, a cross-section of a population in such an environment shows a decline in the share of farm income with an increase in income level. The rural population shifts to high-productivity or high-wage activities.

The pattern tends to reverse itself in an environment where growth is faltering. Here, the share of non-farm income rises in the face of falling income. A comparison of the shares of farm income between 1974-5 and 1985-6 in rural Botswana is a good example. The poor are considerably diversified in such an environment but are funnelled into low-paying income activities.

Figure 1: Relationship between Household Non-Farm Income and Total Income

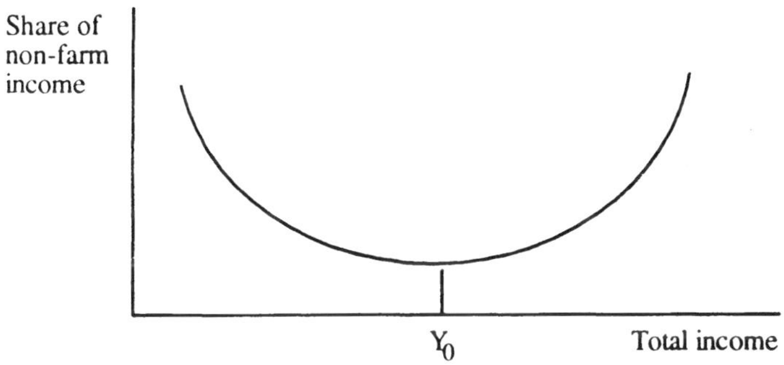

In general, there is a U-shaped relationship between the share of non-farm income and income levels as shown in Figure 1. In this figure, Y_0 is an initial income level. Income to the right of Y_0 represents an improvement in income level and the diversification process is accompanied by a shift to a higher-productivity non-farm income source. An income level to the left of Y_0 represents faltering income growth which is accompanied by diversification into low-paying activities. Thus, the poor are not necessarily more diversified than the non-poor, but they are more active in marginal low-paying occupations, especially in an environment where the rate of economic growth is insufficient to absorb the growing labour force in productive employment.

Within African farm households, the division of work shows regular patterns which are nonetheless changing over time. Time budget studies reveal that a large percentage of rural men, especially those in the prime working age group, are engaged in income-generating activities. Female participation is lower, due to their heavy involvement in home production, which for various reasons is usually treated outside the realm of economic activity. In general, adult males concentrate on high-return activities. A recent study in East Zambia showed the dominance of female labour in crop production, but significantly less among technology adopters (Kumar 1992; Celis and Holleman 1991). The share of male labour was relatively large in the case of hybrid maize as compared to male labour in local maize production. A 1989 household survey in the fertile Ufipa plateau of Tanzania also revealed an association between the profitability of crop production and gender-specific division of crop activities. Men are increasingly participating in crop production due to the benefits of higher cash returns (Beier et al. 1990).

Source of Labour Supply and Variation

National level labour force surveys in rural Africa show low rates of unemployment and 'visible underemployment' defined as those who work less than the full work norm and seek additional work.[2] For example, rural unemployment averaged 2.1 per cent for males and 2.3 per cent for females in Tanzania in 1990-1 (Bureau of Statistics undated) and 1.0 and 0.2 per cent respectively in Kenya (Republic of Kenya, Bureau of Statistics 1990). The highest rates were recorded in rural Botswana which averaged 18.8 per cent for males and 27.4 per cent for females during the drought year of 1984-5 (Botswana Central Statistical Office 1986). A study of rural Tanzania also confirmed that the margin of labour surplus was in the range of 10 to 20 per cent (Collier et al. 1986).

Such a tight labour supply situation is akin to the steep segment of the labour supply curve in Figure 2 (in the area where the demand curve D_2 intersects the supply curve S). The availability of labour is a significant co-determinant of rural employment, unlike the case of a perfectly elastic labour supply W_0S_0 where a shift in labour demand fully determines the level of employment.

Figure 2: Wages Rates and Labour

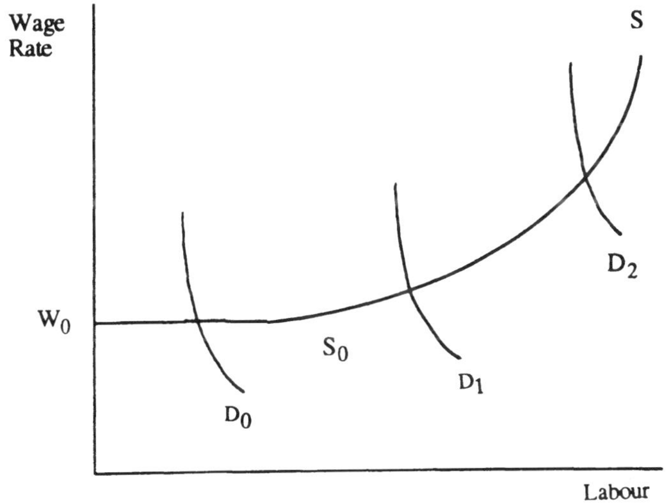

The labour scarcity phenomenon arises particularly in periods of peak farm labour demand related to the agricultural calendar. For example, a road works programme in Kenya failed to meet its employment quota during the busiest months of agricultural work. A study in Nyeri district showed that only 41 of the required 80 workers appeared for work in May 1989 which was at the peak of the planting season. The number reached 74 in the months of August and September, but then dropped to 53 in October 1989 as harvesting was underway (Teklu 1994).

Micro-level studies on the effects of seasonality (Kumar et al. 1993; Kumar 1992; Foeken and Hartog 1990; Delgado and Ranade 1987; Mueller 1985), technological change (Kumar 1992; Celis et al. 1991) and commercialisation of agriculture (von Braun and Kennedy 1994) on labour use in rural Africa show sizeable variations in employment due to shifts in labour demand. For example, the 1974-5 rural Botswana survey showed a decline in the unemployment rate for adult females from 43 to 17 per cent and for adult males from 24 to 13 per cent between the peak and slack farm seasons respectively (Mueller 1985). The same survey showed that the male labour supply in villages with access to employment on large commercial farms is higher (46 per cent of total time allocated to economic work) than the male labour supply in non-commercialised small villages. A study of the technological effect on labour use in East Zambia shows that farm households that adopted the most advanced technology had a greater labour supply than households that adopted simpler technology (Kumar 1992; Celis et al. 1991). The same pattern was also observed in Tanzanian villages in 1989, especially among male adult family members (Beier et al. 1990).

Such demand-induced labour responses within households are consistent with near full employment if the additional demand for labour is met through increases in non-family labour and/or switching between activities. In an environment of near full employment, switching between activities is the only source of family labour supply. However, evidence indicates that sources of family labour supply are not limited to the displacement of labour from other activities, i.e. the 'substitution effect', but also include a 'scale effect' manifested in a change in labour force participation rates by altering the duration and intensity of work of household members. For example, the rural Botswana survey shows that the increase in the male labour supply in response to increased farm labour demand was met partly through replacement of non-work with farm work. Thus, the opportunity for employment on commercial farms prompted time allocated to non-work to drop from 60.2 to 48.6 per cent of adult male time. Similarly, the increase in farm labour arising from technological change in East Zambia was met largely by an increase in family labour. Households which adopted a more advanced technology used 53 per cent more male labour, 20 per cent more female labour and 80 per cent more child labour than non-adopting households. Findings from a 1977-8 rural Kenya survey noted that the periods of peak labour demand coincided with an increase in the family labour supply of the young and the old who were outside the labour force in the slack seasons (Mott and Shapiro 1984). Although there is an inverse labour substitution between youth labour and adult labour in the low-demand season, they both rise during the peak labour demand season.

The fact that the sources of family labour supply come from both labour switching and scale factors suggests that the labour supply is neither perfectly elastic nor inelastic. That is, the rural labour market operates mainly where the supply curve is in S_0S_1 segment in Figure 2 and suggests that labour demand and supply factors co-determine net employment outcomes in rural areas. The effect of additional demand for labour on net employment only diminishes when the demand curve shifts to the steep segment of the labour supply schedule during the peak farm labour demand season (i.e. as the demand curve shifts from D_1 to D_2). Herein lies the potential explanation for the low rates of unemployment and underemployment that are given in the national surveys. These surveys reflect the situation when the labour supply is on its steep segment (close to S_1). At other times of the year, such low rates of unemployment cannot necessarily be assumed to apply to labour supply conditions in most rural areas.

Rural Employment Programmes: Design and Practice

The application of the concept of labour-intensive public works programmes started on an experimental basis in the 1970s. For example, the rural access roads programme in Kenya was initiated in 1974 and the special public works programme in Tanzania began in 1978. The programmes expanded in the 1980s, particularly in countries with volatile demand due to weather fluctuations exemplified by the 1982-7 drought relief programme in Botswana. Some countries also integrated these programmes into their structural adjustment programme to serve as a social safety net.

Typically, these programmes have dual objectives: asset creation and employment generation. Some tend to give more emphasis to asset creation, e.g. road works in Kenya, Botswana, and Ethiopia. Others, like the Tanzanian special public works programme focus on employment creation. The 'special' programmes which function to provide a safety net place emphasis on the stabilisation of income and reduction of transient poverty, e.g. the 1982-7 drought relief programme in Botswana and programmes in Ethiopia and Niger in the 1980s. The relative emphasis attached to these programmes, therefore, varies across countries and between projects within the same countries.

Provision of employment through public works represents an intervention in the labour market. When a household has access to a public works scheme, this sets in motion an adjustment in the household labour portfolio. This manifests itself through: 1) changes in the labour force participation rate (entry of household members into the labour force), 2) a shift of time from non-work to work (increase in labour supply of those already in the labour force), and 3) a substitution of activities due to changing terms of trade across activities. The household labour supply, at a given wage rate, is derived from a combination of these sources.

Recent evidence from a sample of African countries, notably Kenya, Tanzania, and Botswana, shows that eligibility for employment in most of these projects is open to all adults who are able to work (Teklu 1994; Teklu 1996). Most of these programmes do not explicitly take into account the seasonality of farm work. Wages are fixed by the government and are uniform regardless of the type of work, season or inter-personal variations. These programmes thus implicitly assume that:

- there is sufficient unutilised labour in rural areas readily available at some subsistence wage rate,
- the subjective price of labour is the same for all rural households and is below the official wage rate,
- the labour surplus is sufficiently large so that labour can be transferred between activities with little displacement effect across seasons, and
- that it is the creation of labour demand, and not labour supply, which is instrumental to employment creation in rural Africa.

By and large, such unconstrained labour supply behaviour has only been witnessed in countries which experienced severe declines in farm employment due to adverse weather such as the drought years between 1982-7 in Botswana or the 1982-4 drought in Ethiopia and Sudan. Jobs had to be rotated in Botswana to ensure an equal share among the rural population.

A growing body of evidence contradicts aspects of the programme design assumptions. First, rural labour markets in Africa, albeit small in size, are active. These markets are strongly linked to agricultural seasons and wage rates vary across space and time, largely due to factors that affect labour supply and demand factors for agriculture, or due to variations in food prices. Second, because of the non-uniformity of real wages, the labour supply varies across regions, seasons and household groups. Labour supply falls short of prescribed employment quotas when projects operate during peak farm seasons, or where project wages are too low compared to wages in areas located close to major villages and towns, or are insufficient to cover the transaction costs of the labour mobility entailed in labour force participation. The latter is due to the high cost of transportation to the workplace, especially in low-population density areas. Third, 'reservation wages', i.e. the wage levels below which people are unwilling to be employed are unequal among rural workers. Programmes, therefore, tend to hire more workers from low-income families who have relatively lower reservation wages, probably contributing to the self-selection of poor households in some of the study countries.

The programmes appear to reach largely the poor, but the current employment design of the programmes accentuates the shortage of labour in these households. The poor have low labour endowment because of high child-adult labour ratios and/or poor health and nutrition conditions. As the recent study in Kenya shows, poor households be they landless or near-landless, are less likely to withdraw from road work even in a peak farming season. Their common labour supply strategy is to spread the family labour between farm and project work. Adjustments in labour allocation often involve working longer hours, pooling family labour into farm work, including the young and the old, engaging in an exchange system of village labour pooling in order to benefit from economies of scale and the temporary hiring of labour. The burden of such reallocation often falls on mothers and young children.

These examples illustrate the general failure of these work schemes to synchronise their employment and wage designs in line with the actual labour supply conditions of rural households. The assumption of an unlimited labour supply, where the main source of labour adjustment is through scale factors, is unwarranted. Under certain conditions, especially during agricultural labour demand peaks, additional labour demand through work schemes has little net effect on total employment. Where the wage is considered as a viable targeting mechanism, it is necessary to determine wage rates which are likely to encourage the poor to participate in these schemes. Setting such wage rates requires an understanding of rural labour markets and this in turn would go a long way towards improving the design of employment schemes.

Conclusion

While self-employment in agriculture is the dominant economic activity of most rural dwellers in Africa, labour in rural areas is increasingly diversified. At present, wage labour accounts for a small share of the labour market and is more pronounced where land-labour ratios are high. Although the poor are not necessarily more diversified than the non-poor, they follow distinct labour supply strategies that often involve the diversification of employment into low-productivity activities.

The characterisation of the rural labour force as fully employed or as a 'reservoir' of idle labour simply represents a misinterpretation of labour supply conditions in rural areas. The venues for labour supply come not only through the pure substitution effect as in the case of a fully employed labour force, but also from the scale effect. To the extent that additional labour demand operates in family labour supply zones where such scale effects exist, it contributes to new employment. It is only when the demand curve approaches the steep segment of the labour schedule, i.e. where further adjustment in the labour supply is only possible through substitution, that additional labour demand has little net effect on employment.

The main drawback of current labour-intensive public works in Sub-Saharan Africa lies in the formulation of policies that poorly reflect the functioning of rural labour markets. This is revealed in the design of programmes where, for example, wages are uniformly set regardless of variations across seasons, regions and worker characteristics; or, activities are scheduled without accommodating the seasonality of agricultural labour. The assumption that labour is readily available in rural areas at a low cost implies that the absence of labour demand is the main limiting factor for the generation of employment in rural areas. This assumption is particularly unwarranted during the peak farm season, especially for the poor households which the programmes are mainly intended to benefit.

If public works programmes are to adhere to their goal of targeting the poor, it is crucial that they adjust their employment and wage designs in line with rural household labour supply conditions. Where the wage rate is considered to be a viable targeting mechanism, it is necessary to determine wage levels that encourage the participation of the poor. Setting such wage rates requires an understanding of the dynamics of the rural labour market, especially variations in rural wages and employment across household groups, seasons and locations.

Notes

1. Measure of wage income may not be uniform across countries and studies because of differences in how non-local off-farm wage income is treated. Some of the case study countries have included remittances as part of the transfer income component, e.g. Botswana, Rwanda, and West Sudan.

2. The 'current labour force' in the Kenya survey comprised those aged 8 years or more who had worked in an economic activity for at least one hour during the past week, or did not work but reported themselves as the head of a family farm or had looked for work during the past year. A similar definition was adopted in an Ethiopian survey with one variation: those who performed a minimum of one day of productive work in the past year. Productive work excluded time spent on wood and water collection, which was part of economic activity in the Kenya survey. Botswana adopted a broader definition: those above the age limit and engaged in any work or reporting themselves as available for work but not working, or looking for work, or having stopped looking for work. The 'unemployed' in the Kenya survey were those who failed to meet the minimum one-hour duration but were looking for work. In the cases of Botswana and Ethiopia, it also included those available for work but who were not looking for work, i.e. 'discouraged workers'. Those who worked below the normal 40-hour-per-week norm and were looking for additional work were considered 'underemployed' in Kenya. Botswana set the limit at 35 hours per week. The 'underemployed' in Ethiopia's survey comprised those who worked less than 3 days per week regardless of an expressed desire to work more, those working over 3 days and who

expressed a desire to work more, and those who had a farm but were temporarily out of work due to seasonality or social reasons.

References

BEIER, M., C. M. FALKENBERG, N. NJEMA & A. ZEWDIE 1990, *The Southern Highland Development and the Food Security Needs of Tanzania: The Case of Rukwa Region*, Study prepared for GTZ, Division 426, Berlin

BEVAN, D., A. BIGSTEN, P. COLLIER & J. GUNNING 1988, 'Incomes in the United Republic of Tanzania during the "Nyerere" Experiment', in W. van Ginneken (ed.), *Trends in Employment and Labour Income*, Geneva, International Labour Organization

BOTSWANA, REPUBLIC of, CENTRAL STATISTICAL OFFICE 1986, *Labour Force Survey 1984-85*, Gaborone

____, 1988, *Household Income and Expenditure Survey (HIES): 1985-86*, Gaborone

BRAUN, J. von & E. KENNEDY (eds) 1994, *Agricultural Commercialization, Development, and Nutrition*, Baltimore, Johns Hopkins University Press

BRAUN J. von & R. PANDYA-LORCH (eds) 1991, 'Income Sources and Diversification Strategies of the Malnourished Rural Poor, *Quarterly Journal of International Agriculture*, vol. 31, no. 1

BRAUN, J. von, T. TEKLU & P. WEBB 1992, 'Labour-Intensive Public Works for Food Security in Africa: Past Experience and Future Potential', *International Labour Review*, vol. 131, no. 1

CELIS R., H. T. MILIMO & S. WANMALI 1991, 'The Effects of Adopting Technology on the Household Use of Labour', in R. Celis and C. Holleman (eds), *Adopting Improved Farm Technology: A Study of Smallholder Farmers in Eastern Province, Zambia*, Washington, International Food Policy Research Institute

COLCLOUGH, C. & P. FALLON 1983, 'Rural Poverty in Botswana: Dimensions, Causes, and Constraints', in D. Ghai and S. Radwan (eds), *Agrarian Policies and Rural Poverty in Africa*, Geneva, International Labour Organization

COLLIER, P., S. RADWAN, S. WANGWE & A. WAGNER 1986, *Labour and Poverty in Rural Tanzania*, Oxford, Clarendon, Press

DELGADO, C. & C. G. RANADE 1987, 'Constraints to Oxen Cultivation in the Sahel', *American Journal of Agricultural Economics*, no. 64

____, 1987, 'Technological Change and Agricultural Labour Use', in J. W. Mellor, C. L. Delgado & M. J. Blackie (eds), *Accelerating Food Production in Sub-Saharan Africa*, Baltimore, Johns Hopkins University Press

ETHIOPIA, CENTRAL STATISTICAL OFFICE 1985, 'Rural Labour Force Survey, April 1981-April 1982', *Statistical Bulletin*, vol. 51, Addis Ababa

FOEKEN, D. W. J. 1990, 'Aspects of Seasonality in Africa', in D. W. J. Foeken and A. P. den Hartog (eds), *Seasons, Food Supply, and Nutrition in Africa*, Leiden, African Studies Centre

KENYA, REPUBLIC of, Central Bureau of Statistics and Long Range Unit 1990, *Rural Labour Force Survey 1988-89*, Nairobi, 1990

KUMAR, S. K. 1992, *Adoption of Hybrid Maize in Zambia: Effects of Gender Roles in Agriculture, Food Consumption, and Nutrition,* Washington, International Food Policy Research Institute, Draft Research Report

KUMAR, S. K., H. NEKA-TEBEB, S. TAFESSE & T. DEMISSE 1993, *Public Works Projects in Ethiopia: Potential for Improving Seasonal Food Security and Agricultural Productivity,* Washington, International Food Policy Research Institute, mimeo

MOTT, F. L. & D. SHAPIRO 1984, 'Seasonal Variation in Labour-Force Activity and Intrahousehold Substitution of Labour in Rural Kenya', *The Journal of Developing Areas*, vol. 18, 449-463

MUELLER, E. 1985, 'The Value and Allocation of Time in Rural Botswana', in C. Dov, R. E. B. Lucas & E. Mueller (eds), *The Household Economy of Rural Botswana: An African Case*, Washington, World Bank Working Paper 715

REARDON. T., A. A. FALL, V. KELLY, C. DELGADO, P. MATLON, J. HOPKINS & O. BADIANE 1993, *Agriculture-Led Income Diversification in the West African Semi-Arid Tropics: Nature, Distribution, and Importance of Production-Linkage Activities,* East Lansing, Michigan State University and Washington DC, International Food Policy Research Institute, mimeo

TANZANIA, BUREAU of STATISTICS, *1990-91 Labour Force Survey-Mainland Tanzania*, Dar es Salaam, mimeo, undated

TEKLU, T. 1994, 'Labor-Intensive Rural Roads in Kenya, Tanzania and Botswana: Some Evidence on Design and Practice', *Ethiopian Journal of Economics,* vol. 3, no. 2

____, 1996, 'Labor-Intensive Public Works: The Experience of Botswana and Tanzania', in J. von Braun (ed.), *Employment for Poverty Reduction and Food Security*, Washington, International Food Policy Research Institute

VII

CONCLUSION

14

De-agrarianisation: Blessing or Blight?

Deborah Fahy Bryceson

The previous chapters have provided a rich menu of survey findings and historical evidence from diverse cases throughout Sub-Saharan Africa, reflecting different types of farming, differing degrees of urbanisation, and varying assessments of the effects of structural adjustment policies on economic performance. The common thread has been a focus on non-agricultural diversification and changing forms of rural and urban labour. This concluding chapter draws together the emerging lessons. The first section reviews the underlying causes of de-agrarianisation, followed by a consideration of its historical nature and as yet indeterminable final result. Welfare consequences are discussed before considering the growing obsolescence of prevailing models of African development and policy implications.

Forces Propelling De-agrarianisation

Three main forces leading to the growing prevalence of non-agrarian activities on the part of peasants have been highlighted: 1) environmental degradation; 2) economic pressures undermining peasant agriculture; and 3) economic and political opportunities, specifically liberalisation policies realigning peasants' expectations and orientation towards occupational pursuits.

Environmental Constraints

There is widespread awareness of environmental degradation in the semi-arid regions of the African Horn and the Sahel. Less well appreciated is the fact that large semi-arid parts of Eastern and Southern Africa are experiencing similar changes, where destocking and measures to improve water management cannot keep up with the pressure of human population growth. A growing land shortage has led increasingly to the drainage of wetland areas and their incorporation into agricultural production with severe long-term consequences. The threat to regional drainage patterns and climatic stability is likely to affect the farming potential of large areas of the continent (Denny 1991).

The force of environmental degradation is most salient in El Bashir's, Yohannes Habtu's, Meagher and Mustapha's, and Bank's chapters on Sudan, Ethiopia, northern Nigeria, and South Africa. In Sudan, migration has historically been a coping mechanism to counteract low returns from agriculture during the off-season and drought years. Recently, the scale of migration and its increasing internationalisation to Libya and the Gulf States marks a qualitative movement away from reliance on local agriculture. Bank illustrates similar forces at work in the South African highveld, where people had started migrating from their semi-arid home areas to work on white farms as early as the 1930s, with this out-migration continuing until the 1970s.

In Ethiopia, as Yohannes Habtu shows, migration has not been a central factor. The Mengistu government's land reform aimed at resolving land hunger, but within a generation landlessness reappeared, especially amongst the young, marriageable population. In part because of the legal uncertainty of land access itself, the landless have not turned to migration in any great numbers, but have rather resorted whenever possible to indirect land access through sharecropping, casual wage labour, and fixed farm labour contracts. These makeshift labour contracts could be the beginning of a permanently disenfranchised landless class which does not have the same opportunity to move into rural non-agricultural activities as elsewhere documented in this book. Currently, agriculture in these areas of Ethiopia does not generate even the modicum of rural purchasing power necessary to support non-agricultural service activities.

The Zimbabwean communal areas that Gaidzanwa writes about illustrate another dimension of environmental degradation. Here, the agricultural base is over-extended with a surfeit of peasant producers trying to eke out an agrarian subsistence. As in Sudan, these areas have traditionally depended on migration and remittances for household livelihood. Now however, the combined impact of post-independence efforts to redress the racial imbalance favouring white farmers, as well as the government's economic liberalisation policies, have led to a decline in remittance income. Instead many communal area farmers are attempting to engage in commercial agriculture. Grain sales in particular have risen dramatically in the good harvest years since independence. However, there are severe economic and temporal limits. As Pedersen shows, roughly 10 per cent of communal area farmers contributed 50 per cent of the marketed surplus while 40 per cent had deficits. A ban exists on the sale and rental of communal land, but the increasing number of tiny, unviable farm units arising from population growth and land subdivision make it unlikely that such a ban could continue indefinitely. The lifting of the ban and growing landlessness will engender changes in labour contracts to accommodate the land/labour imbalance, as demonstrated by the Sudanese and Ethiopian cases.

Population pressure on land and environmental resources is relative. The carrying capacity of land is subject to prevailing technologies. Current improved agricultural technology consists of standardised fertiliser and seed packages that are recommended by regional agricultural research centres and imported wholesale from outside local areas. Even these packages are not available in many parts of rural Africa. In other areas, their long-term cumulative effect on soils is unknown. In any case, since they represent considerable investment on the part of peasant producers, these packages have been viable only when subsidised by government or donor agencies.

The question of cross-subsidy within peasant households does arise, being mentioned especially in the Nigerian case studies of Meagher and Mustapha, and Iliya and Swindell. Well-to-do farmers are able to use non-agricultural earnings to subsidise their investment in fertiliser/seed packages. The authors emphasise that this is not a generalised pattern, but rather involves small groups of peasant farmers who are moving upward into large-scale commercial farming. Meanwhile, a far larger number of peasant farmers are losing their agrarian assets.

This vortex leads many rural dwellers to turn to non-agrarian activities as a lifeline. Sometimes their meagre resources result in activities which reverse the cross-subsidisation. Non-agricultural activities are pursued at the expense of the agrarian base. El Bashir cites firewood and grass sales by poor rural people in Darfur, Sudan, as major contributors to desertification. Meagher and Mustapha note that many non-agrarian activities extract too much from the local agrarian resource base, thereby accelerating environmental degradation. Livingstone makes the telling point that environmentally degraded semi-arid areas, where peasant farming is increasingly unremunerative and where non-agrarian incomes are most needed, are in fact areas where non-agrarian incomes are difficult to generate. A rich natural resource base may be as necessary for rural non-agrarian activities as it is for agriculture itself.

Economic Realignment of Sub-Saharan Africa's Position in the World Market

For over two decades, African national economies have been in a state of crisis. The 1973 and 1979 oil price rises dealt severe blows to African countries, with the exception of the large oil producers like Nigeria. African commercial peasant agriculture, characterised by household production of relatively low volumes of cash crops collected from far-flung areas, was necessarily premised on low transport costs. The unavoidable and intractable costs of transporting peasant cash crops long distances overland to reach their shipment points severely restricted any restructuring of national economies in the wake of the oil price rise. In danger of economically marginalising vast constituencies of peasant farmers, African governments resorted to transport and input subsidies and guaranteed producer prices. These measures raised consumer food prices for politically-sensitive urban dwellers. The resulting budgetary deficits brought about heavy external criticism of African governments' 'urban bias', rent-seeking, and inefficiency. In the ensuing debate, both the criticising western donor agencies and the criticised African governments failed to confront the unpalatable fact that energy costs and rapid technological developments were setting the pace of change internationally, making geographically dispersed, uncapitalised African peasant producers a historical anachronism. Peasant farming, which had emerged from the colonial period as the continent's ticket to modernisation and industrialisation, was no longer likely to reach its charted destination.

After more than a decade of protracted economic crisis, World Bank and IMF-inspired structural adjustment programmes (SAP) were accepted by beleaguered African governments. Most authors in this book have commented on the impact of SAPs in their case study areas. Bagachwa and van Dijk are cautiously optimistic about the realignment of prices and incentives to informal sector producers. Prior to SAP both Tanzania and Ghana were import-starved economies in which non-agricultural activities were seriously short-circuited by the lack of vital inputs and spare parts. By contrast, Meagher and Mustapha record the opposite outcome in northern Nigeria. SAP actually reduced the level of importation causing a contraction of just such vital inputs. Clearly, oil-rich Nigeria, with its legendary import spending spree during the heyday of the oil price rise, was facing more stringent times.

But has SAP made inroads to restoring African peasant farming's competitiveness in the world market? After all, it is boldly premised on the view that Africa can compete. The question is ***who*** in Africa can compete? Most of the policies are pursued in the name of 'African farmers', presumably peasant farmers, but the Zimbabwean and Nigerian case study evidence reported by Pedersen and Iliya and Swindell demonstrate that SAP policies to date have primarily benefited large-scale farmers. For the majority of African peasant farmers, SAP has amounted to a price squeeze in which the prices of agricultural inputs and consumer goods are rising faster than the prices of agricultural produce. Government cutbacks, resulting in the elimination of producer input and transport subsidies, mean that only large-scale farmers buying inputs in bulk and selling in bulk can overcome the high costs of transport. African traders who have taken over produce marketing from government parastatals in rural areas cannot offer cost-effective marketing services to all far-flung, small-scale peasant producers. They must concentrate on bulk producers.

Furthermore, the continued decline of international prices for Africa's major agricultural exports has undermined the few SAP success stories that the World Bank can cite. Ugandan coffee and Ghanaian cocoa revivals, hailed in the mid-to-late 1980s to be the positive response of African peasant farmers to SAP, are no longer mentioned. Farmers in both countries are now trying to find alternatives, be they agricultural or non-agricultural, to avoid producing such unremunerative crops (Bigsten and Kayizzi-Mugerwa 1995; Sowa 1996). Despite the encouragement given to non-traditional crops such as horticultural products, spices, and flowers in official SAP-inspired policy, only very limited success has been recorded, and then only in Zimbabwe and Kenya. Here again transport is key, specifically producers' proximity to a reliable international airport for the export of perishable, high value agricultural products. Significantly, these products are almost exclusively grown by large-scale, capitalised farmers who rely heavily on wage labour.

The dual theme of transport costs and large-scale production is further illustrated in Iliya and Swindell's case study. The booms and busts of the Nigerian economy over the last 25 years led to rapidly changing agricultural fortunes for those residing in the urban peripheries. During the oil boom, Nigerian agriculture was heavily undermined by massive imports of agricultural products. In today's leaner times the agricultural potential of the urban periphery is well appreciated. Earlier property speculation in the zone has progressed to a point where a number of people with large land holdings can embark on highly remunerative agricultural production for nearby town consumption. Meagher and Mustapha note the same process in Hausaland. Large-scale farmers have taken advantage of nearby urban markets or lucrative cross-border trade which capitalises on currency fluctuations. The converse of this process is the majority of widely dispersed peasant farmers, not so conveniently situated near consumer markets, whose agricultural production is increasingly unviable vis à vis domestic markets, let alone international markets.

South Africa, for different policy reasons, has been the precursor of the pattern of agrarian capital concentration now taking place throughout the continent. During the early part of this century, racially-biased policies had already concentrated land and agrarian resources in the hands of a small number of white farmers relative to the broad masses of African peasants. Africans' commercial farming efforts took the form of sharecropping or wage labour. But agrarian concentration and concomitant peasant de-agrarianisation went a radical step further when white farmers mechanised their holdings and expelled African labour from commercial farming. Bank does not discuss the motives behind this, but one can surmise that it was both a white supremist response to the problems of labour control within the country as well as a response to keeping up with international competition. As large-scale American farmers of the prairies and deep South mechanised due to the high cost of labour, so did the South African large-scale farmers. In turn, so will large-scale farmers in other parts of Africa.

Opportunities under National Policies of Economic Liberalisation

The role of the world market is increasingly pervasive. SAP has laid to rest the post-independence agenda which attempted to nurture national production behind high tariff walls. The continent's industrial production, despite heavy investment during the first two decades after independence, has been in long-term decline ever since. Even at its height, Sub-Saharan Africa contributed less than one per cent of the world's manufacturing exports (Riddell 1990). Meanwhile, African peasant agriculture has also declined. Thus, the service sector provides the main arena for channelling the energies of people disengaging from peasant agriculture.

Up to now emphasis in this chapter has been placed on the 'push' factors forcing rural producers to increasingly forego their peasant mode of existence, but it is equally important to recognise that de-agrarianisation is generated by 'pull' factors, especially since the initiation of SAP policies. Economic liberalisation and 'democratisation' policies advocated by donors have been implemented with the implicit promise that they can deliver economic prosperity, which most Africans equate with western standards of living. Many African youth, in particular, have thrown themselves wholeheartedly into the spirit of western consumerism. The acquisition of fashionable clothes and consumer durables has become a major preoccupation, which people enjoy all the more given their still vivid memories of the pre-SAP years of consumer goods scarcity experienced in so many countries.

Western consumerism is antithetical to many of the traditional values that are lodged in African rural areas. Thus urban residence is part of this lifestyle quest.

This attitude of mind provides a counterforce to the attractions of rural agricultural production that were projected by the advocates of SAP. As Meagher and Mustapha note, urban dwellers have not migrated back to rural areas of northern Nigeria in any great numbers.

However, it is wrong to conclude that rural and urban areas are polar opposites. Rural-urban patterns, as Iliya and Swindell argue, can be misinterpreted if the dichotomy between the places is mistaken for a dichotomy between rural and urban individuals. A wide array of human accommodations can be observed arising from changing opportunities in rural and urban areas. In Zimbabwe, Gaidzanwa identifies the tendency for circular migration to abate. Those who go to urban areas intend to stay, while others no longer bother to migrate because of new economic opportunities in rural areas.

In coastal Kenya, Foeken observes the contrary. The long-established pattern of youthful urban migration is complemented by a return migration of the middle-aged. Many male returnee migrants have capital to establish lucrative businesses. This circular migration pattern shows no sign of waning. The deeply entrenched antipathy to agricultural work on the East African coast, dating back to the slave period of the last century, leads those who have the opportunity to escape agrarian drudgery to take it. SAP-inspired incentives to agricultural producers have literally fallen on infertile ground in this semi-arid area of Kenya.

In general, non-agricultural activities, particularly trade, are highly alluring especially for youth because they are flexible and can be pursued in both rural and urban areas. Trade by its very nature gives one a large circle of contacts, both customers and suppliers, and an ever-increasing awareness of business opportunities in different products and locations. Trade can be both the avenue and the final destination of people's quest for an improved lifestyle in Sub-Saharan Africa.

Functionally, western consumerism, a largely unattainable dream for the majority of the population at present, serves as the overarching ideological force propelling individuals to seek alternatives to peasant agricultural production. Western penetration in various forms has tended to stimulate a desire for changes in consumption more than offering career possibilities. The insidious spread of video films, pop music and television enhances the youthful population's appetite for western standards of living and non-agrarian forms of livelihood. In this attitudinal milieu, well intentioned donor-funded small-scale enterprise projects offer project recipients a lucky break in the form of income and sometimes useful training until the project ends, but do not provide career prospects. Follow-up studies of skills-training programmes suggest that finding waged employment is the exception rather than the rule (Narman 1994). Job opportunities are extremely limited. The alternative, self-employment, requires adapting to the volatility of commodity markets. Previous training may or may not be relevant. Work undertaken tends to be selected on the basis of immediate returns and capital requirements rather than training qualifications as illustrated in van Dijk's Accra case study. Given these circumstances, it is not surprising to find the individual's sense of direction is largely determined by lifestyle aspirations rather than by an occupational vocation.

Analysing a Selective Historical Process

In Chapter 1, the process of de-agrarianisation was defined as a long-term movement away from peasant modes of existence. It has been stressed that there is no specific route nor fixed stages through which a society progresses nor any predetermined outcome. The process itself is but an accumulation of individual and collective actions on the part of actors whose approaches are constantly being strategically revised and refined to fit the prevailing context.

What makes the process of de-agrarianisation so difficult to disentangle is the fact that de-agrarian options are selectively pursued by certain people and not others, producing patterns that are usually quite localised. Overall, a profound but seemingly formless change is being witnessed that Geertz (1995) describes:

> It is not history one is faced with, nor biography, but a confusion of histories, a swarm of biographies. There is order in it all of some sort, but it is the order of a squall or a street market; nothing metrical.

While it is tempting as social scientists to try to construct aggregate pictures replete with spatial and temporal delineations and prescriptive models it would be far too presumptuous to do so. Only the direction of the de-agrarianisation process is certain, a general movement veering away from peasant modes of existence. What is being formed in its place is as yet too indistinct to be classified and periodised. There are however some discernible patterns in the directional movement. Comparison of the growing body of case study material facilitates identification of critical features and thresholds of the de-agrarianisation process.

From the case study material presented in this volume, four major trajectories of the de-agrarianisation process may be posited, namely: 'labour flight', 'rural non-agricultural labour diversification', 'gain or loss in rural labour autonomy' and 'labour drop-out' (Figure 1). These trajectories, by no means mutually exclusive, represent social actors' efforts to both mitigate economic constraints and seize new opportunities. They can be viewed as notional currents of rural transformation rather than hard and fast rules of social change.

'Labour flight' refers to migration away from rural environments which is undoubtedly a calculated strategy on the part of those involved, because it involves considerable initial expense and risk. Whether migration is circular, staged or straight-line, it is more than just physical relocation. Exposure to new places and people of widely different backgrounds engenders attitudinal change and access to vital information and skills. In this volume, the 'labour flight' trajectory is most salient in the case study material from Sudan, Nigeria, Kenya, and Zimbabwe.

'Rural non-agricultural labour diversification' is perhaps less of a physical jolt to the individuals who choose this route, but has major opportunity costs and financial risk as well. It too may bring about attitudinal change. Certainly, it raises the question of occupational identity. This trajectory has become a sign of the times, propelled by forces of economic exigency and opportunity during the prolonged crisis of the past two decades and the implementation of structural adjustment programmes. The content of all the chapters of this book, to a greater or lesser extent, exemplify this tendency.

The third trajectory, 'gain or loss in rural labour autonomy', involves resort to alternative agricultural labour forms and is best illustrated in the Ethiopian, Sudanese, Nigerian and South African case studies. It represents both positive and negative movement away from peasant farming. In the latter, it is invariably a result of constraints rather than opportunities, with the exception of those who engage in wage labour in off-agricultural seasons. It signifies declining agricultural assets, as well as a lack of mobility and alternative non-agricultural opportunities. It is strongly associated with what Lenin (1956 (1899)) termed the 'Prussian road' to denote rural areas experiencing a concentration of wealth in the hands of a few while the broad masses are dispossessed. This he contrasted with the 'American road' in which the bulk of peasant producers gradually transform themselves into capitalist commercial farmers, gradually outgrowing their peasant origins. Economic differentiation of the Prussian road creates growing awareness of relative impoverishment and class consciousness. With the American road a sense of relativity arises more with respect to time, the 'before' and 'after' successful transformation away from peasant production. Only localised and incomplete examples of this emanate from African case study material, e.g. Cowen's middle

Figure 1: Major Occupational/Residential Routes for Peasant Producers in the De-Agrarianisation Process

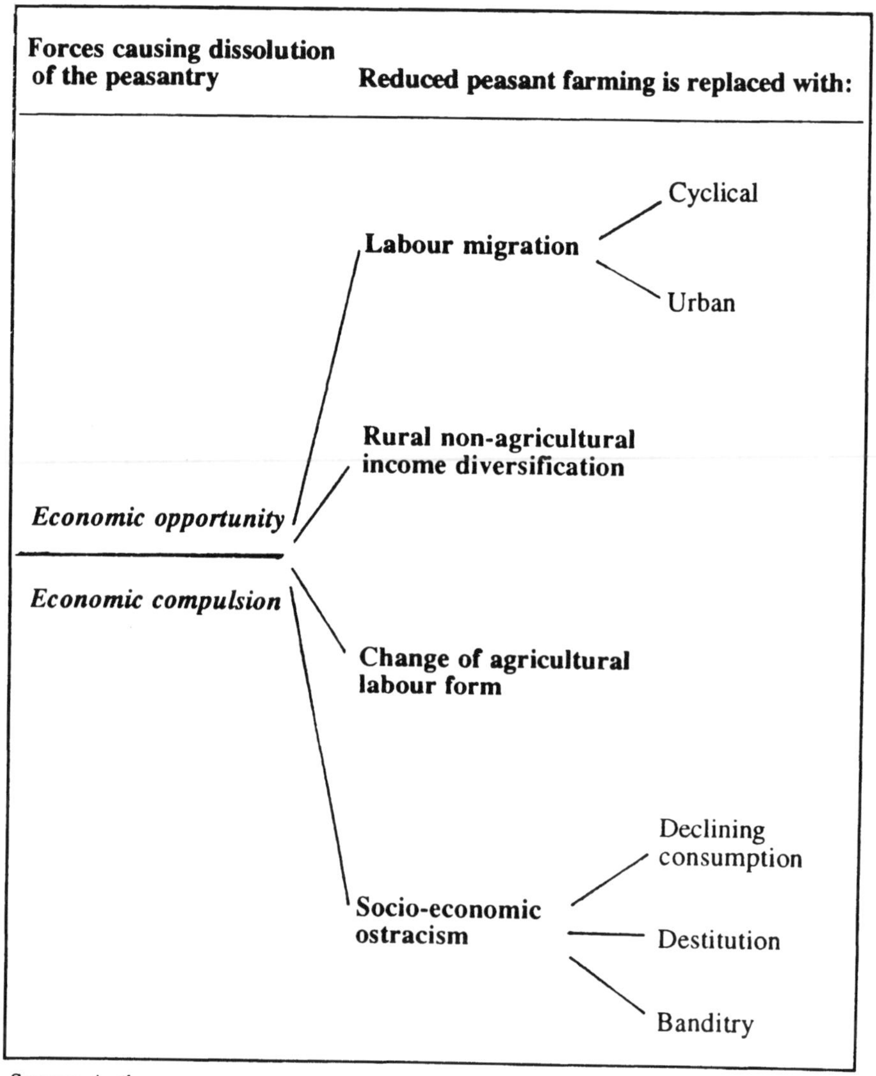

Source: Author

peasantry in highland Kenya (Cowen 1982). Examples of the broad and complete transformation of an African peasantry to capitalist farming have yet to surface.

The final trajectory can best be termed the 'labour drop-out' route since it involves those socially and/or economically marginalised vis-à-vis their peasant societies of origin, who seek or by default are part of 'non-labour' solutions which are not sanctioned legally or socially in any other sphere of the national economy. These include the extremes of the social spectrum. On the one hand, there are the old and the infirm who are no longer productive nor adequately cared for in peasant communities and face declining levels of consumption. On the other hand, there are youth, particularly male youth, who are also not productively engaged, but are by no means destitute. Rather they have discovered the power of the gun and opportunistically live off rural and urban producers by the threat or actual exercise of violence. Their numbers have grown in the various destabilised war-torn economies of the continent which include at present vast areas of Liberia, Sierra Leone, Somalia, Burundi, Rwanda, and Zaire. From the individual's perspective, the drop-out route is similar to the other three trajectories in terms of minimising economic constraints and maximising opportunities. It is merely that the minimising/optimising actions of the individual are not sanctioned by the peasant society of origin nor the wider national political economy.

The delineation of these trajectories facilitates intersocietal comparison. Furthermore, within any individual case study different levels of analysis can be linked to produce a composite picture of interrelationships. Levels of individual action, that of the household, village, province, nation-state, geographical region, or continent can be linked to the central trajectory and subsidiary trajectory to reveal interesting patterns.

For example, various questions arise with respect to the interrelationship between individual and household action in the de-agrarianisation process. To what degree do rural households act as collective decision-making units with strategies to optimise overall household welfare or the welfare of select members of the household? Or in the absence of joint decision-making, to what degree do individual household members nonetheless seek to maximise the welfare of their natal or conjugal households as opposed to their own individual interests? Obviously, the answers to these questions will vary from case to case. Bank documents that Qwaqwa households following a 'rural non-agricultural labour diversification' trajectory successfully ventured into 'deadstock' shopkeeping on the basis of the use of family labour, notably of women and youth, who were subject to the decision-making power of the male head of household.

Iliya and Swindell describe a less corporate family strategy with respect to non-agricultural diversification, but one that nonetheless depends on tacit cooperation between extended family members in the hinterlands of Sokoto and Gusau towns. Here, adult male sons involved in 'labour flight' seek non-agricultural employment in urban centres, but nonetheless feel a strong sense of responsibility to their natal homestead because they retain a vested interest in its rural land holding. However, not all non-resident offspring send remittances back to rural areas. Only those who can afford to do so - i.e. whose earnings exceed the urban cost of living - are able to fulfil their extended household responsibilities and earn approbation as dutiful sons.

Meagher and Mustapha document that the prevailing tendency in rural Hausaland is towards a decline of familial exchange. People still feel a sense of filial duty, but the protracted economic crisis has left them with little disposable cash or even time to spend on gift-giving to relations beyond their nuclear families. Elsewhere in rural Africa, Tesfaye Teklu refers to similar stress leading to the disintegration of people's traditional economic and social fallbacks, especially for people involved in 'loss of rural labour autonomy'. In these contexts, public works programmes become vital to rural welfare.

Assessing Welfare Outcomes

The process of de-agrarianisation is creating a number of new welfare outcomes, both positive and negative for those involved that are not necessarily accommodated by existing cultural constructs and socio-economic institutions. Differences in welfare relate to who participates directly or indirectly and are affected by the four trajectories outlined in Figure 1. The distribution of benefits and costs results in large patchworks of relative advantage and disadvantage by gender, age and class. Furthermore, the aggregate welfare outcome of the de-agrarianisation process becomes evident at the level of the nation-state, raising the policy question of what forms of de-agrarianisation should be actively encouraged as opposed to those forms which government policies might seek to suppress. The following subsections briefly consider welfare outcomes at these various levels.

Gender/Age Bias

Economic migration provides the clearest example of the unevenness of benefit distribution. In northern Sudan, coastal Kenya and communal areas of Zimbabwe, as well as in many other African rural locations, it is men, particularly young men, who migrate to obtain employment. The indirect beneficiaries are those receiving remittances. El Bashir refers to the fact that while migration is a historical constant, its welfare outcome has changed over time, because it now engages more male youth for longer periods, while their net incomes, i.e. earnings minus living costs while away, have been eroding. The latter is partly because the youth now spend their income on consumer goods, i.e. fashionable clothing, radios, cassette players, etc. which 'those left behind' consider non-essential. Thus, the rural community loses its most able-bodied labourers with negligible compensation.

The welfare outcomes arising from the recent rapid growth of non-agricultural work in villages and nearby rural towns are only now coming to light. Gender and age differences figure prominently. Meagher and Mustapha report that protracted economic crisis has necessitated women's involvement in non-agricultural activities despite their secluded status. But contrary to western feminist theories, such engagement in productive work does not enhance female decision-making power. To the women concerned, their new non-agricultural activities are merely extra work in an already long work day, as well as a diminution of their right to depend on men for household provisioning.

Gender bias takes a different form in the Zimbabwean case cited by Gaidzanwa. Here women were eager to pursue non-agricultural activities shoulder to shoulder with men, but the informal implementation of municipal regulations discriminated against them. The disadvantage women face in African rural labour markets is salient in Tesfaye Teklu's chapter. Women's willingness to work for below-market wages in public works suggests their lower opportunity costs relative to men. This can be read in various ways: either they have little to do and are willing to work for low wages; or they are discriminated against in other income-earning activities in rural areas; or they have greater needs for income than men. The fact that female heads of households figure so prominently in the public works labour force may suggest the latter since they rarely have other household earners to rely on (Bryceson and Howe 1993).

Class Formation

It is impossible to ignore that the de-agrarianisation process is a major contributing factor to class formation within rural localities, within nation-states and within the continent as a whole. Firstly, changes in rural assets, especially in relation to peasant land, set off a chain of events whereby some are dispossessed or voluntarily relinquish their peasant means of livelihood whereas others transcend peasant agriculture to become capitalist farmers. Secondly, and less well documented, those who seek alternative forms of non-agricultural livelihood in the process of de-agrarianisation are caught up in impoverishing or wealth-enriching economic activities which ultimately give rise not only to new occupational categories but also new economic classes. Class consciousness begins with a vague but ever sharpening sense of relative disadvantage as documented by van Dijk in Accra.

To what extent has income diversification been a route to enrichment? The case study evidence presented in this book relating to the interplay of non-farm activities and economic differentiation suggests that better-off rural households are not necessarily monopolising particular non-agriculture activities, nor do they have special diversified activity portfolios. On the contrary, they tend to be involved in activities that are similar if not identical with their poorer neighbours. The main difference is that they operate on a larger scale. With more resources at their disposal, be it capital or labour, they gain higher returns and more reliable income streams.

Iliya and Swindell stress that reliability of income is just as important as diversification. It is indeed the stops and starts of income flows which plague the poor. El Bashir documents the declining reliability of remittances from family members who have migrated. Yohannes Habtu demonstrates the lack of year-round wage labour opportunities for the landless poor in rural Ethiopia making underemployment and unemployment notable features of the countryside.

There are signs of deepening rural wealth differentiation on a generational basis. As land becomes scarce, it cannot be passed down in the traditional manner to the next generation. Many youth miss out as observed in Sudan and Ethiopia. Since generational transfers are a two-way process, this short-circuiting of land inheritance may contribute to the low level of remittances that youthful migrants send back to their natal villages. But it is not only land which is the sticking point. Similarly, a non-agricultural inheritance is passed on to the younger generation, which is gaining in importance. Naturally, its content and size reflect household assets. Iliya and Swindell document that the wealthy offer their offspring a better education, inroads to salaried employment, and contacts and capital for starting diversified multi-occupational careers with higher earning power. Yohannes Habtu finds wealthier households harbouring landless sons who are availed access to oxen and ploughs, making it possible for them to sharecrop or rent land.

Critical land scarcity preventing a large portion of the next generation from combining agricultural and non-agricultural activities is likely to usher in a hardening of the options for the disinherited. As long as people can combine the two, there is not only flexibility but also a subsistence fallback. The land affords some degree of livelihood, however small. When land availability becomes highly restrictive, opportunistic income diversification and labour experimentation may be severely curtailed. It is at this point that 'flexibility' of rural livelihood strategies is replaced by 'fragility', to borrow the phraseology of Meagher and Mustapha.

Virtuous and Vicious Cycles of National Economies

Whole nation-states get caught up in impoverishing or enriching economic cycles of de-agrarianisation and class formation which lead countries to diverge from one another. Nigeria provides a striking example. During the oil boom, the county's rural peasantry were eager to migrate to urban areas and enjoy the material benefits of the country's high import capacity. In so doing, agricultural production declined nationwide. This would have been unproblematic if the international price of oil had stayed buoyant, or if Nigeria had meanwhile developed alternative high-value non-agricultural exports. This was not the case and over the past fifteen years Nigeria has witnessed the development of nodes of commercial capitalist agriculture in geographically advantaged areas to provision urban food markets. This has been in place of a peasant agricultural revival. Thus, Nigeria continues to experience de-agrarianisation but the process has changed from an emphasis on urban migration to capitalist agriculture and non-agricultural diversification.

Other patterns of de-agrarianisation emerge elsewhere. Rural populations in Sahelian countries, with their dwindling arable land resources, have had fewer opportunities for wealth-generating forms of de-agrarianisation within their own countries. Not surprisingly, they have tried to benefit from the oil boom second-hand through labour migration to the Gulf States. International migration may be the future for many de-agrarianised peasants throughout Sub-Saharan Africa, providing the only means of taking advantage of world market opportunities that are otherwise inaccessible to them in their home countries (Bryceson and Howe 1997).

Occupational Specialisation versus Diversification: Finding the Right Policy Track

African de-agrarianisation is a continental phenomenon which takes place under the influence of local factors as well as broad parameters set by the world market. Whereas de-agrarianisation is relatively new in Sub-Saharan Africa, it is not a new process in world history. In fact, its occurrence in Europe inspired the work of such early political economists as Adam Smith, David Ricardo and Karl Marx. The theme of occupational specialisation arose in their work and has prevailed as a fundamental theme in development economic literature and influence on industrialisation models during the past forty years. Yet, as has been argued in this book, several aspects of African de-agrarianisation appear to run counter to the growth of specialisation at present. There is extreme diversification on the part of African non-agricultural producers. Occupational specialisation, which developed with rapid urbanisation in the context of the 1960s and early 1970s has been declining since the mid-1970s. The question is when and where will the tendency for specialisation reappear? Is it out of place in Africa? Or is it generally obsolete in today's global economy?

Latin America and Asia have succeeded in specialising through industrialisation, while Africa has not. The success story of the 'Asian Tigers' is held up as a model for African development. But even a cursory glance at Asian industrialisation reveals that the skill base and organisational features prevailing there are far removed from those characterising Sub-Saharan Africa. Africa will of necessity have a mode and pace of development different from Europe and Asia. It could be argued that Africa may be charting its own course through population nucleation, occupational experimentation and service sector expansion. These tendencies are little understood because current development models have clouded their perception.

The concept of de-agrarianisation has been advanced as a means of focusing attention on these tendencies, and providing a conceptual framework for identifying socio-economic interlinkages and patterns. However indistinct the picture is currently, it is becoming increasingly apparent that the polarising welfare outcomes of the on-going de-agrarianisation process warrant policy attention. Like so many complex historical processes, de-agrarianisation can generate negative or positive welfare outcomes in terms of the broad masses of the population. It is becoming imperative to understand the process sufficiently to gain predictive powers and devise public policy measures to curb its negative tendencies, while encouraging its economic growth potential. Achieving the means of effective action is all the more critical given the protracted economic crises in Africa. The neo-liberal economic mood of the times has ruled out recourse to the old policy intervention package of trade protection, price control, and welfare subsidies. On the other hand, over the last ten years, the alternative neo-liberal policy package has yet to be proven very effective.

Several authors have hinted at what may be coalescing as a form of de-agrarianisation which positively affects broad sections of the population, namely the growth of non-agricultural diversification in the service and manufacturing sectors of urban areas. Iliya and Swindell refer to a tried-and-tested traditional pattern of rural diversification and urban craft specialisation in Northern Nigeria. Livingstone, Gaidzanwa and Pedersen all remark on the importance of the urban development of non-agricultural activities. Jacobs (1969) argues that cities are central to economic development given the intrinsic proliferation of the technical division of labour which can only successfully take place under conditions of urban agglomeration.

Pedersen, however, emphasises the importance of pursuing non-agricultural activities with the right scale of urban development. Both Pedersen and Livingstone agree that many non-agricultural activities are unviable in rural areas, where purchasing power, infrastructure and the availability of natural resources are all limited. On the other hand, large urban centres go too far in the opposite direction, causing an overconcentration of population and investment-draining infrastructural requirements. Small towns, sometimes referred to as 'rural towns' because they are highly accessible to the hinterland rural population are considered the most promising, offering economies of scale for non-agricultural enterprise, as well as the necessary modicum of transport and productive infrastructure.

Individual occupational experimentation is currently taking place on an unprecedented scale in Sub-Saharan Africa, particularly in urban areas. Van Dijk documents how individuals in Accra move rapidly between radically different types of activities. Often their training bears no relation to their current work. They move from occupation to occupation on the basis of pragmatic considerations including the physical accessibility of the workplace and financial returns. In the process they acquire a wide array of on-the-job training, gaining valuable experience and flexibility for their future working lives. The evidence presented by Pedersen, Gaidzanwa and Livingstone regarding the high turnover of small-scale enterprises is further demonstration of the widespread experimentation taking place, and points to the highly competitive environment that most firms currently face within Africa, let alone outside the continent.

Now and for some time to come, most non-agricultural activity will be directed at non-tradables. Livingstone cites survey evidence showing expenditure elasticities are highest for services. Pedersen identified the tendency for market segmentation to be based on differences in delivery services rather than product specialisation. The provisioning of goods and services tailored to the mobility and time constraints of local customers is key. Service sector expansion rather than industrial development will be paramount. African industrial and agricultural products face stiff international competition, whereas the service sector catering for local markets affords more room for experimentation and development of skills and production techniques that can be later fine-tuned for export.

Viewed in a positive light, the amorphous nature of African non-agricultural diversification can be seen as an enormous training ground for the future, perhaps analogous to a sort of bubbling gene pool from which African specialisations could emerge. When they are subjected to world market competition, they may then not only pass the survival test, but also serve to enhance the world market itself with new, creative skills, techniques of production and products. However, for this to take place, more structural support must be lent to the African skills training process. On-the-job training must be supported by better formal skill-training, building on the use of locally-available materials (Bryceson and Howe 1997). Local and national governments need to build more incentives into their education, zoning and tax policies to form nodes of specialised non-agricultural activities.

Other institutional issues arise. Small-scale enterprises are operating in the context of extreme infrastructural disadvantage and savage competition. The importance of establishing professional organisations along occupational lines to contend with these problems cannot be overstated. Just as European medieval towns had guilds which were highly instrumental in establishing the ground rules of fair trade in the early days of city formation and later facilitated the capture of markets in world trade, so too professional organisations currently have a formative and regulatory role to play in African non-agricultural enterprise development, particularly in view of the huge skill training needs of the continent.

So far concentration in this section has been on non-agricultural enterprises in urban areas, but this is not to suggest that non-agricultural activities have no place in rural areas. As Livingstone points out, they have far more limited economic scope in rural areas, but their function in surplus labour absorption and training is vital. In those areas, where non-agricultural activities have not appeared and agricultural livelihoods are threatened by climatic extremes or protracted deterioration of the natural environment, public works programmes outlined by Tesfaye Teklu which incorporate a strong skills training component have a vital role to play.

Conclusion

Since the European 'scramble for Africa' at the end of the 19th century, African peasantries have been gradually created and moulded as independent semi-subsistence agriculturalists producing in household units and subjected to the world market and colonial government taxation. In the post-colonial period, African national governments and also the international donor community have continued to espouse policies consciously directed at fostering peasant agricultural production. At present, the policy approach remains the same, but the context, both the world market and the physical and attitudinal milieu of peasant producers themselves, is serving to undermine peasant agricultural production. We are witnessing a period of erosion, not recovery of African peasantries. The process of de-agrarianisation represents the historical reversal of almost a century of African peasant formation. The objective of this book has been to identify and begin to understand this process and its welfare outcomes for the African rural populace and their urban counterparts.

In the context of world history, the occurrence of de-agrarianisation in Africa is far from being an unexpected phenomenon (Singh and Tabatabai 1993). To consider it a 'blight', an obscure force which is harmful or destructive, as many development theorists and donor agencies do, is to ignore the inevitable. Like their colonial predecessors who abhorred the appearance of the 'de-tribalised' native, many present-day policy makers would prefer to have an inert peasantry, Marx's proverbial 'sack of potatoes', rather than an economically and socially mobile population seeking new occupational niches. This is because the outcome of de-agrarianisation in Sub-Saharan Africa is so uncertain and potentially destabilising by virtue of its uncertainty. Some would favour its postponement for fear of the consequences.

Change offers opportunity as well as posing danger. The 'blessing' de-agrarianisation harbours is the possibility of unleashing the largely latent creative potential of a continent. But this necessitates enlightened intervention, particularly with regard to the encouragement of formal and informal education and skills training. In the meantime, African policy prescriptions continue to recommend 'specialisation' in agricultural exports to the global economy. This is the continent's legacy not its future.

References

BIGSTEN, A. & A. S. KAYIZZI-MUGERWA 1995, 'Rural Sector Responses to Economic Crisis in Uganda', *Journal of International Development*, vol. 7, no. 2

BRYCESON, D.F. & J. HOWE 1993, 'Women and Labour-Based Road Works in Sub-Saharan Africa', in B. Johannessen (ed.), *Labour-Based Technology: A Review of Current Practice*, Geneva, ILO, pp. 140-53.

____, 1997, 'African Rural Labour and the World Bank: An Alternative Perspective', *Development in Practice*, vol. 7, no. 1, 26-38

COWEN, M.P. 1982, 'The British State and Agrarian Accumulation in Kenya', in M. Fransman (ed.), *Industry and Accumulation in Africa*, London, Heinemann, 142-69

DENNY, P. 1991, 'Africa', in M. Finlayson and M. Moser (eds), *Wetlands*, Oxford, Facts on File

GEERTZ, C. 1995, *After the Fact*, Cambridge, USA, Harvard University Press

JACOBS, J. 1969, *The Economy of Cities*, New York, Random House

LENIN, V.I. 1956 (1899), *The Development of Capitalism in Russia*, Moscow, Foreign Languages Publishing

NARMAN, A. 1994, 'Education/Training for an Invisible Reality', Paper presented at the De-Agrarianisation and Rural Employment Workshop, Afrika-Studiecentrum and International Labour Office, Leiden

RIDDELL, R.C. 1990, *Manufacturing Africa*, London, James Currey

SINGH, A. & H. TABATABAI 1993, 'Introduction', in A. Singh and H. Tabatabai (eds), *Economic Crisis and Third World Agriculture*, Cambridge, Cambridge University Press

SOWA, N.K. 1996, 'Adjustment in Africa: Lessons from Ghana', *ODI Briefing Paper*. 3

Notes on Contributors

Mboya S.D. Bagachwa Until his death in April 1996, Mboya Bagachwa was Professor of Economics at the University of Dar es Salaam and Director of the Research on Poverty Alleviation Programme. He was an internationally renowned scholar, deeply involved in economic policy research in Tanzania and Africa more generally and the author of many publications and books.

Leslie Bank is a research fellow at the Institute of Social and Economic Research at Rhodes University, South Africa, working on the topics of gender and households in the Eastern Cape as well as urban land reform and environmental management. He is a research associate in the Afrika Studiecentrum's De-Agrarianisation and Rural Employment Programme.

Hamid el Bashir Ibrahim is a social anthropologist working for UNICEF in Khartoum where his special area of interest is the extension of the Sudanese educational system to cater for the needs of pastoralist children.

Deborah Fahy Bryceson is a research fellow at the Afrika Studiecentrum in Leiden. Her research activities have concentrated on issues of food marketing, urbanisation, gender, and rural transport and mobility patterns. She is presently coordinating the De-Agrarianisation and Rural Employment Programme which is concerned with rural employment and land accessibility in Sub-Saharan Africa.

Meine Pieter van Dijk is working at the economic faculty of Erasmus University and the Institute for Urban Housing Development Studies (IHS) in Rotterdam. He is a research associate of CERES Research School, Utrecht. His research focuses on the role of small enterprises in developing countries.

Dick Foeken is head of the Environment and Society Theme Group at the Afrika Studiecentrum in Leiden. For the last fifteen years he has been involved in research projects in different parts of Kenya related to food security, seasonality, labour patterns, and politics. His current area of concern is urban farming.

Rudo B. Gaidzanwa is an Associate Professor of Sociology at the University of Zimbabwe and has published on gender issues in agriculture, industrial workplaces and rural development. She has carried out consultancy work in the SADC region on gender, rural developmen and skilled labour migration.

Yohannes Habtu is working on Ethiopian food security and crisis prediction systems for CIDA in Addis Ababa. His former position with USAID included work on food policy as well as on land tenure and employment issues.

Mohammed A. Iliya teaches in the geography department and is Director of Consultancy Services at Usmanu Danfodiyo University in Sokoto Nigeria. His research interests lie in farm labour studies and agricultural development systems in north-west Nigeria.

Vali Jamal is an Industry Specialist for Agriculture, Plantations and other Rural Sectors at the International Labour Office in Geneva. Between 1976 and 1984 he was based in Addis Ababa with the ILO's regional employment team for Africa, Jobs and Skills for Africa, and between 1994 and June 1997 in Bangkok with the ILO's East Asia Multidisciplinary Advisory Team.

Ian Livingstone has been Professor of Development Economics in the School of Development Studies at the University of East Anglia since 1978. He has served in teaching and research capacities in several African universities and carried out extensive consultancy work in Africa and in other developing countries, particularly in small industry development but also in a wide range of development areas.

Kate Meagher is a lecturer in the Department of Agricultural Economics and Rural Sociology at the Ahmadu Bello University in Zaria, Nigeria. Her recent publications include work on food security and cross-border trade, with special reference to grain trading with Nigeria's neighbours and its impact on agricultural production in Nigeria itself.

Abdul Raufu Mustapha is currently a lecturer in politics at Queen Elizabeth House, Oxford and formerly lectured at Ahmadu Bello University in Zaria. He is a research associate in the Afrika Studiecentrum's De-Agrarianisation and Rural Employment Programme.

Poul Ove Pedersen is the Research Director at the Centre for Development Research in Copenhagen. He has written widely during the 1990s on regional development and transportation, with special focus on the development of rural towns in Eastern and Southern Africa.

Ken Swindell has served as a senior lecturer in geography at the University of Birmingham and has more than 20 years' research experience in rural development issues, particularly rural labour issues.

Tesfaye Teklu is currently coordinating an African agriculture policy research network. He previously held research positions at Iowa State University and the International Food Policy Research Institute in Washington D.C. He has carried out extensive research in agriculture, food security and famine policy issues in Africa.

Index